ANA ROŠ SUN AND RAIN

Text and recipes by Ana Roš
with Kaja Sajovic

Photography by Suzan Gabrijan

FOREWORD

By Kaja Sajovic

Introduction to Ana Roš

People often ask, 'Who is Ana Roš?' Even in her homeland of Slovenia, she's often seen as a somewhat enigmatic figure. If you ask her, though, the answer is straightforward: she is a mother first, a chef second. Then all the rest – a wife, an ambassador of Slovenia, a traveller, a rebellious soul – comes after.

There are numerous articles written about her, and the story is an inspiring one, for sure; that of a self-taught chef, of a woman who gave up her lucrative diplomatic career to follow her heart. Born on the last day of 1972 in Šempeter pri Gorici in what was then Yugoslavia to a journalist mother and a doctor father, Roš often ecounts that as a child, she was never really allowed to underperform; a high achiever at school, she was also an accomplished dancer and had an unmistakable talent for alpine skiing, which landed her a spot on the Yugoslavian junior Olympic team. Even though she wasn't fluent in Italian, she decided to study diplomacy across the border in Gorizia where she worked hard and excelled. Next stop: Brussels. But alas, to the great chagrin of Ana's ambitious parents, it wasn't to be.

During one of her outings she re-met a man named Valter Kramar, whose family owned Hiša Franko, a countryside inn in Staro Selo, a tiny village close to the Italian border. She had first met him during the summer when she was home on holidays the year before she graduated. And the rest, as they say, is history. In that same month, Ana moved in with Valter and never looked back. Her parents expected her to take a job at a European commission in Brussels. This new chapter heralded the beginnings of a new career in the kitchen. It was a nightmarish outcome for Ana's parents – or so it seemed at first. It took them quite a long time to accept that their oldest daughter was now focusing her ambition on becoming a chef, and most likely it took almost the same amount of time for Ana herself to get a handle on this new position. She worked with Valter on the new concept of Hiša Franko. For the first few years she was managing the restaurant and working as a server, cleaning tables, helping out her parents-in-law Joži and Franko in the kitchen. And she had never attended any culinary schools, or completed a stage in an esteemed restaurant. In 2002, only three years later, Ana took over the kitchen.

Ana's true mastery came from observation. She would copy, then fail, then observe again. And afterwards, she would taste, taste and taste again. In this frame of mind, she travelled the world with Valter, and continued to do so after the births of her children Svit and Eva Klara in 2003 and 2004 respectively; she even multitasked by eating a tasting menu at Heston Blumenthal's The Fat Duck while breastfeeding Eva Klara. And she learned, developing a very unique and personal way of cooking, because she did not have a lot of occasions to follow the trends. Dinner by dinner, dish by dish, bottle of wine by bottle of wine, year by year.

But Ana was always one to stand out and break ground – she was doing it her way, ignoring the people who said she should stick to the basics, who thought she was aiming too high, and queried why she was experimenting so much with flavour combinations. She wasn't interested in being 'just a cook'. If she was doing this, she wanted to make an impact.

And so she did. During an event in Italy, the renowned food critic Andrea Petrini noticed her, and was intrigued by her story of a little house in the valley. He immediately took her under his wing, and soon after, she found herself at an event in New York City, where she was the lone female among male chefs – but truly, it was her food that stood out. Shortly afterwards, she found herself at a Cook it Raw event in Poland; again, the only female chef, and again, her dish was the star of the show. She knew at this point there was no turning back. Hiša Franko was put firmly on the culinary map, even though the vast majority of those immersed in the food world have never set foot in this mythical place, where a turquoise river runs through the gardens, and the towering mountains rise above the pink-coloured restaurant.

Fast-forward to 2015, and Ana receives an email from Netflix. The *Chef's Table* team wants to come and make an episode about her story and Hiša Franko. Ana ignores the email, oblivious to the hype surrounding the series. But the producers were persistent and persuasive, so eventually she and Valter agreed to open their doors – and their lives – to the filming crew. That decision changed everything. Overnight, people from all over the world were calling for bookings, completely taken by those 43 minutes of lush green countryside in this fairytale-like place called Slovenia, where the pristine rivers, old ways of making cheese, saving the marble trout, and love that can move mountains made Ana change career paths.

Ana followed up her Netflix success with the title of Best Female Chef in 2017, the same year Hiša Franko entered the top 100 of the World's 50 Best's list, leaping into 69th place. Despite these accolades, nothing could have quite prepared her, Valter and the team for what was to come. In 2017, she boarded 150 flights, and gave no less then 515 interviews. Everybody was calling her, from CNN and Bloomberg to the BBC and *Forbes*. Her voice seemed to resonate; her experience was one shared by a lot of female chefs, a lot of whom were also struggling to balance their careers with motherhood and marriage. In 2018, Ana was named as one of the 10 Most Influential Slovenians by local editors, journalists and CEOs and in 2019, Hiša Franko peaked at the 38th spot on the 50 Best list.

Ana was on top of the world, but it's fair to say that in her own country, she is somewhat of a polarizing figure. However, she's never shied away from speaking her mind, from striving to be better, from trying to make the Slovenian gastronomical scene better. In a place with hearty, peasant food where people have historically not been used to dining out, and which is now trying to promote itself as the hottest new food destination, Ana is trying to seize the moment. Some view fine dining at Hiša Franko as a yuppie extravagance, not as an excellent way to promote the local environment, to revive old traditions, to jump-start gastronomic tourism of Slovenia and bring attention to that particular, very remote part of the country.

Indeed, young, aspiring cooks from Switzerland, the United States, Canada, Colombia, El Salvador, Serbia and Croatia have come to Hiša Franko, declaring it as a place on the CV that can open many doors, despite having to give up urban comforts and move to the countryside. These are people with ambition – and Ana herself has plenty of that. You cannot build an establishment like Hiša Franko without it, and you certainly cannot move onto the 50 Best list without it. What this area of Slovenia lacks in modern convenience is certainly made up for with natural resources, unspoilt produce and natural born storytellers, hiding in vineyards, fields and farms. At the time when a 'back to nature' trend swept across the global culinary scene and celebrity chefs had to take a step back and find their roots, Slovenians and Hiša Franko didn't need to adjust anything or do a U-turn in their approach, because they were never really very far away from it.

But in truth, Slovenia could use a few more people like Ana who want to shake up the sleepy, self-conscious rural producers who sadly have come to believe that a tourist would rather eat shop-bought yogurt than their sour milk; to show them how to market their produce and how to proudly display them for the foreign and domestic visitors to appreciate them, and tell the world about it. And as Slovenians, Ana believes it's up to us to champion the incredible food culture at our fingertips.

Putting Hiša Franko on the Map

A tiny, chicken-shaped dot on the world map, it can be easy for the eyes to miss, easy to mistake for some other nearby Eastern European countries. In Slovenia, nothing seems too far away – Venice is only a two-hour drive, and Vienna four; we can swim in the Adriatic Sea and hike in the Alps all in the same day. It's a special kind of luxury that is easy to take for granted, but it's our unique geographical position that separates us from the rest.

It's also a cacophony of different cultures; wild, untamed Balkan soul crashes hard with the polished, reserved Germanic character and hedonistic, temperamental Italian spirit. We're a nation shaped by our struggles with bigger, stronger nations and civilizations that tried to subjugate us. The Romans, the Ottomans, the Austro-Hungarians, the Italians. . . Unsurprisingly, this also left a mark on our food and culinary traditions. What is a truly Slovenian dish? It entirely depends on which part of the country you are in as to the answer you will get.

Soča Valley, where Hiša Franko is located, is a world entirely of its own. Even by Slovenian standards, it's remote. The restaurant is situated in the extreme northwest part of the country, right by the Italian border. It's far from the motorways, far from cities and industry, far from the capital – at least as far as anything in Slovenia *can* be. It's where the Alpine climate and air masses melt with the Mediterranean ones, creating thermal conditions that are perfect for paragliding, but it also brings in a lot of heavy rain; the valley is one of the wettest spots in Europe, hence the verdancy and lushness. It's also a place where the sea breeze that reaches the tops of the Alpine plateaus from the Adriatic, changes the minerality of the soil and thus creating subtle differences in the ingredients Hiša Franko uses in the kitchen. From the nearby hill of Kolovrat, you can see the lagoon where Ana gets her clams, squid and sea urchins; wine country is just around the corner; trout is abundant in the Soča river, which winds through the entire valley, and above it are the hunting grounds where Ana's father goes on the lookout for deer and chamois. A small stream runs past the house, right under the last row of tables, separating the restaurant from the meadow where Ana's kids play and her staff pick wild herbs. Hiša Franko is part of this area – it grows with it and it shares its history and struggles. And there were many struggles. More than anything else, historically, this is the area of borders. In the past 500 years, there were ten different national borders here. And with that, ten different regimes, and ten different methods of intimidation and suppression of the local inhabitants.

World War I still defines this part of Slovenia. The hills are pierced with old military tunnels, and gravel on the hiking trails is mixed with rusty pieces of grenades and shells. Some of the bloodiest battles were fought here; lives lost counted in hundreds of thousands, their stories made immortal by Ernest Hemingway's *Farewell to Arms*, with Kobarid as the setting. The country's history is full of mobilized men who never returned from the slaughterhouses in the East, with those who did doing so broken. In 1915, the Italians evicted whole villages – thousands and thousands of people were shipped to camps in Italy, and upon their return they were left with nothing – their houses burnt down, their land destroyed. 'Starting over' seems to be something that people from this region got used to doing. After the briefest period of post-war delirium, hard times hit again – first with fascism that oppressed these parts for a quarter of a century, then with World War II, and finally, a series of devastating earthquakes. People have learned to live with constant struggles, and with poverty that has forced them to use all the natural resources, of which luckily, the area has plenty. The first thing that strikes visitors about the Soča Valley today is how incredibly beautiful it is. 'The nicest compliment I hear is that it's prettier than a picture,' says Katja Roš, Ana's mother, sitting in the holiday retreat that she owns with her husband overlooking the lush green landscape and milky blue river. She named the property Heaven, and it is indeed very apt. Katja fully realizes that the very thing that made life in this valley often painfully hard – remoteness, underdevelopment, lack of industry, lack of infrastructure – is the same thing that now makes this part of the world so alluring. Kobarid and Soča Valley seem to be frozen in time. There are no international supermarket chains here, but they do however have an agricultural co-op with a large village store, owned by Dairy Planika, where you can find everything from yogurt to rain boots, from cow bells to underwear.

And then there's the nature. The sheer force of it defines the lives, livelihoods and mood of the people here. When the sun shines over the valley, it's the most beautiful place on earth; at the point in the day that the light hits the spectrum of greens and old barns that are scattered on the foothills of the towering mountains just right, it looks more like an oil painting, less like real life. But when the clouds gather and hunker down for days on end, and when the November wind change ushers in endless rain, depression hits hard. It hangs over, like a thick layer of doom and gloom that drags everyone down. The same mountains that in the summer are bursting with wildlife, mushrooms and edible berries now feel barren and oppressive. Living here is a rollercoaster, a wild ride that shapes the people, the products, the mentality and the region itself. It's a place of complex people; of pain and joy; a place of sun and rain.

Kaja Sajovic is from Ljubljana, Slovenia and after many years of writing about international politics, she became a food and wine journalist. She is published widely and also works for Television Slovenia.

Bread
&
Milk

Ana Roš

My Life

I was 30 years old when I became pregnant for the first time. I was also a young, unseasoned cook; a few months earlier I had taken over the kitchen of Hiša Franko. At this time, a friend of mine, a young director, Jan Cvitkovic, was launching his debut feature film. It was called *Kruh in Mleko* (*Bread and Milk*), and the premiere was screened where the film was set; the little town where I was born and where I had lived for the most of my life. So many of us gathered that evening – friends from school, friends from the streets, old boyfriends, forgotten first kisses. We all knew each other. The film itself was very moving; a true story of people migrating from the beautiful, lonely, mountain villages to the artificially constructed little towns without soul and empty prospects. The story begins with a man who leaves the house to buy bread and milk for his family. He is unemployed, his life devoid of joy and motivation. He has just promised to stop drinking and behaving abusively towards his family, a scenario that is all too common among disillusioned and vulnerable people. With a loaf of bread and a bottle of milk in his hands, though, fate has another idea when he crosses the path of an old friend. It only takes a few minutes for him to abandon his resolutions to live a better life, and a few hours later, he is drunk again. It stuck in my mind as that evening, I realized something was wrong; I hadn't felt any movement from my baby in a few days. Hours later, my doctor confirmed the death of the child. I was nine months pregnant. A few weeks after that, the film *Bread and Milk* won a Golden Lion at the Venice Film Festival and launched Jan Cvitkovic, and our narrative, into the stars.

I was born into a very intellectual and ambitious family. My father was a doctor, and in the Slovenian countryside, this is a very highly regarded position. My mother worked as a journalist for the biggest Slovenian newspaper. Her side of the family is particularly colourful, and according to my mother's mother, we are related to the Austro-Hungarian empire. As a child, I would go to sleep listening to my grandmother's stories about her growing up in Šibenik on the coast of Dalmatia, in one of the richest families of the south; her bohemian mother-in-law was an art collector who helped a whole generation of promising young artists during World War II.

My parents met as students in Ljubljana, but they soon moved to Tolmin, a little countryside town in the west, for my father's career, where he got a job as a pulmonologist. By all accounts, it was not an easy decision to move to the mountains, especially for my mother, who was so much used to her Mediterranean way of life, and was devoted to the sea. She is always saying that our years in the Soča Valley are just a short stop – a temporary solution for the family.

But my father never searched for another job – he totally assimilated to mountain life, and joined a group of local hunters, passing all of his time off high up between the clouds.

My mother, meanwhile, managed to feed her childhood nostalgia by cooking fish: sardines, seafood, anchovies, mackerel, clams, mussels. The flavours of olive oil, garlic and parsley will always remind me of our time together as a family.

First Crossroad

I was three years old when, as I was playing 'doctor' with my younger sister, my right ear drum was perforated by a long nail. My hearing never really returned to normal, and I needed to wear a hearing aid for many years. It made me feel very insecure and vulnerable; I was asked to leave music school because of lack of relative pitch, and years later, no one could believe that I was trained as a professional dancer for twelve years, simply by following my intuition, and not my ears. Around this time, I was also scouted by the local skiing club, and a year later I started attending classes of contemporary and classic dance. My life seemed to move quickly; soon I was selected for the Yugoslav national ski team, but I refused to quit dancing. Between the ski slopes and dancing stages and studying hard at high school, before I knew it I had turned 17, and I was beginning to grow into a rebel, somewhat of a wild child. I never spent my time at home; I never cooked with my mother or with my grandmother. I simply considered food as a fuel for my extremely active body.

Second Crossroad

One October morning of that same year, I told my father that I wanted to quit skiing and dedicate my life to dance. Surprisingly, he never opposed my decision. The pressure of dance aesthetics made me hate my athletic body. My English teacher was the first to notice that I was losing weight too quickly. In those days, anorexia was more of a taboo; no one knew how to talk about it, let alone treat it. Six months after quitting skiing, I was admitted to the central Slovenian hospital having lost 30 kilograms (66 pounds) and shattered a dream. I knew I could never dance again.

Third Crossroad

Fast forward six months, and I was on the road to recovery, but with no clue as to what to do with my life; everything had slowed down. I was skipping classes at school on a daily basis, and even though my grades were still excellent, I was almost kicked out. I needed direction, and finally decided to study international science and diplomacy at the University of Trieste in Italy. It was just after my first trip to Africa; our family friends had moved to Tanzania and our family spent three months travelling with them around the country with locals, learning all about their lives. The experience made me want to contribute to the world being a better place to live for everyone. It was also the site of my first true food memory. Tina, the daughter of Tanzanian family friends, was celebrating her birthday and she invited my sister and me to the slums of Dar es Salaam to the simplest Ethiopian restaurant. If I close my eyes, I can still see the red bucket full of cold water to clean up before sitting down, smell the spices, feel how it was to eat with my hands, and watch the graceful movements of the people who were cooking and serving. The food was incredible, and since then, I've never stopped travelling.

Fourth Crossroad

In the last year of university, I met Valter. The story is brief; I fell in love and followed my heart. His family had a simple countryside restaurant, 20 kilometres (12 miles) from my hometown. Despite graduating with fantastic grades, my mind was made up – I wanted to follow him back there, and my desire for a career in diplomacy came to an end. My parents were upset, of course; there was a conversation between us that I will never forget, where my mother said, 'You are not going to cook, right?' I answered angrily, 'No, Mum, I do not know how to cook.' My parents at that time considered cooking as a second-class, manual job that was far removed from the intellectual world.

Fifth – but not final – Crossroad

To everyone's surprise, not least of all mine, a few years later in the summer of 2002, I took over the kitchen of Hiša Franko , and I started from the beginning. I was 30 years old and pregnant.

Milk

Katja Roš

Two Anas

During the 20th and 21st centuries, Slovenia has experienced every style of government that there is to offer – a few monarchies, a few versions of socialism, and two or three derivatives of capitalism, to name a few.

I have had two Anas in my life – my grandmother and my daughter – and they've each lived in different centuries. One in the monarchy of Mittel-Europe, the other in the Socialist Federal republic of Tito's Yugoslavia. Both, in their own ways, separated from the crowd and wandered off into unchartered waters.

Birth of the Past

On December 18, 1890 in Szászrégen, at that time under Austro-Hungarian, monarch-led rule (now Reghin in Romanian Transylvania), the Frenchwoman Eugenie Peroux went into premature labour and gave birth to her daughter, Ana. Eugenie had to fight hard so that the tiny creature survived. Meanwhile, her husband, cartographer Rudolf Schmit from Vienna, had a soon-to-be fatal accident. Eugenie made all the necessary arrangements to bring her dying husband to her parents in Šibenik. On this long road to Dalmatia, she transported tiny Ana in a shoe box padded with cotton wool. The family was reunited; Rudolf soon died in Šibenik, while Ana grew into a spirited child. She spent her childhood in a sophisticated environment, surrounded by art, culture and science, in the company of a much-respected family, Šupuk.

Birth of the Present

Eighty-two years later, on December 31, 1972 in Šempeter, then Yugoslavia, my daughter was born: her name was Ana. Nothing about her birth was planned, from the awkward timing of New Year's Eve, when most staff were on holiday, to the huge Birds of Paradise flowers her father decided to bring to the hospital – you could barely fit a cup of rose hip tea on the bedside table because of them. It might have been there and then that overcoming the unexpected became the theme in Ana's life. In those days, there was a lack of prams, and by order of the socialist government, babies were sent off into life with a cardboard box to sleep in and a package of nappies. For Ana's journey home, I covered the cardboard box with a pastel-coloured blanket, crocheted by her Great Grandma Ana. Expecting a nice New Year's Eve spent with Bojan, my husband, in our high-rise apartment block, I had baked a Malakoff cake (an Austrian dessert made with cream and rum) following Grandma Ana's old and complicated recipe on the eve of the unexpected delivery. Suffice to say, we ate the New Year's Eve cake well into 1972.

Born in a socialist era, this was the framework within which Ana carved her unpredictable path. Socialism, to us, was just a word. Our kitchen was always full of friends and relatives, always celebrating something; the smell of good food mixed with cigarette smoke; instead of cocoa and juice, children drank Benko, instant chocolate powder, and Cedevita, orange vitamin drink powder. Television had no role in the lives of children who were running in the courtyards, jumping the hoops and collecting stickers for the Sandokan album. In that environment, we craved many things, but our spirits were free. At times, we laughed at our own – and Socialism's – expense, at our financial limitations and diminished personal freedom, but truly, life was one big *joie de vivre*! That's how it was, and it will never be the same.

Family of the Past

Grandma Ana was bright and handy. She wanted to study, but she was instead married off to Jakob Klemenc, an officer with ambitions to become a general. He was from a family of wine merchants from Karst and his uncle was Julius Kugy, a famed Triestino merchant of colonial goods, a legendary climber and a wonderful writer; a boon for the family, who profited from his supply of Oriental sweets, exotic spices, teas, coffees and wine. Sadly, his life was cut short in World War I, during which time Ana gave birth to my mother, Olga. War and the collapse of the Austro-Hungarian empire turned her world upside-down. Gone were the benefits of Jakob's military rank. Gone was the comfort and the ease. The family were forced to move around, and fought for a decent life. Ana had a habit of quoting phrases, sometimes in French, sometimes in German, often in Italian, but rarely in Croatian or Slovenian. '*Un chagrin accepte...*,' she said of her life: 'you suffer less if you accept fate.' She often referenced Jean-Jacques Rousseau. When she had to raise three children, she got herself a copy of *Émile, ou De l'éducation*. She couldn't get the French edition, so she ordered the German translation. Instead of the first and second book, they sent her two copies of the second. For the rest of her life, she wondered what mistakes she had made when raising the kids because she couldn't get hold of Rousseau's first book.

Family of the Present

In our little family – myself, Ana's father, Bojan, and her little sister, Maja – everyone was naturally active and creative. Bojan was a doctor by trade, but he was also a passionate hunter, forester and butcher. I was a journalist, writing for *Delo*, the biggest Slovenian newspaper, and working almost seven days a week. As expected in those times, I was also a diligent housekeeper; the girls were good students, talented athletes, sociable and fun-loving. Despite the fast pace of living, I made sure we always had dinner together, even though at the time, the girls found it a bit tyrannical. We ate simple food, Mediterranean in its influence. In interviews, Ana often talks about her first oyster – the one that tasted like her future. Nothing would be the same after that oyster.

Ana's first word was *tnto*, which means 'light'. When her sister was born, Ana was one year and fifteen days old. Soon after, she started walking – it was as if she wanted to show who was in charge. Ana doesn't like authority – she is a dissident by nature. I suppose it wasn't easy for Maja. She had to adapt. And she did. We all did.

Possessiveness isn't part of my philosophy. When the girls were small, I tore myself to pieces to get them what they needed for healthy development and growth. When they started walking, they had to walk independently. I focused on providing curiosity and excitement. But as a child, Ana's enthusiasm for life never strayed towards cooking. The only thing I can remember her cooking was a crappy cake made of Cedevita and Benco. I learned to cook from my mother, and she from her mother, Ana. The skill was expected to pass from one generation to another; *mousse au chocolat, wiener schnitzel, pasticcio di maccheroni, ratatouille, créme brulée, tarte au citron, tarte tartine, kaiserschmarrn, tranches de langue de boeuf, escargots, pieds de porc cuits. . .* I thought Ana was going to be the first one to break the tradition.

The first sign that Ana was ready to fly the family nest was the drastic haircut in her teenage years. She chopped off her mane of amber curls – the curls I always told her were her treasure – and dyed the remains platinum blonde. When I saw her like that, I just turned and left, speechless. And Ana cried, and then told us that she was leaving. And so she went.

Grandma Ana was often asking us, her grandchildren, who we thought she was. Austrian by her father; Italian, French and Dalmatian by education; Romanian by place of birth; Yugoslavian, Slovenian and Croatian by nationality. But in fact, it was this cacophony of heritage that defined her. She was the living joke of Mittel-Europe, the historical centre that the West thought of as East, and the East thought of as West. She chose to escape this chaos through creativity. She took photos and developed the films in her giant rococo closet. Camera obscura, lanterna magica: she mastered it all. She always had her paints and paintbrushes ready to make puppets for miniature theatre. Balls of wool were waiting for patchwork ideas. Her oasis was a large writing desk, surrounded by ornamented oak wood furniture. Her legacy was a stack of notebooks, filled with tiny, pretty handwriting, filled with thoughts.

Ana-the-daughter always carries notebooks in her purse. The handwriting is different though, larger and less tidy than Grandma Ana's. She writes down whatever crosses her mind. That's how she creates her own landscape.

Like Grandma Ana, little Ana was also raised when the times were changing. Capitalism was already peeking through the curtain of Socialism; times called for adaptation as we went along, and with adaptation comes creativity. Maybe that's why Ana is like a burst of gunfire. She wanted to become a star skier, then she wanted to become a prima ballerina, followed by a diplomat, a president, an ambassador, even a queen. Jumping from one to another. That wasn't part of her upbringing – it was something intuitive. A bit overwhelming. With Ana, you got a feeling that it's okay if life serves you injustice and failures. When you get up, you are softer, more agile, better.

Our family holiday destination was Serbani, a tiny Istrian village with a medieval infrastructure and warm people. We felt very much at home there among the fields of tomatoes, vineyards of malvasia grapes and groves of old olive trees. In Serbani, my almost city-like girls settled among the free-range chickens and piglets in the stone stables. They learned the dialect of Istrian Italians, and a deep respect for the people who persevered with working the rocky Istrian soil. I believe it's why Ana is so sincerely fascinated by the generation of farmers who returned to the soil and the old ways of their ancestors. Today it's to Ana's great advantage that she lived this experience in her childhood.

Christmas Red Cabbage → p. 211

The Path

Only once did our family trade the Istrian summer for another destination – Tanzania. In the scorching heat of Dar es Salaam, Ana's eyes opened to the world. No turning back. You have to know that the time of Socialist rule was also was a time of immense yearning. Beyond borders were pieces of our dreams. In Ana the seed of these dreams began to sprout in the colourful community of young people in Dar es Salaam. And life was never the same. She was adamant that she would go and study in Paris, which for us was financially impossible. She ended up in Gorizia, in the old university building my father used to attend. That's where his path to becoming a lawyer started. He was also an athlete – a member of the Yugoslavian Olympic fencing team. History was repeating itself.

Ana was a brilliant student. She graduated with honours, but she hated the idea of burying herself in the grey of paperwork in the offices of foreign ministry. What now? She did something Grandma Ana never dared to. She turned off the path she had marked for herself. She followed her heart, her love, and subsequently found a path to the kitchen.

Hiša Franko

Ana's life at Hiša Franko began with rebellion – firstly, against its traditional decor. She decided to paint the dining room a dream-like, almost apocalyptic shade of red. Local painters protested, saying they never work with those colours. Little did they know that Ana is stubborn by nature. 'In red, I say. Let the adventures begin!' When she started cooking and constructing dishes, the kitchen staff were stunned. They didn't trust her at first; in fact, she mostly found her early support from the guests. Her cuisine was unpredictable, yes, but everything she produced made sense in the end. 'Learn and it will happen!'

Ana had to accept that she lacked knowledge. So she studied the books, studied the cooking vocabulary, studied the techniques. 'Learn and it will happen.' And it did. She learned the craft and developed it into an art form. Being an artist is an adventure, but it also involves risk. Sometimes it works out, sometimes it doesn't. But Ana wasn't stressing about that. She was doing it her way, no matter the consequences.

She wanted her dishes to make people to think. At first she composed the recipes following well-known formulas, but then she spiced it up. Dandelions in tempura with yogurt and honey. Local mash made into a sorbet. These were my first experiences with my daughter's cooking style. I was cautious because of these novelties. I didn't understand that a restaurant plate can be a cultural event. I didn't anticipate that my daughter was crossing the threshold of global recognition, that she was riding a wave. 'Ana, your plates are beautiful like Picasso's paintings. But you cannot eat Picasso,' I quipped. I worry I am becoming ascetic with age.

The Travels of Grandma Ana

Grandma Ana was in her 80s and long widowed when she began travelling every year from Ljubljana to Rome, Rome to Ljubljana, Ljubljana to Belgrade, Belgrade to Ljubljana. Trains, porters, wool coat, a hat with a veil across the eyes, *a tracolla* purse with random items – a whistle, a rope, a flashlight. Little Nona, as we called her because of her frail figure, was admitting her helplessness. That was her logic. If anything happens, if there's an accident and I find myself buried in ruins, in debris, I won't yell, I will whistle, I will crawl out with the help of my rope and my flashlight will light the way out.

The Travels of Daughter Ana

Even after twenty-plus years of a career on the world stage, now and then somebody, usually in mean spirit, will call Ana a hillbilly. And if by that they mean she stays faithful to her valley, to her villages, to the pastures and the forests, in time of rain or in time of drought, then I suppose they are right – she is a hillbilly. It's a matter of heart and pride – you have it or you don't. Ana has it. She has a real force. With it she avoids the grips of control, manipulations and hegemony. And we've observed this in her indignation for a long time. Here is one such example:

Day One

Ana: 'In three days I have an event in Paris. Do you want to come with?'

You: 'Oh, I don't know, I have work. But maybe I could do it.'

Day Two

Ana: 'We fly to Paris day after tomorrow!'

You: 'Oh, my, I'm not sure yet if I can.'

Day Three, the Day of Travel

You wake up in your bed. Ana's not there. You call her, angrily: 'Where are you?'

Ana: 'Oh, in Paris, I had a 4 a.m. flight from Venice and didn't want to wake you.'

Valter

Kaja Sajovic

The Natural Wine Guru

'You have to try this, it's insane', says Valter, sparks in his eyes, a smile from ear to ear, as he hands me a glass of amber-hued, cloudy wine. We are at Border Wine, a small natural wine festival in Cividale, a half-hour drive from Hiša Franko across the Italian border. This is Valter's playground. After 25-plus years working as a sommelier, he still gets excited about wine. The wilder, the better. Radical, uncompromising, extreme wines with high acidity – juicy wines bursting with life. Even though there's a lifetime of bickering between Valter and Ana about the oh-so-thin line between crazy and too crazy wines, my guess is it's no coincidence you can describe Valter's favourite wines with pretty much the same descriptors as Ana's plates.

'To this day I'm still not quite sure if Ana's dishes developed to this level of intensity because of the wines we drink or not,' wonders Valter. 'And her plates, they have a lot of character, so it's only natural the wine we serve has to have character and spunk as well, otherwise it would fall flat with her dishes.'

He stops mid-sentence as he hugs yet another friend he runs into at Border Wine. With piercing blue eyes, olive skin tan, wild hair, natural charm and a certain magnetic presence, he's a striking figure. He is – apparently – the kind of person that you leave your lucrative career in diplomacy for and move full-time to one of the most remote parts of the country with, as Ana did.

He's an adrenaline junkie, and grins when he talks about how he survived a *salto-mortale* (acrobatic sommersault) on his motorcycle, or crashing through the Hiša Franko roof, breaking his back. He hates structures and rules, and sometimes the most common question you hear asked at Hiša is: 'Do you know where Valter is?' He's unpredictable and spontaneous to the point he once went out drinking to Kobarid and woke up in Bosnia. When I asked him once which winemaker were we going to see that weekend, he replied, 'Someone in Romania' and I wasn't really sure if he was joking or not.

Unlike Ana, Valter was born into the world of cooking and hospitality. When his father Franko bought the house to be known as Hiša Franko in the 1970s, they were on a tight budget. The available workforce in the valley was close to zero, so the entire family had to pitch in and help. Valter's parents lived, breathed and almost tore themselves apart for the restaurant; for 25 years they pulled 18-hour shifts, struggling to pay the huge bank loan. It was hard work – hard to the extent that the three Kramar kids were soon completely put off by the restaurant business. Valter was the only one who persisted and managed to find an area of the industry that truly excited him: wine. And this passion seemingly was awoken in him at an early age. When he was ten years old, his father put him in charge of wine decanting and he always secretly slurped a few small sips. 'I knew it was wrong, but I just couldn't resist it,' smiles Valter.

Franko Kramar paid quite a lot of attention to the wine part of the restaurant, and was always buying it from small farmers, not from large co-ops. But Valter's thirst for exciting wines and high-level gastronomy soon surpassed his father's, and when he started hanging out with his like-minded peers – ambitious, promising young cooks and wine connoisseurs – they soon started to talk about bringing their passion to the next level. At that time, Valter met Joško Sirk, the well-known Michelin-starred Slovenian chef and hotelier based in Italy.

Sirk took Valter under his wing, and on Mondays, let him come behind his kitchen counter at La Subida, where Valter developed a passion for fine dining. Sirk became like a father figure to Valter; he paid for his first sommelier class, and introduced him to a whole world of biodynamic pioneers – Joško Gravner, Stanko Radikon, Valter Mlečnik, Nicolo Bensa, Edi Kante, Ivan Batič – an entire generation of progressive, visionary and stubborn-as-a-mule winemakers. 'They were the key people in my life and people who taught me everything – about wine philosophy, about terroir, the land, cultivating of the vine . . . the secret of wine that doesn't need corrections in the cellar,' explains Kramar. 'They were the most important factor in my personal growth.'

When you tour Valter's wine cellar, you can see how big a part this generation of pioneering Slovenian winemakers played in shaping his taste and shaping the collection he boasts today. Mlečnik's chardonnay 1992, Radikon's rebula 1999. . . with Slovenia being a very boutique wine producer, it's not easy to amass older vintages, and some of the wines Valter has in his cellar even the winemakers themselves ran out of.

His collection is also a testament to the fact that Slovenian winemakers, especially those on the Italian border, were making the now oh-so-trendy orange and natural wines way before they found their way to back-to-nature orientated Noma, Septime and Le Chateaubriand restaurants that co-contributed to their almost mythological status among the hipster crowd. Ninety percent of approximately 600 wine labels in Hiša Franko's cellar are natural, ecological or biodynamic, and the crazier they are, the more Valter loves them. 'I have fun with the crazy. I think my body really responds well to them. They are great for digestion, and they don't make me nervous, unlike conventional wines,' he explains.

At a certain point, his ode to natural wines almost sounds like he's describing a drug. 'When I'm completely down, drained and burnt-out, but I still need to be functional and up-and-running, it's best to open a bottle of Organic Anarchy (*Aci Urbajs*) and it lifts me up all the way to the sky. In that state, if I had a glass of conventional wine, it would only wear me down more,' But for Valter, wine is not just a momentary pleasure, it's something to soothe your soul, it's the product of winemakers' philosophies, work and environmental awareness. 'I know that for those who decide to go natural, their approach to soil, to land, to preservation of nature is completely different. Their heart beats in a different rhythm, one that's not tuned to the sound of money,' he adds.

Bottles of Slovenian natural wine with funky aromas weren't always selling for 70 Euros (£60/$80) in wine shops of Paris, London and Brooklyn. Twenty-five years ago, when Valter was slowly introducing them to sceptical clientele at the old Hiša Franko, they weren't featured on wine lists of Michelin-starred restaurants, and sometimes Valter would have to spend hours with a larger party at a table, trying to bring them closer to his vision of wine as a living, breathing thing. With Netflix's *Chef's Table* and the attention Hiša Franko received in the past few years, those kind of personal engagements with the guests became less spontaneous. Valter and Ana are celebrities of some sort in this world, and everyone who dines there wants to meet them, take a picture with them, have a chat with them. But Valter is not a fan of formal obligations – he lives in the moment. He might still drink with you and talk to you until 2 a.m., sharing the very last bottle of the oldest vintage in the cellar, but is as likely to retreat and not set foot in Hiša Franko for the entire evening, depending on his mood and state of mind. 'The biggest art form is how to let the guest know politely that you have only three minutes for him and not the entire evening,' he ponders. That said, the thought of leaving the restaurant world never crosses his mind. 'No chance in hell, it's way too much fun, if you accept this business the way it is,' he shakes his head.

Of course, running a business with your wife, especially one so strong-willed as Ana, can be a challenge, and their characters sometimes make for an explosive combination. But the story of Hiša Franko and what it has become today is really the story of Valter and Ana, and the sheer power of their will that in tandem has turned into a winning combination. 'Of course, we're different. She likes to have things planned, I prefer to deal with it as we go. In the end, the result is the same. That said, we're both extremely passionate people. With the energies we possess, we could move the world. And in a way we have – at least this part of the world.'

It was a mutual attraction at first sight, a love story that involved a lot of road trips, inter-continental flirting and spontaneous spur-of-the-moment decisions. 'We knew each other from before a little bit, when I was still married. But then one time at a local discotheque, I ran into her and we were glued to each other for the entire night. Nobody else existed,' remembers Valter. Soon after, he went to South America for six weeks, and she went to Spain for eight weeks. 'Every two, three days I was calling her and somehow, she was never there. Every time I called, her roommate was like, "Sorry mate, again, no luck, Ana's out.' Can you imagine, calling Europe from Bolivia all the time? My God, I must have spent half of my travel budget for long-distance phone calls!' After he returned, Ana showed less restraint, and she moved into Valter's flat practically immediately, even before they were officially a couple. Ana pitched in at the restaurant, started working in service, then moving to the kitchen where she soon showed a certain assertive approach to running things. 'Even though I had a lot more technical knowledge and cooking skills at that time, she never wanted my advice, always wanted to do it on her own. Stubborn as hell. It was quite frustrating, to be honest,' laughs Valter.

With Valter, Ana travelled the world, ate in the best restaurants, tried every exotic and extravagant ingredient, immersing herself in a world that was up until then unknown to her. They soon came up with ambitious new ideas for the restaurant and they were very much in sync about what they wanted. Valter's parents, culinary traditionalists with a more pragmatic approach to the restaurant business, were sceptical, but after a while Franko Senior decided to hand over the place to Valter and Ana. And with that, Hiša Franko, once a popular village restaurant where people were lining up outside to have some of Franko's famous English roast beef and a spritzer, entered a new chapter.

After their trip to the Tunisian desert, Ana and Valter painted the restaurant in bright, bold colours; they separated the bar from the dining room, sanded down the glossy, outdated tiles and removed the heavy curtains. It was then that Valter started fulfilling his long-time dream of having a wine and cheese cellar. Cheese, something the diet of the locals here is pretty much based on, always played an important role in Valter's life. 'When we were kids, every Monday when the restaurant was closed, our father picked us up from school and took us to a nearby mountain pasture where we would pick up a supply of cheese and cottage cheese and dragged it down to the valley on a wooden sleigh. On our way back, the kids on the back seat, would always devour more than half of it. These memories stayed with me forever,' recalls Valter. His father was one of the first people to start ageing the local cheese for longer periods of time, but he never went to the extremes that Valter can afford to go to now. When he was redesigning Hiša Franko, the wine and the cheese cellars dug under the gardens became the focal points, and every other place in the renovated house was built around it.

At that time Valter, a respected sommelier, was making good money with his workshops in Italy, so he was able to buy larger quantities of cheese from the local shepherds – part of it was used in the restaurant fresh, part of it he kept in the cellar and left there for a year, or two, or three. Simultaneously, Joško Sirk across the border was himself working on a cheese story at La Subida, ageing it in hay and grape skins. Inspired by the *formaggio di fossa*, cave-aged cheese from the Italian region of Emilia-Romagna, he came up with the idea that he and Valter could start doing the same thing with the local cheese from Kobarid. So now, every year, they drive south to the underground pits of Sogliano al Rubicone with a four-month aged Slovenian cheese and leave it there for another four months.

Standing still, even if it's in a dynamic place like Hiša Franko, doesn't seem to be an option for someone like Valter. He's always full of ideas, ideas that aren't necessarily always directly linked to the growth of Hiša Franko, but always to the growth of local produce and local environment. He loves fine dining, but first and foremost, he's someone who understands that people in these parts aren't really Hiša Franko's customers. And that's how the idea of creating something more accessible to the general public came about. The idea of a small taverna with good, hearty, local food, the kind his mother used to make at the old Hiša Franko, wasn't something new – he'd toyed with it already a decade ago, but back then, it turned out to be financially unfeasible. Years later, the stars aligned, and in 2017 Valter partnered with two local caterers and became involved in a local craft brewery, now called Feo, and a pub in the centre of Kobarid called Hiša Polonka. He decided to expand it, adding a selection of natural wine to Feo beer on tap and a menu based on the food they used to serve at the old

Hiša Franko. If some people close to Valter think Polonka is a place where he can be more himself than at Hiša Franko, he denies it assertively. 'Absolutely not. Nothing can replace Hiša Franko, nothing. But at the moment, I do have to be constantly present at Polonka to establish a certain standard and service that we set out to have.' He leaves me at a table in the corner, with a glass of sparkling wine from the nearby Vipava Valley, as he tends to customers. It's midday and Polonka is packed with locals, tourists, hikers and cyclists. Valter emerges from the kitchen with trays of Franko's signature roast beef that's now featured prominently on Polonka's menu. He carries them to the main dining room, occupied by elderly revellers who came to celebrate Valter's uncle's 70th birthday. This was the old Hiša Franko clientele with whom, back in the days, Valter always needed to pull back on his wine preferences and offer them something more conventional. 'They would kill me if I had served them anything cloudy,' laughs Valter, knowing full well it takes a special kind of skill to change the mindset – and the palate – of an entire generation of drinkers; to read a guest and subtly introduce them to wines they might be extremely sceptical of.

Alen Audič, head sommelier of Hiša Franko, with whom Valter has worked for the past few years, concurs. 'As a mentor, Valter has always stood by me and taught me that the most important thing in this line of work is to sense what the guest wants, and never ever impose on him your own taste or the taste of Hiša Franko. You can, however, suggest he maybe try a sip of wine that might not sit well with him on the nose, with the accompanying dish. Seventy percent of them will understand that, thirty percent won't, but we're here to please them, not to please me or Valter,' explains the young sommelier. Asked if Valter was the one who sparked his enthusiasm for organic and biodynamic wine, Alen shakes his head. 'He didn't enthuse me – he showed me the difference between natural wine and 'made' wine. The latter, you can't really believe in them, you can't feel them, they're not alive.' He does, however, believe that first and foremost comes the dish – the wine only complements it and lifts it up. 'It's like chemistry between a girl and a guy – if they're attracted to each other, they will kiss and it will be very pleasing. And that's exactly the feeling you must get when you pair the wine with food,' explains Alen, who obviously inherited Valter's penchant for colourful analogies.

It's late afternoon and Valter has disappeared somewhere again, nowhere to be found. His phone is ringing outside the storage room, next to his motorcycle. 'He'll show up eventually, he always does,' shrugs Alen just as Valter emerges from the house, with a wheel of cheese in one hand and a bottle of wine in the other.

Joško

Kaja Sajovic

The Role Model

'Look at that. I just wanted a vinegar cellar. But because of my damn megalomaniacal inclinations, instead of making a small acidic coop, I've built myself a sour cathedral that I'm still paying off,' jokes Joško Sirk, showing off the huge, impressive temple, dedicated to his acidic passion. Sirk is a legend in these parts. He's respected and admired by Slovenians and Italians alike, not just for what he created with La Subida, but also for his quick wit, sharp tongue and strong will. He can be the funniest, most endearing host, but cross him and you will learn first-hand why Slovenians living on the Italian side of the border have been able to survive and keep their identity so strong all these years. 'He's my ideal man, my dream man. He gets me,' said Ana as she sent me off to La Subida in Collio, a 45-minute drive from Hiša Franko. How can you argue with that?

La Subida, a sprawling estate centred around a fine dining restaurant called Al Cacciatore (Hunter's), is an institution. Al Cacciatore has one Michelin star, and technically that makes Joško (at least at the time of writing) the only Slovenian with that accolade. Sirk, with his knowledge, understanding of food and the need to bring the traditions and terroir to the forefront of haute cuisine, quickly became a mentor to many young local chefs and hospitality workers in the 1980s, among them Valter Kramar. 'He was almost like a father figure to me. He really took extra special interest and spent hours and hours at the time teaching and mentoring me,' explains Valter. And so it was only natural that Valter decided to take Ana on their first real date to Al Cacciatore. Well, things didn't exactly go according to plan – Valter left Ana waiting for two hours and when he finally arrived, Ana was pissed and furious and picked a fight with Joško 'within two seconds'. When I ask Joško if he remembers, he just grins widely. 'It's very easy to pick a fight with me, as it is with her. If she was waiting for Valter, she was nervous, that I didn't stand a chance is obvious, so all of the elements were there!' Joško starts laughing so hard that the guests at Subida's trattoria quickly notice him. He's hard to miss, really, although he has had a slight makeover since the last time I saw him – now he's sporting a silver goatee to go with his moustache. He has just returned from a biker road trip, 6,000 kilometres (3,700 miles) down Route 66, and apparently the goatee is just as mandatory for these kinds of things as a leather jacket. His wife, Loredana, the embodiment of patience, is less thrilled. 'She told me she didn't want me like this and that it was time I sober up,' laughs Joško, and immediately takes a sip of delicious local vermouth.

After lunch, he shows us around the estate's twenty holiday houses, including one where you sleep on the hay and one in the forest where you sleep amidst a sea of ferns. And, of course, his famous hunting room, the one Al Cacciatore got its name from. But Joško being Joško, he likes to reinvent things, bring them closer to modern days. Even hunting. So gone are the in-your-face trophies of deer, chamois and mouflon – Joško took a bold move and remodelled them into modern pieces of art that are easier to swallow for a younger, more squeamish generation. He was the one who, back in the 1980s, brought 'luxury stay with a concept' to this area and Subida is still a role model for many who are trying to set up something similar in the wine country of Collio/Goriška Brda. But even though some local celebrity winemakers are now driving expensive cars and live in gigantic mansions, this is still a pretty traditional environment and throughout the years he has struggled to convince the local people why places like Subida help to boost the entire region. And still, to this day, when he gets together with his hunting friends, he sends them dining any place other than Al Cacciatore, 'because they will be disappointed and my family embarrassed'.

It's a very similar situation to what Ana is often dealing with at Hiša Franko. Like Al Cacciatore, it's a culinary institution – but it's not exactly a local favourite. Trout sashimi is no match to plum dumplings. 'We still get a lot of older customers coming in, but simply because they are in love with my wife. And she makes them something simple, hearty. The day Loredana stops working in the dining room it's the day these customers stop coming in,' explains Joško. 'But so far, she's still very much involved. Too involved. She's from a very Catholic family where their whole life is considered to be one gigantic penance. And she is doing the repentance. I am too, but I still treat myself to a spoonful of Nutella!'

Joško gets how specific these parts and people are, and he understands Ana's battle to push through

and stick to her guns in an environment that is not necessarily always the most supportive or receptive. But he quickly shuts down all insinuations of the potential frustrations of being someone who stands out in an environment like that. 'Let's not be modest – that is exactly why we tried, worked and fought so hard. To stand out.' Even though they had a rough start, Joško says he immediately saw Ana had a 'fox-like' mentality; natural intelligence, the need to be at the forefront, and that she's destined to become something more, but he also knew Valter who, as he puts it, 'was no less intelligent – or no less of a saint. And that's why he was able to present himself to her in a way that she fell for. And at that moment, for her, it was really a very simple decision. Because the itch was just too strong,' winks Joško. When I ask him if he thought back then that they made a good couple or a potential disaster – or a little bit of both, he laughs again: 'A *lot* bit of both! Because if a couple is that great, it often risks a lot. The mediocrity is the one that lasts in the long term.'

And while Joško's relationship with Valter was always warm and full of mutual respect, his relationship with Ana, to his own surprise, developed to a full-blown friendship, one full of admiration and lately, as he puts it, tenderness. 'Before, I saw her as a colleague. Now I see her as a woman,' he smiles.

He also sympathizes with her and the struggle to combine a meteor-like career, family and relationships. 'I'm very much familiar with these internal battles, being split between the role of a protagonist and all the personal stuff going on around you. And on one hand, these battles make you stronger, they build character; on the other, they don't give you that easy-going demeanour that when someone stings you, you laugh it off, instead of being so tense that when the bee stings, you go and knock down the hive,' he says and references Ana's hot temper and feistiness that sometimes feels like a hurricane for those around her. 'I would like to help her carry that burden, I would like to give her the energy like in *Avatar* where they were sharing energy with their tails, but I can't. Because she chose to carry that burden and it's also the engine of her success.' When I ask him if he can identify with the whirlwind Ana's life has become lately, he shakes his head. 'No, I've never had that kind of success, because I've never dared to dream so big. Ana is living proof that the higher you fly, the more challenging is the flight.' That said, he's absolutely certain there's no risk of her crashing down. 'No. She's not a crazy risk taker. She's very capable and so incredibly sure of what she's doing that she'll always have ideas, the energy and the courage to go on.' Not one to spoil the party, but I can't help but ask him what I've been asking myself for the past year: once you reach the top, once

you're crowned best female chef, what's left? How do you deal with the limelight turning from you to someone else? 'Yeah, that's hard. Only a very strong character can play this game, because you will get the bill afterwards. And you have to have character for that bill as well. Or,' he pauses, 'she can shoot even higher – best chef.' He also believes that he and Ana are not enough to change anything in the long-term. The key, he says, is to work on the development of the region. 'Once you're gone, what's left behind you? The territory. Most of the first-generation winemakers from Collio are gone, but what's left? Collio. That's why every successful individual should dedicate part of his time and resources to development of the territory. Not because of some poor lazy schmuck next door, but because it pays off for him in the end. It pays off for his children.'

He's also quite blunt about the need to pass the torch on to the younger generation and he really admires Valter's father, who back in the day decided to step aside and pass Hiša Franko to Valter and Ana. 'Euthanasia in this sense is necessary. The problem is only who decides when to pull the plug,' he laughs and offers me a piece of *formaggio di fossa*. The next morning, a text message wakes me up. 'Food for thought: Ana's power doesn't lie in her hands, but in her head. That's why, *ce la fara sempre* (she'll always make it)! Good luck, Joško.'

Wild Plants and Joško Sirk's Vinegar p. 34 → p. 212

Bread

Ana Roš

The Magic World of Bread

Did you know that bread is a living thing? Just like mankind, bread needs the rain just as much as it needs the sun. I look to the sky every time I think about it.

In the Bible's book of John, Jesus declares, 'I am the bread of life; whoever comes to me shall not hunger, and whoever believes in me shell never thirst'. Bread is both literally and metaphorically a human staple. Along with water, it is always the first thing on the table. I love the idea of huge loaves being shared among family or friends; indeed, 'breaking bread' means coming together, both at a meal and in society. Making bread requires a lot of time and a lot of attention.

My mother never had the time and patience to bake. Her food was delicious and creative, but always prepared at the last minute. So my first memories of homemade bread are from the hot summers spent in our little stone house in Istria, a peninsula in the Adriatic Sea shared by Croatia, Slovenia and Italy, and not from home. Our neighbour there was an elderly woman who seemed to be the mother of most of the men in the village. I used to call her Nona Efa, even though this wasn't really her name. Every Sunday, the intense aroma of freshly baked bread woke me up, and, half asleep, I would walk downstairs and knock on her door. In my little pyjamas, I would wrap myself around her legs until she cut me a large slice from the loaf. I still miss her, and the bread. Many years later, when I started dating Valter, his mother Jožica baked bread for the restaurant, and the nostalgia came flooding back. Her bread was different; likely more sophisticated. She baked every day, kneading it by hand. She used to say that working the dough with your hands gives the bread energy, love and life. When I took over the kitchen, I wanted to keep this tradition. I developed three types – rye, buckwheat and corn – and our guests loved it so much that they were even asking to take it home with them. We hired a young guy called Đuro to help us out with it; he had a lot of problems in his home life, and I sometimes wondered whether the bread was so good because of his strong hands, or because he worked the dough harder than most to get rid of his anger, bitterness and disappointments.

One day the police called – Đuro had been involved in a terrible car accident. He had been drinking throughout the night, celebrating the birth of his first child. Early in the morning, still drunk, he was driving to the hospital to see the baby and was involved in a collision. A woman died in that crash and Đuro never returned to the restaurant. As a result of that tragedy, I had to go back to the drawing board with this particular chapter of the book.

Made with fresh beer yeast and loads of butter and cream, those breads were like a shortcut to (bread) heaven. But really, I wanted bread with a story – bread rooted in tradition. I wanted to understand how people in remote mountain villages would make it hundreds of years ago, when relatively expensive items weren't on hand to help. I decided to ferment apple peels – this being the only fruit available in the valley in winter time – with flour and spring water. When I baked my first loaf a few months later, it was full of mistakes: hard, chewy and too sour. My children begged me to just give them 'normal' bread. I brought a loaf to my mother-in-law. She did not discuss the quality, she simply asked me how I made it. She smiled. Without ever asking, I knew I had begun my journey to bring her grandmother's bread back to life. After four years of hard work and dedication, and with the love of Francesca, an Italian woman who takes care of the bread – four years of looking to the sky – we have one of the most incredible breads I've ever tasted. It is now rooted deep in strong traditions, but with the eye to the future.

Francesca was the first person in the house who really felt the sourdough. She was not a professional (this came two years later with Nataša Djuric), but she was passionate about what sourdough bread really needs. This is why her bread has been really affected by sun and rain. To control all the temperature changes, humidity variations and pollen in the air in the countryside, you even need more than passion. Nataša is now one of the most important people in modern baking in Europe, and even she fails sometimes.

Bread p. 41 → p. 212
Nataša Djuric and Her Spelt Bread,
Cultured Butter p. 40 → p. 212

Hotel Moo

Ana Roš

Svit

It is June 14, 2018: Svit's last day at primary school. Svit is my son, and he has just turned 15, and even in my wildest dreams, I could not imagine all he has grown to be. Parents, relatives, teachers and even the local mayor are silently sitting in the community hall in the centre of Kobarid, watching our boys and girls saying goodbye to their childhood.

Svit is given an award as best in class for his athletic achievements – he has just broken two school records in running, and he was the football player of the year. He also receives prizes in literature, mathematics, Italian and English language. As I watch him on the stage, I realize he looks so much like me at that age; as he walks up, he is smiling, but looks so humble at the same time. While granting him all those prizes, in front of all of us, the head teacher asks him what he wants to do in his life. I am surprised by the question, especially because I have never dared to ask him the same myself. I always thought he was too young to know the answer.

I can sense the intenseness of his embarrassment, and for a moment the room becomes painfully silent in anticipation of his answer. I have a strong feeling he is searching for my eye contact, for my approval. 'I want to be a farmer,' he finally says. At first the silence becomes even more intense but then it releases into laughter that echoes across the room, followed by loud cheering. I search my soul for disappointment, but I cannot find it.

Ana

When I was Svit's age, school was invisibly divided into two very separate groups: children of farmers, and children of non-farmers. I can still remember the intense aroma of a stable, a warm, almost umami smell that clung to the hair and clothes of my schoolmates – boys and girls from farming families who probably had a much earlier start than me, milking their cows and helping to tend to the animals far before catching the bus to school. Being a farmer at that time did not have the same status as being a farmer today; sadly, it wasn't celebrated as something to be proud of. Thankfully, times have changed.

Anka

I used to say I never had a hero. But today, I do, and it is Anka. You would guess at Anka being 40 by the way she looks, even 30 by her energy and charisma, but in reality she is probably closer to 60. She wakes up every day at 5 a.m., covers her curly, reddish hair with a headscarf, puts on her rubber boots and spends her first waking moments milking her cows. She knows every single one of them by name and age; she knows all about their characters. An hour later, she leaves the house, often in Chanel-style suits and bright-red high heels. Her makeup is perfect, and not one hair is out of place. Half an hour later, she is sitting in her office, holding meetings, making big decisions and managing a company of hundreds of employees. Somewhat of a '*femme fatale*', a strong woman, a manager, a proud farmer, a great mother and a brand new grandmother. Anka is a true woman of the Soča Valley. Anka and her extended family were the first to introduce me to the luxury of Hotel Moo. And yes, Hotel Moo really exists. It is a tiny collection of stone houses overlooking the stunning Tolminka Valley. There is always a wooden barn covered with a sheet metal roof, there is a huge stone sink full of cold water, and there are lush green pastures. Did you ever read the story about Heidi?

Sometimes when I am in a dreamy mood, I can still bring back the picture of my younger self trying to fall asleep on a stinging hay bed, covered with clean white sheets and smelling of the intensely deep aroma of dry plants; listening to my parents quietly talking to shepherds in the pitch-black kitchen by the fire, frying potatoes and cheese recuts in pork fat, roasting them into a delicious soft-crunchy *frika*. Early in the morning while my father was still hunting, we would pick varieties of mushrooms and cook them with fresh eggs for breakfast. My mother once cooked bull's balls for breakfast and tried to convince me I was eating fried parasol mushrooms. I try the same trick with my children.

Shepherds

The shepherds always looked forward to seeing the two little doctor's girls, Maja and Ana. They often had special gifts for us; old Čufer used to say that his chickens had to prepare to go without food when the two of us arrived to the mountain; offcuts of *obribini*, a cheese with an incredible milky, salty flavour, were usually saved for them, but not when we were around. I used to call it dairy chewing gum.

The shepherds would secretly spoil me also with freshly made, still-warm cottage cheese that we were allowed to eat with our hands from huge wooden barrels. We needed first to climb steep steps to reach the top, and we often failed (and almost fell in) to reach the cottage cheese because the barrel was new and there were just a few layers of cottage cheese inside, right at the bottom. Ah, fermented cottage cheese – to me, it's the spice of our mountains. Our valleys are very low, usually not more then 250 metres (820 feet) above sea level, and the mountains where the pastures and meadows lie are more than 1,400 metres (4,500 feet) high. The paths to reach them are steep and dangerous, and this is why in the summer months, when the cows are at the highest pastures, the shepherds are not able to make the journey to the valley very often. Whey cheese is one of the most important products in the industry; 1,000 litres (220 gallons) of milk only makes 20 rounds of cheese, and a lot of primary whey is created, with which we make cottage cheese. In turn, this meant a lot of cottage cheese, and people needed to find a way to preserve it because of its short shelf life, especially in areas where refrigeration was challenging. The only way to store the product was fermentation.

Farmers used big wooden barrels with holes in the bottom in which they would put freshly made cottage cheese with a layer of salt on top. Additional layers of cottage cheese then pressed the water out of the cheese below, creating ideal conditions for safe lactic fermentation. Our cellar at home was always full of it. You can see the ageing by its change in colour from shiny white to almost yellow, but really, it's the aroma that defines it. The older, the stronger; it is a lot more intense than any French or Swiss cheeses I have ever eaten. Traditionally, we would serve it simply with lightly scrubbed, boiled new potatoes; my children also love it over their tomato pasta.

In 2005, Valter opened his cheese cellar – he had a dream of creating the greatest cheese in the world. Since then, he's learned that the freshest Tolminc cheese isn't necessarily the best; it needs three to five years at the right temperature and humidity to get there. This cheese is not only the most important part of our local diet; it is like a gift from the people of the Soča Valley.

Srečno (Good luck)!

Čompa s Skuto → p. 213

Kaja Sajovic

Cattle

It's early morning, mid-May – so early that you only catch the hints of the rising sun and its bright hues behind the towering mountains when we meet up at Anka's farm stay in the village of Zatolmin, a twenty-minute drive from Hiša Franko. Anka is a powerhouse of a woman – a cattle farmer as well as the CEO of Dairy Planika, one of the most successful Slovenian companies with the highest buying price of milk in Europe. Anka runs the business with the utmost respect for the farmers from whom she buys the milk. It comes as no surprise, as she herself is one of them. And she knows that if she falters – if the dairy falters – dozens and dozens of families will feel it first-hand.

The cows are getting anxious back at Zatolmin, ready to head up to the alpine grazing pastures. Anka hands us wooden sticks to nudge the less enthusiastic ones, and off we go. The majority of the cows are *Cikas*. The only autochthonous Slovenian cow breed, they have brownish fur with white patches, are sturdy and adaptable to traditional ways of cow breeding methods, thus suitable for ecologically minded farming. They are very active and regularly change pastures and altitudes. Being dairy cattle, it's also one of the reasons why people in this region have never consumed much beef – the meat of dairy cows is tougher, chewier, less fatty and thus less suitable for consumption than breeds raised specifically for meat produce. Cikas are known for their longevity – a modern dairy cow lives up to six years, on average, but a Cika's life expectancy is a whooping 15 years. Even though the light is still dim in the valley, some of the villagers get up to see the shepherds off on their annual transhumance. In the second half of May, livestock is moved from the valley to higher grazing ground where it remains until end of June. Then, it's moved even higher, where the grass hasn't been grazed yet. It remains there until September when it's moved back to the middle ground where it eats until no grass is left, roughly October, and the circle is closed. As Ana and I hike higher and higher, the air gets fresher, filled with just the slightest scents of mountain dew, elderberry flowers and forget-me-nots. Thick, marshmallowy clouds of morning mist cover the valley floor, the idyll only interrupted by the strong smell of manure

that's being sprayed heavily on the path by the cows in front of us. In this pristine environment, far away from the busy sea-bound roads and the influx of tourists in the valley, the 3,000-year-old traditions that date back to the times of Celts still live – and now thrive, with no small thanks to Ana and Valter, who buy the shepherds' cheese in bulk and age it in Valter's cellar at Hiša Franko or in the underground pits in Italy's Emilia-Romagna region. Formaggio di fossa, they call it. Pit cheese. The first stop on our pilgrimage comes after about two hours of strenuous walking, when we reach a pasture with an old stone cabin, where those with more cooperative herds are already making celebratory toasts with strong local liquor. 'Mountain life is hard, you have to start the day with a shot of schnapps,' proclaims Anka as she pours one for Ana. They toast, their faces flushed and sweaty, as they take in the glorious, warmly lit scenery. Then they pour another glass.

One could easily forget how much blood was spilled here if it wasn't for the ubiquitous reminders of the war, now serving random purposes such as the grenade shell used as a vase on the window sill, or a rusty gun barrel that Anka uses to fan the fire in the cabin's old 'black kitchen'. This is where milk is heated in a closed stone kitchen on a natural wood fire, which becomes black and smoky. The outside wall is adorned with a stone plate of an unknown fallen soldier, moved up here from the makeshift war cemetery right below the cabin. Sandi, Anka's husband, sets up a large pot of coffee on the open fire to give Ana and me the energy for the last stretch of the journey. We hit the trail once again, with our sights firmly set on the elusive Mount Medrje, where the cows will stay for a couple of weeks before moving even further up to the ungrazed pastures of Mount Sleme, and back to Medrje again. We drag ourselves to Medrje, where the cattle are already happily grazing the pristine green alpine meadows full of fresh spring grass, herbs and mountain flowers. 'Welcome to Hotel Moo!' Sandi says joyfully as we reach a larger complex where young shepherds Aljoša, Erik and Samo are already on their third beer – eyes blurry from the combination of hard work, lack of sleep and early-morning alcohol. The point of high-mountain cattle breeding isn't just to keep the animals healthy and get the freshest,

The Cow in the Hay → p. 216

healthiest and most nutritious milk and meat possible, there's a practical reason for it. If the farmers kept the cattle in the space-limited valley, there wouldn't be enough grazing ground for it, and the stock would have to be much smaller. About forty percent smaller, to be exact. But with cows up in the mountains, the farmers can use the grass in the valley for hay they feed the animals with in the winter. The same hay Ana uses to bake potatoes in. Because of transhumance during the summer, Dairy Planika loses about 4,500 litres (1,000 gallons) of milk per day, but they make that up during the winter, which is why it's also in their interest to live in a kind of mindful synergy. The way the things are set up within the co-op is that each week or so, another family is in charge of the high-altitude shepherding, milking and cheese producing. When they bring the cheese down to the valley it gets distributed in the old, retro-looking Dairy of Zatolmin, each family getting its cut of the cheese, depending on the number of cows they own. The old lady behind the half-a-century-old typing machine weighs and meticulously documents each wheel of cheese before she writes down the receipt on a piece of paper and hands the cheese over to Valter, who comes to pick it up with his SUV then ages it in his cellar for up to four years. This socialistic system works perfectly here, an area of no less than 35 active high-mountain pastures where the population has traditionally relied heavily on the milk industry, and the diet has always been dairy based. Tolmin cheese or Tolminc, as they call it, is arguably the most famous food from this part of Slovenia, and the oldest – first written mentions of it date back to the 13th century. Back then it was used as a currency to pay taxes to feudal landlords. And it was solely due to the stubbornness and perseverance of local people that the art of making Tolmin cheese survived in the times when traditional cheesemaking in Slovenia almost became extinct because of migration to cities. They also survived a 19th century initiative from the cheese market experts in the Austro-Hungarian empire who wanted to persuade Tolminians to make Emmental cheese instead of Tolminc. But the wheels of Emmental would be way too heavy to carry them down to the valley, so they stuck with Tolminc, of which they produce 100 tons a year. Until recently, Tolmin cheese was eaten more or less fresh – a couple of months old at most – as ageing was considered too big a luxury. Valter and Joško from La Subida started experimenting with ageing the local cheese, but most still prefer to eat milder versions.

Times have changed in the valley. Nowadays, most farmers don't have enough cows to live solely off cattle breeding and selling cheese. Like Anka, they alternate between the mountain and valley life. For a few weeks

each summer, they get up in the middle of the night to milk the cows, tidy up cow dung, herd the cattle up and down the grazing pastures and produce the cheese. When they return to the valley, they work as teachers, veterinarians, foresters, even doctors. Most of them are highly educated – educated enough to realize how important keeping the old traditions alive is. 'Cheesemaking is in our genes. Without it, we would lose ourselves,' Anka tells me a few weeks later when we meet at her office on the first floor of Dairy Planika. 'The other day they asked me – what's more difficult, being a farmer or being a CEO? Being a CEO is a lot harder because you carry the burden of knowing how many farms and livelihoods depend on the success of the Dairy.' She adds, 'We are cheese makers. Born and bred. And cheese makers we will remain. And we are proud of that.' Two months later, we head up to Mount Sleme for a sleepover with the shepherds. Ana presented the whole thing as a raucous affair filled with late-night schnapps and sturdy, solitary mountain men. Long story short, the shepherds were all joined by their girlfriends and parents, and by mid-July the schnapps was all gone.

We hiked up one sunny afternoon, but midway we were caught in a heavy downpour. After three-plus hours, the sky finally cleared just enough to be able to appreciate the majestic views of the very last stretch of the trail. We arrive to the shepherds' compound, a dog bark greeting us before we could even see the big German shepherd owned by the Bončina family, from the tiny eco village of Čadrg, who were occupying the residence at the time of our visit. Aljoša emerges from the ground floor of the building where they make and keep the cheese, looking tired. His girlfriend Špela greets us with the little energy left in her from the eight days of staying up on the mountain; she offers us the last drops of blueberry brandy, and we hand over a package of coffee. Their day is slowly coming to an end, and they are finishing their last chores before sitting down for dinner in the pleasantly warm kitchen. The girls gather what's left of the food supplies – some cold cuts from their farm, tins of pâté and tuna, pickled mushrooms and slices of bread, toasted on the old oven over which they dry their wet, rain-drenched clothes. 'The weather is horrible this year, not summery at all,' says Špela. 'But then again, better that than that summer a few years back when it was so dry we couldn't shower for eight days.' The house is rainwater powered and they use the generator to charge their mobile phone batteries. The kitchen window overlooks the towering mountain of Migovec that harbours one of the largest alpine cave systems in Europe – 36 kilometres (22 miles) long with 1-kilometre (½-mile) deep chasms. They only let experienced speleologists in like Aljoša, who also works as a

Cinnamon and Apple Rosette, Sheep Cheese → p. 218

caver and is in charge of mapping out the extensive and haunting underworld, aptly named 'parallel universe'.

The term Hotel Moo is used in Slovenia to describe spending the night in a hayloft above the stables high in the mountains. The upper floor of this stable had bare walls, some patchy looking with exposed isolation panels, a dozen or so stained mattresses from Yugoslavian times set on the floor, and a natural heating system coming from the cows downstairs. At 4 a.m. our alarm clock goes off and the rain is coming down heavy again; it's pitch black, but the smell of freshly brewed coffee is already coming from the main building. It is time for the men to gather the cows and bring them to the milking room under our bedroom. It's a relatively long and monotonous process, and by the time they are finished, the sky clears up a bit and the mists rise so you can see down all the way to the wooden Holy Spirit church on the hilltop of Javorca, dedicated to the fallen Austro-Hungarian soldiers, built by their compatriots. Andraž, a student of eco farming from the capital, is spending his mandatory internship here in the mountains. He is using a steel pestle for hitting the gigantic mortar, hanging on the side of the house. Another remnant of the great war. After eating leftovers, the family heads to the ground floor to light the fire under a huge, hundred-year-old copper vessel where they still make the cheese. It's hard to find good copper craftsmen these days, so most of the families use these old vessels.

The procedure of making traditional Tolminc cheese, one of four Slovenian autochtonous cheeses, changed slightly throughout its history, but the basis remains the same. They heat the raw cow milk with rennet to just 36 degrees Celsius (96.8 degrees Fahrenheit) – basically the natural cow body temperature. The reason for not boiling the milk is very simple. It used to be impossible to get the firewood to light under the copper pots. Also, by keeping the milk at just below simmering, it keeps all of its natural properties and it coagulates into a sweet, custardy substance that Aljoša then slowly cuts with special strings and stirs for 40 minutes. Phil Collins' Against All Odds blasts from the small radio. Špela is quietly sitting outside, her second cup of coffee in one hand, and a joint to replace the schnapps they ran out of in the other. When the cheese paste is coagulated enough, Aljoša takes off his T-shirt and starts scooping it with a large gauze, holding two of its edges with his teeth. He hands the dripping package to Nastja and Špela. They squeeze the cheese mass into moulds and pat it down to drain the liquid, then they use the wrench to press it for twelve hours. From 1,000 litres (220 gallons) of milk, they can only make 20 wheels of cheese, each weighing about 3 kilograms (7 pounds). They transfer the cheese to brine water where it rests for 24 to 48 hours until it's taken out and moved to wooden racks in the ventilated cellar next door, where for weeks they regularly wipe the cheese wheels with cloth and turn them so that they dry evenly. Nothing is added, nothing is taken, it's a completely natural process that they replicate in Dairy Planika as well.

The whey, left in the copper vessels, is used to make ricotta or albumin cottage cheese, as it's called in Soča Valley, a zero percent fat byproduct of the cheesemaking process, often fermented so it keeps longer. That day, the Čadrg crew threw out the whey. 'We have a lot of ricotta left and there's simply not enough interest for it, unfortunately,' shrugs Aljoša. No matter how good, pure or cheap the product is, it's no match for the imported spreads full of additives and artificial flavouring people buy in supermarket chains across Slovenia. 'No, Marija, I'm driving!' Valter tries to turn down Aljoša's mother, who offers out generous portions of fruit schnapps when we visit her eco farm Pri Lovrču in the village of Čadrg within the boundaries of Triglav National Park, a narrow, steep and winding road leading up to it via the Devil's Bridge. 'Oh, hush, one is like none!' Marija rolls her eyes and hands Valter the glass. It's heaven here, above the gorges of the Soča river, and I sip the fiery liquid while a gaggle of geese with their goslings waddles past. Čadrg, a settlement that has always survived on cattle breeding, came close to dying out back in the 1970s when the population fell to 22 inhabitants, but thanks to the visionary that is Marija Bončina, it's now experiencing a renaissance of some sorts. There are five families living in the village, comprising 45 inhabitants, all dedicated to ecological farming and cheese producing. Čadrg is also home to Don Pierino's community for treating drug addicts, and the entire village works as some sort of police-free autonomous zone. On one side of the village there is a chicken coop next to a pigsty under the old walnut tree, on the other a small stand where they sell ricotta, fermented ricotta, Tolminc cheese, apple vinegar and eggs. One time, a massive delegation of security guards and policemen descended upon the tiny hamlet. Nobody knew what was going on. Top secret visit, they told the inhabitants. Then two helicopters landed directly on the meadow above Marija's farm, and with the first one flew in the U.S. Secret Service.

With the second helicopter, Mariel Goss, the wife of Porter J. Goss who, at the time, was serving as the director of the U.S. Central Intelligence Agency. It turned out Mrs. Goss had a keen interest in eco farming and the villagers showed her how to make natural anti-insect spray from stinging nettles and field horsetail. Mrs. Goss was so impressed she picked a bouquet of stinging nettles from Čadrg and took it back home to the United States.

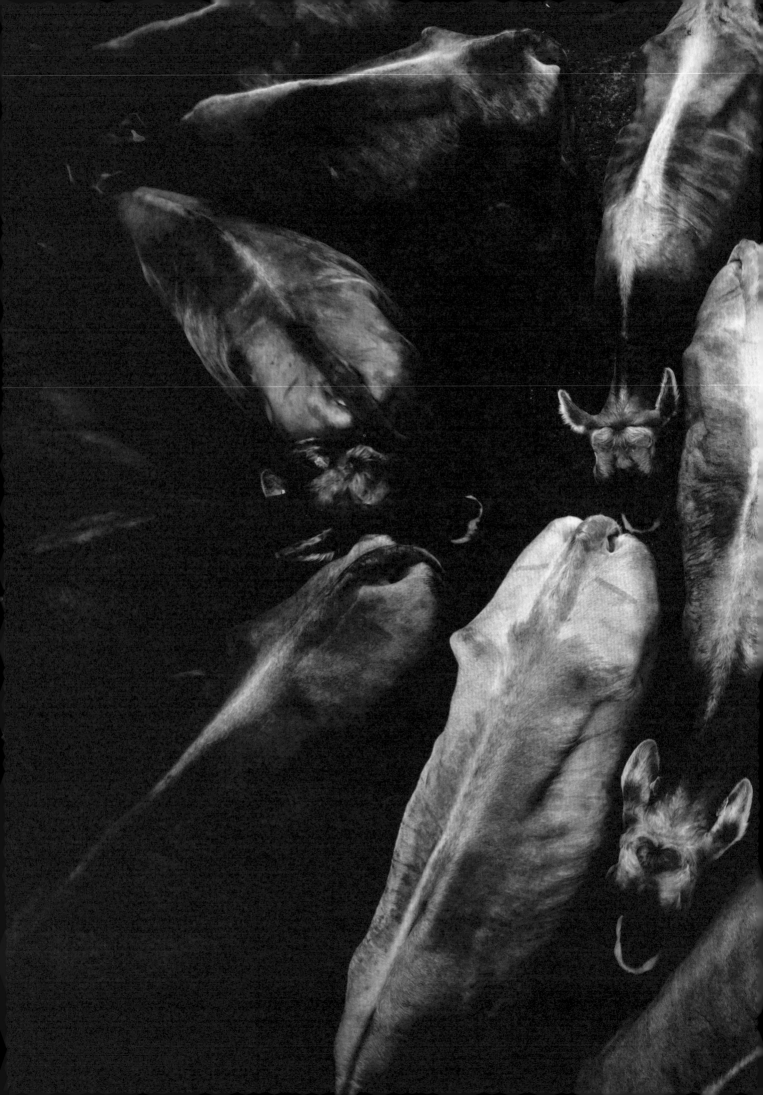

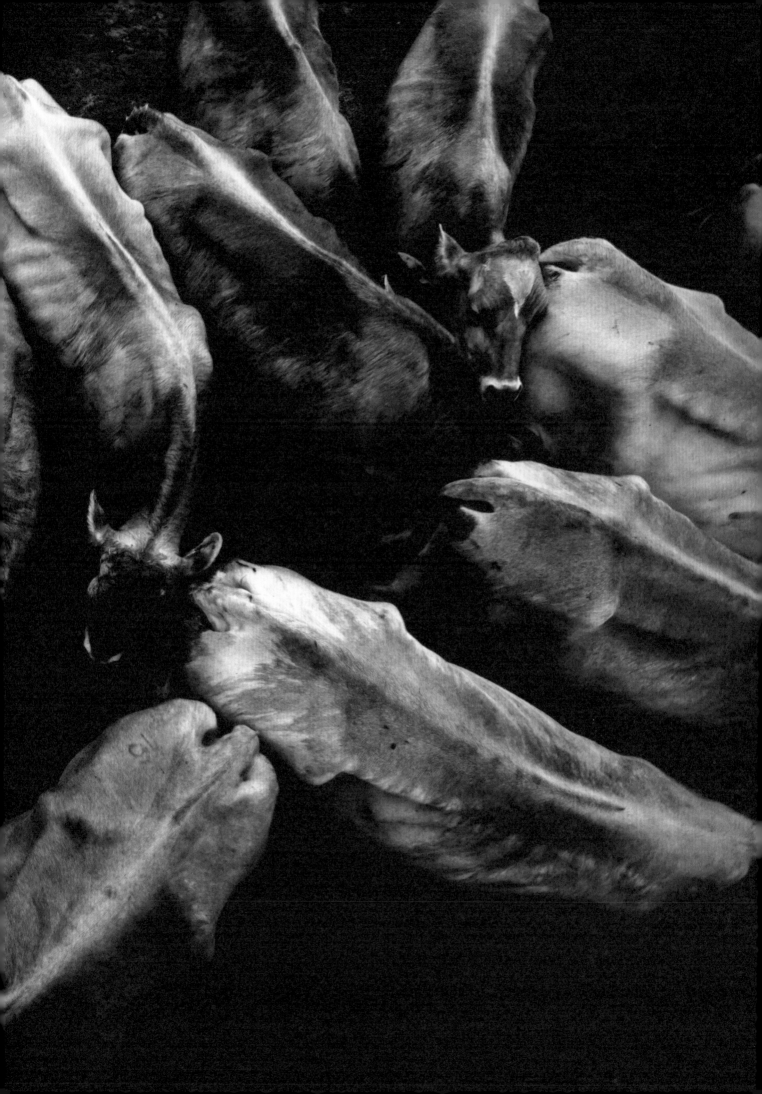

Land of Living Waters

Ana Roš

To Soča

Krasna si, bistra hči planin,
Brdka v prirodni si lepoti,
ko ti prozornih globočin
nevihte temne srd ne moti—
krasna si, hči planin!
Tvoj tek je živ in je legak
ko hod deklet s planine;
in jasna si ko gorski zrak
in glasna si, kot spev krepak
planinske je mladine—
krasna si, hči planin!
Rad gledam ti v valove bodre,
valove te zelenomodre:
temna zelen planinskih trav
in vedra višnjevost višav
lepo se v njih je zlila;
na rosah sinjega neba,
na rosah zelenih gora
lepoto to si pila—
krasna si, hči planin!
Ti meni si predraga znanka!
Ko z gorskih prišumiš dobrav,
od doma se mi zdiš poslanka,
nesoča mnog mi ljub pozdrav—
Bog sprimi te tu sred planjav!...
Kako glasno, ljubo šumljaš,
kako čvrsto, krepko skakljaš,
ko sred gora še pot imaš!
A ko prideš na ravnine,
zakaj te živa radost mine?
Kaj trudno lezeš in počasi,
zakaj so tožni tvoji glasi?
Težko se ločiš od hribov,
zibelke tvojega valovja?

You are splendid, limpid daughter of the heights,
You are graceful in your natural beauty,
When your transparent depths
Are not disturbed by the
Wrath of darksome storms,
You are splendid, limpid daughter of the heights!
Your course is lively and gentle
Like the walk of highland girls,
You are serene as the mountain air,
You are loud as the vigorous
Chant of the highland youth –
You are splendid, daughter of the heights.
I like to look into your lively waves,
These green-blue waves;
The dark green of highland grass
And the cheerful azure of the heights
Have flown together with delight;
From the dew of the blue skies,
From the dew of green mountains,
You have drunk your beauty –
You are splendid, daughter of the heights.
You are my most dear friend!
When you rustle down from mountain woodlands
You seem a messenger from home,
Carrying plenty of dear greetings –
May God welcome you amidst the plains! . . .
How dearly and loudly you murmur,
How stalwartly and soundly you bound
When you still flow through the mountains!
But when you clatter down to the flatlands,
Why do you lose your lively joy?
Why do you flow tiredly and slowly,
Why are your voices sad?
Is it hard to part from the mountain range,
The cradle of your waves?

Simon Gregorčič

To Soča

Simon Gregorčič (1844–1906) was a Slovene poet and Catholic priest. He is the first lyric poet of our Realists and the most melodic. He was born in the small mountain hamlet of Vrsno above the Soča river, and for the most part, his poems were patriotic in nature.

'To Soča' is a poem that all the school children in Slovenia must learn by heart; the same was required from their parents, and their parents before them. In the poem, written in 1879, Gregorčič praises the beauty of the Soča, the emerald Slovenian river. However, behind the description of its magical beauty (*The Chronicles of Narnia* was filmed along the river) looms something sombre: a dark premonition that some day the crystal-clear river will turn into a river of blood. Today, this is seen by many as a prophetic announcement of World War I, written more than three decades before it broke out.

Vera (Faith)

I am happy to live in one of the most stunning corners of the world. Never-ending green forests and pure waters make the Soča Valley really a magical place. Our rivers are home to a true queen of fish – the magical marble trout. Let's call her Vera. This is her story:

Vera is a wild animal, very fast, intelligent and difficult to catch. I can spot her sometimes during my long walks along the river. To live, she needs the cleanest, coldest waters, and a lot of oxygen. But Vera and her kind were almost gone. A man was convinced he was wiser than nature. He did not understand that Vera needed her own space where she could live, hide and catch. He wanted more fish in the river, but he made a bad decision. He populated the waters with rainbow trout. Vera was a better fighter, wilder and more beautiful, but the genes of her new rivermate were stronger. In the following 50 years, Vera disappeared from the Soča river. She was almost gone. But then a wise man came. He wanted Vera back. He was searching for her everywhere. One sunny day, he finally found her. She was old like the Mother Earth, and had managed to survive since the Ice Age. The greedy man could not harm her because she was hiding between two waterfalls, which, as the cleverest guards, stopped the rainbow trout to steal her home. The wise man was very clever, he did not want to rush. With patience and intelligence, he convinced her to go back.

Today the Soča river is a home to a lot of Vera(s). In the Slovenian language, Vera means faith.

I can only hope that my children will read this story to their children. And you can read this story to your closest friends, brothers and sisters. We really don't want Vera to leave us again.

Respect

We, people from the Soča Valley, deeply respect our rivers. We are almost afraid of our wild waters. Most of us do not kayak. Most of the people from the valley never fish. Most of the people from the valley never eat a trout, grayling or arctic char. For us, the rivers are sort of magical, mythological places.

Kaja Sajovic

The Trout Kingdom

If there's one thing that immediately strikes visitors to the Kobarid region, it's the Soča river. Before they notice the towering mountains, before they smell the pure alpine air, before they are impressed by Hiša Franko's cuisine, they fall in love with the Soča. How could they not? This wild river that changes colour with the seasons, from milky blue, still hazy from the melting snow, to striking summery turquoise, is almost surreal. It's the combination of river microorganisms and limestone river basin that paint Soča in the most unique colour. No wonder the international fishermen who descend upon the area in large numbers are blissfully happy just to throw their hooks amidst such jaw-dropping scenery – catching fish is just the icing on the cake.

The best way to get to know the river is on a raft. The Soča Valley in general is an adrenalin junkie's heaven, and descending down the crystal blue rapids is a must for every visitor. Kobarid's go-to-guy for everything sports related is Blaž, who owns a small but busy bike, raft and kayak shop in the centre of the town with a strategic position that overlooks not one, but four bars.

The rafting season here starts early, in March, and can last until early November, depending on the year. In peak season – mainly August – they can get so many tourists in a day that Blaž's crew can barely keep up. They are on the water 24/7, tanned like vetted seamen, with the flair and cool of surfers. We stop at a roadside shack where they hand each one of us a wet-suit, a life jacket, a helmet and a paddle. A local river guide called Kevin takes us to our boat and quickly explains the basics. 'I'll count to three. On two, you push the boat into the river. On three, you jump in.' Kevin continues handing out instructions: 'If you fall in, swim with your legs up, so you don't get caught in the fallen tree trunks. Always keep your hand on the handle of the paddle so you don't hit someone with it. You wouldn't believe how many broken teeth I've seen.'

Our first stop is a calm part of the river where you can go for a swim. It's mid-July, which is a perfect time for a jump in the Adriatic Sea – less perfect is the 12 degrees Celsius (54 degrees Fahrenheit) Soča river. We wade to the riverbank where a small stream trickles down to the Soča, where we refresh ourselves with some spring water; it is so clear that you can drink from the same water you swim in. We row and glide towards the next stop – a large boulder in the middle of the river where the crew turns our raft sideways so it works like a waterslide. The first part of the river was the easiest. The second part is more technical, with a lot of rowing back and forth, with the water turning wilder and the boulders seeming dangerously close to the sides of the raft.

For a different perspective on the river I headed over the old stone bridge, built under Napoleon, to the Tolmin gorges on the southern end of Triglav National Park. Here, the Soča carved gorgeous natural formations in the limestone, creating deep, twisted hideaways in moss-covered rock and bluffs. One of the many caves through which the waters of the Soča glacier flowed is called Dante's – it is almost a kilometre and a half (one mile) long and 45 metres (150 feet) deep. It is said that at the beginning of the 14th century, Dante Alighieri visited the cave and it inspired his 'Hell' chapter of the *Divine Comedy*. It is perhaps a fine line between heaven and hell, especially in untamed nature, but the Tolmin gorges definitely look more heavenly than anything else. The vegetation is lush, almost tropical, from all the precipitation. The Devil's Bridge leading to the remote village of Čadrg offers a head-spinning view over the river, filled with rainbow trout and the elusive marble trout that after World War II came very close to extinction. The man co-credited with the salvation and preservation of marble trout is Dušan Jesenšek, long-time member of the Tolmin fishing community. He knows the story of the marble trout inside out, from the early days when it used to be the only kind of trout in Soča, to near-extinction, to becoming an integral part of the Hiša Franko menu.

The destruction of the marble trout began with the opening of the quicksilver mine in Idrija in the 19th century. The Austrians built dams and blast furnaces on the river and the water wave destroyed the fish, so they started introducing rainbow trout to Soča and its tributaries. During World War I, hungry soldiers were pillaging rivers with hand grenades, and after the war, the Italians were running commercial fishing in the valley, adding even more rainbow trout. The practice continued after World War II, and it wasn't until the late 1960s that they realized marble trout were rapidly disappearing.

Jerusalem Artichoke Flower → p. 220
Marble Trout Roe, Rosa di Gorizia, Yeast p. 70 → p. 219
Trout Skin p. 71 → p. 218

Unable to rely on the state, the fishing association of Tolmin set out its own project of saving the marble trout in the late 1980s, when they discovered a larger, naturally preserved colony of them in the small, difficult to access river of Zadlaščica in the Tolmin gorges area. Experts from the French institute Tour du Valat became intrigued and joined the project, which turned out to be a huge success. With genetic testing, they were able to discover seven preserved populations of pure, uncrossed marble trout that became the basis for the creation of new populations; some were also set aside for eco fish farming.

Dušan introduced the marble trout to Ana in 2010, and she immediately came on board with the idea of adding this unique fish to her menu. The fish grows extremely slowly, so the meat is leaner, therefore more suitable for carpaccio, sashimi and cold smoking than heat treatment, and also about ten times more expensive than the rainbow trout. It takes a skilled chef to get that, so the association only works with a handful of exclusive restaurants, such as Hiša Franko and La Subida. It's the same story with another endangered indigenous Soča fish, grayling. Ana also uses the marble trout for its roe, so in winter, during the spawning period, it is harvested from the live fish, as is also done for reproduction purposes. There was a New Year's Eve menu in Hiša Franko with a glorious starter – a shimmering piece of raw marble trout with chestnuts, tangerines and salty trout roe on top. It was like a splash of the Soča river.

Klemen and Gašper, Dušan's sons, organize fly-fishing trips in local rivers and streams. Even though the locals were never really fishermen and a lot of them considered trout to be a lesser product, fishing has always been an important source of income for the valley; it began as commercial, but later switched to sports. The Soča river is now a global fishing destination and 95 percent of the fishing is done by the catch-and-release method, since the smart phone era enables fishermen to document their prize in the matter of seconds and return the fish to the river. The impact on the environment is minimal, and the fishermen are known to be extremely good guests – they appreciate the nature, they are big spenders, they are respectful and they are not greedy.

For them, one caught fish is often enough to have their whole week complete. 'Fishing is like a fine dining experience, like a tasting menu at Hiša Franko – you don't need to be stuffed full, it's all about the experience of different flavours and being pleasantly sated at the end of the meal,' says Dušan as an analogy of fishing. '*Bon appétit*,' quips Gašper as he teases a big fat rainbow trout with his fly. You can tell which fish are wild and which are 'implants', or 'dumplings', they call them. They are fatter, slower, and they don't put up much of a fight in comparison to leaner, faster wild trout, with which you can battle for up until fifteen minutes. 'I got one!' yells Klemen as he pulls out a slippery, shimmering fish and flips it into a rubbery net where it waits, sunk underwater, to be photographed and released back into the wilderness.

Fishing season runs from April to the end of October. Long gone are the days when the fishing associations were rapidly getting older; it is now extremely popular among the younger population, and the gender gap is closing, too. 'We've been seeing more and more women,' notices Dušan. 'To be honest, patience and skilfulness are more their domain,' he opines. We wade past another fisherman, giving us a slight nod of appreciation for letting him have a large enough area all for himself. 'This place is heaven for foreign fishermen,' explains Klemen. 'First and foremost, there's the nature. Second, is the price – for a day of fly-fishing, you pay 90 Euros (£80/$100) – in Iceland it's 1,000 Euros (£890/$1,130).' Another factor is the visibility and clarity of the water – Nordic rivers are clean, but because of the granite beds, the fish are practically invisible. 'Then, of course, it's the accessibility. In New Zealand or the Russian Kola peninsula, you have to be flown in with a helicopter and hike to the river for hours. Here, you can be on the river in the morning and half an hour later, you can be sitting eating lunch in the 38th best restaurant in the world!' smiles Gašper.

La Regina p. 74 → p. 220   Trout Belly and Rosa di Gorizia → p. 219
Arctic Char p. 76 → p. 220   Baby Trout p. 77 → p. 221

Garden & Forest Witches

Ana Roš

Loredana,
the Garden Queen
in Pink

It was a rainy cold September morning and the whole film troupe of French-German TV production Arte was dressed warmly, complete with mountaineering equipment, ready to start shooting my foraging expedition with Loredana. When she showed up, I could not hide my surprise. She was wearing a pink rock 'n' roll jacket, tight jeans and white high heeled boots from the 1960s. Her platinum blonde curls and blue eyes made her look as though she was in an ABBA biopic. Loredana has a vast knowledge of wild plants, and she used to keep a huge garden close to 1,000 metres (3,280 feet) above sea level. When I walk with her through her garden or in nature, she always surprises me with her incredible sensibility; she even finds plants which can make you high (prohibited, of course) or ones that purport to cure every possible disease. Loredana is our tea blender – good morning tea, spring tea, energetic tea, regeneration tea, digestion tea, summer tea, evening tea, good night tea – they all have more than fifteen different varieties of plants, a mix of foraged plants and those from her garden.

The teas are always colourful, and always fresh.

Joži is a
True Housewife
of Hiša Franko

Ah, my mother-in-law. She is a woman of the mountain, very religious and very nature oriented. She grew up hand-in-hand with the change of seasons, and her childhood meals were whatever was foraged or collected in the garden on that day. Jevšček, her home village, is a tiny group of houses on the Italian border, overlooking the lowlands of Friuli, and three hours walking distance to the valley. The only way the family could survive was to produce their own food. She was one of six children, and it was very much a matriarchal family. Her mother and her sister took care of the entire family, sometimes making huge efforts to feed everyone. Their garden was of huge importance. When Franko and Joži bought Hiša Franko, they built a huge garden at the back of the house. It was not a kitchen garden, but more for their personal use. They would never buy any vegetables for their family meals. When the season of the cucumber was gone, the cucumber disappeared from their daily menu. All the upper gardens of Hiša Franko are still taken care by Franko and Joži. At this time they are in their late 70s, and they still spend every minute of their day taking care of the plants, the compost and the little greenhouse. The lower gardens, right behind the house, were added in 2005 when our wine and cheese cellars were built. They are taken care of by the kitchen team.

American guests sometimes ask us why we do not write on our menus that we only cook biodynamic and organic vegetables. It is difficult for them to understand that respecting the rules of the nature is the only way of gardening we really know. Almost every Slovenian has a garden. Even in Ljubljana, the capital, in the middle of the most densely populated area, you can find green spaces with little wooden houses where people spend their time off taking care of their vegetables. In the mountain area, the gardens are built in terraces. A scenic train ride through Baška Grapa is the best showcase of our gardens; potatoes, beans and cabbages seem to touch the sky.

My Beautiful
Nona Olga

My mother had a very aristocratic mother. She was of Austro-Hungarian blood: a tiny bit Austrian, a bit Italian, a bit Dalmatian. She was one of the few true ladies I have ever met; very beautiful, and always perfectly dressed up. Her life had a lot of repetitive routines, and a lot of those were in regard to her gardens. She lived in a stunning Italian villa on the coast between Koper and Izola, overlooking the whole gulf of Trieste. Her dream house was surrounded by gardens; a berry garden, an apricot garden, a cherry garden, a persimmon garden, a potato garden, a vegetable garden and a huge compost. As a child, I always spent one month of my summer holidays in that magical house. I will admit that I was not always at my happiest with my grandmother and her strict rules of everyday life – they were often too much for my vulnerable soul. When it got dark, I would sit for hours on a little stone balcony counting the lighthouses in the bay of Trieste, looking towards the Julian Alps. When the sky was clear, the snowy peaks would shine so brightly, and I almost felt like I could touch them. In those moments, I missed home so much.

There was always a lot to do in the gardens; before my breakfast of a cheese and ham sandwich with black tea, I had to clean the weeds from the vegetable garden. After the last afternoon swim, I was charged with picking the Colorado beetles from the leaves of the potato plants. Every dinner was served with a huge bowl of bitter summer chicory and steamed vegetables. All the food she prepared was very healthy and freshly picked.

Nona Olga also made a lot of delicious marmalades and jams. She would put a pile of pillows under the fragrant medlar tree to catch the fruit, which in July was full of white-yellow flowers. My sister and I were given the task of slowly mixing the marmalades until cold; it was of course strictly forbidden to lick the wooden spoon or put our fingers into the delicious, sticky jam. After a month at my grandmother's house, we usually weighed a few more kilos, and her famous preserve cellar was reduced to empty sour cherry and apricot jam jars.

Prekomorske Brigade, Tolmin

When I was seven, my family moved to a very modern apartment in a residential area of Tolmin. There were four floors, no elevators, one kindergarten and one hairdresser. It was a very interesting community of people; farmers that moved to the town hoping for a better future, intellectuals and dreamers. And there were gardens. Our children's community was organized into garden 'gangs'. We mostly stole strawberries, redcurrants and plenty of green peas. Every garden even had its own personalized scarecrows. During our night expeditions, it was hard to distinguish them from the angry owners of the gardens. Scarecrows are of course meant to frighten away the birds, but in the gardens of Prekomorske Brigade, they were mostly making a joyful gang of children run fast and far with their pockets full of smashed stolen berries.

The Bees

It is comforting to know that there are still so many things to discover. The bees and their colourful wooden houses are all around us. Our traditional pastry is based on honey, which was the only sweet thing I was allowed to eat as a child. When Valter's mother Jožica offers my children a 'lollipop', they know exactly it is – a spoon of honey. Propolis in our culture is considered a medicine for every imaginable disease, and yet I know nothing about the bees and their life. Writing a book was a good reminder of this gap in my knowledge.

Chickweed Paradise → p. 222
Walnut, 21 Day-Aged Kefir, Pollen and Honey p. 83 → p. 225
Summer Pumpkin and Elderberries p. 84 → p. 222

Kaja Sajovic

What Exactly is (Garden) Perfection

'Oh, I see you got some help with weeding,' remarked Valter's father Franko as he stepped from his apartment on the first floor of Hiša Franko to check on Nac's progress with the small, chaotic garden behind the restaurant. 'What help? She's no help whatsoever, she just sits there,' said Nac, glancing towards me with just a slight grin. I don't know, maybe it's my outfit, which is better suited for cocktail hour at Hiša Franko than getting dirty in the garden, maybe it's the fact I crashed Franko's old Audi earlier in the month and Nac had to tape over the damage – either way, I'm not inspiring a lot of confidence that I can be trusted with tools of any kind. Nac, an architect-turned-Hiša Franko-handyman, was just recently put in charge of the garden that used to belong to Valter's parents, Franko and Joži, but since they're not getting any younger, and they have a huge vegetable and flower garden on the upper slopes of the estate as well, the restaurant team pitched in.

Gardening is about as Slovenian as beef soup and roasted potatoes on Sundays. There's almost an inherent need to remain in touch with the earth, possibly stemming from our peasant heritage. Sometimes the work seems almost masochistic – hardened 85-year-olds, barely walking, but still battling with relentless weeds, rock solid soil and midday sun. Nac, to Ana's despair, isn't one of them. He takes his time, slowly weeding and stopping every few minutes for what seems like a never-ending ponder about the meaning of life, and how it relates to urban landscape. 'I look at this garden through the prism of Socgorod architecture – as a brutalist Russian socialist town that strives for perfection, but never quite reaches it. . .' he trailed off. Nac comes from one of those types of towns in Eastern Slovenia, where a lot of people lost their true selves when they turned from farming to modern ways of living. Nac, although not possessing the most dazzling of talents for telling apart edible plants from inedible ones, maintains that bond with the old ways by spending summers at his grandfather's place by living here in the Kobarid area. 'Damn, these tomatoes are horribly planted,' he cursed, his wild sandy hair peeping out from the mass of far too densely packed tomato plants. Next to them, rhubarb leaves were fighting for domination with tiny chilli plants.

'With this garden, I'd go full Haussmann. You know who he was, right? The architect of modern Paris. He was well aware of the fact that in order to achieve any progress, you have to burn stuff down,' Nac mumbled as he pushed through the rows of overgrown carrots. Hiša Franko has a lot of fascinating and complex characters working in its team – this fatalistic pyromaniac seems oddly fitting. 'Don't look at me like that – it's a fact. If you want to have a future, you have to demolish the past. Haussmann did just that with old, narrow and inefficient Parisian alleys that he expanded into beautiful, broad avenues. And Paris adapted to these avenues like a plant adapts itself to the environment.'

It was a refreshing take on gardening, for sure. For me, though, working in the garden has always been a great way of letting out your pent-up frustrations, your sadness, your anger. Like punching a boxing bag – but with some positive results to show. Well, at least the weeded part. Somehow, I never quite managed to successfully reach the harvesting phase. Gardens also reflect the culture of the nation. French gardens are beautiful, bohemian overgrown patches of paradise; British gardens are often neat and carefully manicured, not permitting much craziness and spontaneity. Slovene gardens are closer to the latter than the former. As a nation, we have this annoying character trait of constantly seeking approval, the need for things to look perfect on the outside, even when they're crumbling on the inside. And gardens are the most obvious sign of whether you're 'hard-working' or a good-for-nothing lazy-ass. An entire book could be written on Slovenian neighbourly rivalry over the nicest-looking garden, flawless in appearance and in perfect order.

Rodrigo is one of Ana's young chefs in charge of the daily picking of the herbs, greens and flowers that she uses so liberally in her dishes. Rodrigo comes from El Salvador, where he studied marine biology and, out of curiosity and practical need, also attended courses in agriculture. His parents own coffee and sugar plantations, and he is a true treasure chest of knowledge about plants, their diseases, their medicinal purposes and their fickle nature. 'So, when we started planting this year, the idea was to divide the garden in accordance with how the plants coexist and interact with each

Holly, Black Shallots, Blue Cheese → p. 224

other. Rhubarb provides shade for smaller plants, beans act as a natural barrier and a host to bacteria that inject nitrogen, which is the main element the plants need to attach themselves to the floor,' explains Rodrigo. He points his heavily tattooed arm towards the herb section of the garden. 'There are some herbs that we plant every year because there's constant need for them in the kitchen.' They also started experimenting with chillies of different heat levels – not just because of the strong South American-Balkan presence in the kitchen team, but also because Ana never leaves the house without a pack of chilli flakes she sprinkles generously on every meal she finds too tame.

With the aforementioned tomatoes currently struggling for space, she makes a tomato water that she uses in a lot of her dishes, and incorporates the leaves into the mix with greens and leaves. Green peas, which were sprawling at one corner of the garden and threatening the thyme close by, were used in snacks, served as an amuse bouche made of smoked bone marrow and *Silene vulgaris*, and the rhubarb in the other corner was cooked into syrup and turned into a sorbet, served with elder marshmallows. Also at their peak were gooseberries, redcurrants and blackcurrants and raspberries used for the bear dish, and at the edge of the garden, next to the wild meadow, was a patch of nettles that was destined to be fried and tossed with tripe and cave cheese.

Rodrigo heads toward the beans. 'See, plants, if they're suffering, they tell you that through their leaves – if they're brown, it means they're lacking phosphorus, if they're yellow, they're lacking nitrogen. And that tomato leaf over there is simply telling you "Help me, please!"' In an area like Kobarid where the weather conditions can change within five minutes from scorching sun to pouring rain, keeping a garden happy is not always the easiest thing. At Hiša Franko, where the abundance of rain washes out the nutrients, they try to help out the plants with natural fertilizers, such as egg shells for calcium, coffee residue for acidity. Ana's mother-in-law also closely follows the moon calendar for planting, so nothing is left to chance. 'A garden is a city on a small scale. And like a city, it needs a vertical. Like every person needs a vertical,' concludes Nac as he wraps up work for the day, fighting his way out of the narrow, pre-Haussmann era tomato alley. The dark clouds of doom gather yet again above Hiša Franko. Someone tell the weather here about the damn vertical.

Where the Wild Roses Grow

'Wait, you've never met pretty Miha? How's that possible?' Ana asks me, incredulously. Even after five-plus years of coming to Hiša Franko, I've only ever heard about and not seen Ana's prodigal forager. He also moonlights as a masseur and personal trainer, and is a basketball coach by day – at this point, the multitasking of the people in this valley does not surprise me any more. My first meeting with Miha is at 7 a.m. on a mushroom-picking expedition at the foothills of Livek, where Ana's parents live. It's one of those gorgeous early summer mornings, the air still fresh, the valley floor covered with marshmallowy mists that envelope the road-side garden patches and creep around tiny chapels that dot Slovenian countryside.

Miha leads the way with his Red Riding Hood-style basket. 'In July, you'll find porcinis on that slope,' he points towards the left side, then heads right where he notices a bare-toothed russula. He moves fast, skipping the bolete he considers too old and shows how to separate an edible russula from an inedible one – one has more yellowy top than the other. For Ana, the weirder the mushrooms are, the better. Almost on the limit of edibility – clustered coral, stuff like that. Miha recites plants and mushrooms he notices along the way in Latin like the skilled botanist he is. 'If you manage to stay quiet enough, you can see so many animals out here. And I've pretty much seen them all. One time, I saw sixteen wild boars, and the other day, a bear suddenly appeared right in front of me. Probably the first time I was genuinely frightened,' he whispers. On the way back, Miha parks the car next to a sun-drenched meadow, overgrown with wild flowers that Ana was using for her trout-whey dish. Every two or three days, Ana's kitchen team hands Miha a long order list with different plants, wild flowers, leaves and wild greens needed. It's a kitchen that relies heavily on nature. 'Ana, no, there's no more acacia flowers left, I'm telling you, I've scoured the entire valley for it,' stresses Miha, but Ana doesn't want to hear it. 'I'm sure you can still find it somewhere. Just today I spotted it on my morning jog, so apparently, there was still some of it left!' Acacia flowers in tempura with kefir and pollen was a popular dish on Hiša Franko's May menu that year, so Ana was having a hard time accepting that there was no more acacia to be found. She switched to elderflowers, but to her, it just wasn't the same, so the dish departed the menu.

A couple of weeks later, Miha explores the area around Drežnica, a gorgeous part of the valley filled with secret waterfalls and dreamy clearings in the middle of the forest. 'You've got watercress over there, milfoil over here. This is broadleaf plantain – if you don't have any mushrooms, you can use this because it tastes the same,' explains Miha as he walks down the pathway. 'Wild lilies, cloves, mint… elderflowers all done, now we're getting close to the elderberry season.' Through

The Peach and the Woodruff → p. 226

his eyes the forest seems like a supermarket set out exclusively for Hiša Franko. Foraging is one of those inherently Slovenian things; everything from blueberries to mushrooms, from dandelion to wild garlic. In skilled hands, it can be a way of life. In unskilled ones, or the ones who view foraging as a new hip trend, it can be deadly. Every year here in Slovenia a couple of foragers who mix up wild garlic with autumn crocus die. Ana walks side by side with Miha, brainstorming about her new menu. 'What do you think would go well with meadowsweet? Boar? Duck?' Meadowsweet grows in marshy areas and has a distinct almond aroma and a kind of healing, aspirin effect. Miha shrugs in an I-don't-know-you're-the-chef kind of way and gets more animated when we make a turn where the trees give way to a big clearing with views over the Soča river on one side, and an almost fairytale-like chalet on the other. 'I love this meadow, it offers you something new all the time. In April you can find morels, in the autumn, huge parasol mushrooms grow like crazy. I often do team-building exercises with my basketball group here,' regales Miha.

The chalet was built by his grandfather Borut in the 1950s on the foundations of an old stone barn. Borut was a doctor, and one of the biggest jazz connoisseurs in Europe – in fact, he was the owner of the largest jazz record collection in Yugoslavia. He spent a lot of time in his forest chalet, reading, playing the flute and eating blue cheese imported from France. Rumour had it that he even hosted the great Louis Armstrong here, but alas, after a little investigation it turned out that even though Dr. Borut did indeed invite Armstrong to Slovenia, the musical icon never actually made it to Drežnica – just to the jazz festival in Bled, where he signed a book to his doctor friend.

On an old table, there's the assortment of homemade drinks – blueberry and cherry brandy, mead and gentian – that Miha pulled from the shelves above the rustic, hundred-year-old stove. There's no electricity in the lodge; the dim light comes from the candles, paraffin lamp and the fireplace where they bake the bread during the longer winter stays. The walls are filled with all sorts of artifacts that reflect the area and Miha's well-connected family – on one side hangs a scary mask of 'the ugly one' from Drežnica carnival, on the other an old painted beehive panel. There are also some orthodox icons and Ana claims that the painted female nude is Miha's aunt, who posed for France Slana, one of Slovenia's most famous painters – and best man at Miha's parents' wedding – but Miha denies it feverishly. 'Every time I try to tell her it's not true, but she just keeps on repeating it. Ana, please, let it go!'

Loredana, the Pink Witch

Sun and rain. Ana has often told me that even the people of this region fall into these two categories. If that's the case, then Loredana is definitely the sun. She greets us in front of her house with pink geraniums on her windowsills, wearing a pink flowery T-shirt, with pink painted toenails. She shows us the way inside and sits us behind a kitchen table adorned with a single pink rose in a vase, overlooking a clock with exactly the same faded pink rose design. 'Want some tea? I just made one of my mixtures with rose petals, mint, raspberry leaves and oregano.' Everything I know about Loredana intrigues me. She used to raise deer and have the most beautiful garden in Livek, and that's how Ana's parents met her. And through them, Ana met Loredana. Even though they don't see each other very often, they 'feel' each other, as Loredana puts it. 'It was heaven up there. I had two herb and flower gardens with rich soil on the high altitude, overlooking the valley, where everything grew like crazy in a completely unspoilt environment. People were coming to see my garden all the way from Italy. I even hosted the Slovenian president there once!' remembers Loredana, with just a hint of sadness in her eyes.

For 32 years, she lived the perfect life with her husband Ivo, Valter's second cousin. It was one of those fairytale marriages – love at first sight, a kiss good night every evening, a kiss goodbye every morning, shared hopes and dreams, a beer in the sun after gardening, never-ending lust for each other. But all of this was ripped away from Loredana in a senseless tragedy. One sunny day in May, Ivo, a statuesque man by all accounts with a spark in his eyes and a gentle soul, took his life after a short battle with depression. Loredana found him deep in the woods east of Livek with the help of a local medium, an herbalist like herself. That was three years ago. Ivo's portrait now hangs in Loredana's living room in the village of Smast, her gardens in Livek lost forever, deserted and overgrown. 'I can never go back. Never. It pains me too much to walk past the plots where Ivo and I used to breed deer, past the footpaths to Matajur where we used to pick thyme, past our hidden spots where we had an afternoon beer or two,' reminisces Loredana as she twirls her wedding band on her finger. 'I lived and breathed for Livek, I was doing tea mixtures for the expectant mothers up there, marigold creams for old ladies, assembling bouquets for local festivals. People don't really get why I can't come back any more,' explains Loredana as she shows us faded photographs of her old garden. She's seen there, younger, blissfully happy, with long blonde hair, standing in the middle of the scarlet bee balm and purple coneflowers in full bloom, mount Krn in the background and butterflies in the air. When she left Livek, she took a couple of plants and seeds with her and planted them on a small patch of land near the school where she works as a kindergarten teacher – something the villagers so kindly donated to her.

She descends down the narrow footpath elegantly, like a forest fairy, to her plot and picks a couple of twigs of chicory plant and red clover along the way. 'I like my gardens lush and wild,' she smiles as we walk past bushes of wild mint, sage, lavender, marshmallow plant, coneflowers and dog rose in full pink bloom. 'That's buckwheat over there; it's great for the vascular system. Evening primrose makes your skin perfect, elecampane is used to treat interior organs and goldenrod is for kidney. Red clover is excellent for hormones, when you hit menopause, St John's wort is good for healing wounds,' she explains. Herbs and healing plants share the small plot with dill, tomato, raspberries and zinnias. 'I put some wool under the soil for the vegetable garden this year – the very last sheep Ivo and I sheared together,' she glances towards the lettuce and courgette patch. 'I took everything that happened to me as some sort of challenge. If someone had told me what would happen, I would have never thought I was going to survive it. But I did,' she replies when I ask her how she managed to rebuild her life. 'I heard somewhere that nature never forgets the heart that loved her. You know, the other day, I was weeding a patch of valerian and I spotted a tiny sprout of oak. Ivo's last name was Oak. I took it as a sign that he's still with me.'

We head back to Loredana's house, looking so perfect with pots of marigold, aromatic everlasting flowers and rosemary. Behind the house an extra fragrant rose bush grows, a gift from her uncle; on the other side, an old rose bush that survived even the disastrous earthquake of 1976. 'What I lost in Livek, I started planting in pots. From 18 hectares (45 acres) I ended up with a pot – see how life turns out,' smiles Loredana. She shows us inside her herbal room, dimly lit with books on herbs and medicinal plants that she's been collecting for the past 30 years, bouquets of dried flowers hanging from the ceiling, and a large cabinet filled with glass containers of all kinds of herbs and petals, tiny tinctures of thyme, and hawthorn soaked in schnapps. 'Smell – this is mallow. It works wonders for people with respiratory problems. These are bean shells; I've been setting them aside for my mother's diabetes. You recognize these flowers probably – they're primroses, they help you sleep at night,' she goes on and on as she showcases the content of her magical jars. 'This is dried dandelion, great for liver and gall bladder, and these are dried birch leaves. I mix them together with elderflower and nettles for people who suffer kidney and gall bladder conditions.' Her husband used to come to her asking her

to heal the men who were working for him, but she was always reluctant, a firm believer that you have to really know the medical history of a patient before you start treating them with the help of herbs. 'See, Perforate St John's wort is used to treat the depression, but if you're on a birth control pill, it can cancel out the effect and you can become pregnant. And if you're taking any pills for a heart condition it's crucial to ask the doctor first if you can take hawthorn which is otherwise by far the best for any heart problems.'

Loredana isn't charging for her help – she is convinced that if you pick and forage for money, it can quickly spoil you. Instead, she's handing out her advice and her packages for free, for good karma. She's been Ana's go-to tea supplier for years now, mixing special blends for Hiša Franko and its guests. The 'good morning' tea is a mixture of scarlet bee balm, elderflower, raspberry and blackberry leaves. For the 'good night' version she uses chamomile, lemon balm, mint, lavender, valerian tincture and wild hops. 'Or a pint of beer works as well,' she laughs. For stomach aches, she offers a tea made of lemon balm, mint, cumin, chamomile and anise, and she gifts new mothers a 'good luck' mixture of raspberry and blackberry leaves, *Alchemilla vulgaris* and rose petals. For aphrodisiac purposes, she recommends rosemary and summer savory. 'There's no magic at work here, it's about using herbs that make the blood run faster. And rosemary and summer savory they do just that.' When I ask Loredana when was the last time she visited a doctor, she shakes her head. 'In 40 years I've never ever taken a sick day – the only time was when Ivo died. This passion of mine is what saves me. And the people that surround me.' She pauses for a second. 'Hmm, I guess I could get myself a cat as well. Witches usually have cats,' she says as she smiles mysteriously.

The Bees

When you drive through the Soča Valley, windows down, letting in the fresh mountain air with the scent of summer flowers, blooming linden trees and freshly cut grass, one of the things you notice immediately is how unspoilt with industry and shopping complexes this area is. Pristine, green, almost primitive. Instead of the soulless, ubiquitous warehouses you so often find in the Slovenian countryside, the landscape here is dotted with colourful beehives. Simple hives, elaborate ones that almost look like small Russian dachas, practical types, ones incorporated into truck frames so they're easier to transport – every kind you could imagine. Traditional Slovenian beehives from the 18th century were works of art, with a number of folk motifs painted on beehive panels – the most popular being women portrayed as vil-

Meadowsweet is a Queen of Summer Fields → p. 225

lains, liars, lousy cooks and repressive witches chasing their husbands from the pubs. Of course, designs have changed a lot since then. And while our historic attitude towards women has clearly been problematic, we've always treated bees as our national treasures, and have always been a nation of beekeepers. We are also the only European Union member state that has protected its own autochthonous honey bee, the Carniola, and in the era of huge international honey scandals, our honey has remained completely traceable. The area of the Soča Valley, where the tradition of alpine dairy farming is still going strong, is especially suitable for beekeeping. The bee association of Tolmin was founded in 1908, which makes it one of the oldest in Slovenia. In these parts, bee products are the third most important, after milk and meat produce, and when the season is good, the area produces up to 40 tons of honey per year.

The star product is linden honey. A symbol of Slovenia, linden trees form the majestic tree alley that leads from Kobarid to Hiša Franko. A tree alley that Mussolini planted, not knowing what it represents. Linden honey has very distinct floral, minty, herbal and nutty aromas, and is praised for its medicinal purposes. We drive up to Vrsno, a tiny hamlet high above the valley where Darinka, Ana's honey producer, owns a couple of beehives and a small village store where she sells pollen, propolis, different kinds of honey and her tea mixtures, composed of herbs, leaves and flowers that she forages in the meadows at the foothill of Mount Krn. Darinka took an interest in bees very early on. When she turned eighteen, instead of a coming-of-age golden necklace or a new pet, she asked for bees. Her parents bought her a small beehive, and ever since her love for bees hasn't dwindled a bit – even when they sting her. 'The swellings, you get immune to in time, the pain – never,' says Darinka as she opens up her beehive for us. 'There are times when I get ten stings a day,' she says, trying to reassure us that on the part of the bees, it's nothing personal. 'In the end, it all comes down to the fact that you have to love the bees. That's the whole secret,' explains Darinka, who quit her day job 17 years ago to become a professional beekeeper. Her hobby has now become a full-on family business, with her eldest son set to take over in a few years. On a good year, Darinka's hives, spread across five locations, produce up to a couple of tons of honey. In mid-July, they gather to decant the honey from the hives into large vessels. Sweet, thick, bright amber liquid oozes slowly, like a vibrant lava running down the slopes of a volcano. Its next destination will be Kobarid's co-op store, Planika, and Hiša Franko's breakfast table, set under a gigantic bouquet of flowers – probably the same ones that Darinka's bees feast on.

My Dad is a Hunter

Ana Roš

Alice in
Wonderland

Soča Valley is a real zoo, abundant with wildlife that lives in the greenest, most untouched natural surroundings. If you step on the terrace of Hiša Franko at dawn, you can see deer and roebuck stealing apples from the trees and wild rabbits eating leaves in our salad garden. There are wild boars, chamois, muflons, bears, snakes, dormice, foxes and weasels.

On my morning run, I often surprise herds of roebuck on the pasture; sometimes I follow rabbits, enjoying their funny little hops and their elegant beauty.

The Wolf
and the Bear

A huge wolf wanders around the valley in spring, scaring people and sheep half to death. Locals say he is looking for a female. If he finds her, the resulting union would be a pack of wolves that would essentially declare war on the local farms. Miha, my forager, came across him with his girlfriend, Ana, who often forages with him. They were heading to the top of Kolovrat to enjoy the full moon; Miha told me that when he saw the wolf, he had never experienced such a rush of adrenaline in his life.

That same evening, while doing his daily 'work out' just a kilometre (half a mile) away, my father stumbled upon a huge brown bear. There have always been a few bears in our mountains but you rarely have a chance to meet them; they can sense us, and always try to avoid humans. He said it was an altogether different experience; he could almost smell his own fear, and the hair on the back of his hands was upright for hours after.

My Father
and the Roebuck

Once I asked my father if he ever dreamed of having a son. His answer was that he was happiest in the company of the three women in his family, but I felt he said it too quick off the mark for it to be honest. I have always tried to make my father happy. I was faster and wilder than all the boys of the school, and sweet sixteen when I cut off my curls for the first time. The connection between us has always been very deep and special; the kind of bond that only a father and daughter can have. As a consequence, my father has struggled with my choice of boyfriends – you could feel the disapproval in the air whenever I tried to bring them over for lunch or dinner. I finally stopped inviting them, but my inner rebel never really gave up. When I started dating Valter, I had to hide him for a pretty long time.

One beautiful autumn morning, my father took me hunting. We woke up far before dawn, and I remember him taking two big guns from the wardrobe in my parents' bedroom, which has only just struck me as a funny place to keep hunting weapons. I was given my own binoculars to help him trace his target. We were walking fast and long and I was not allowed to say a word. How did he know where to find the animal? We lay down, hiding in high grass, and in my head I started counting down minutes:

> 'Pssst! Did you see it?'
> 'No, Father. . .'
> *Baaam!*

All I could smell was the persistent and intense aroma of gunpowder.

> 'Let's go. Let's find it.'

We left the forest with a small roebuck hanging over my father's back. I never wanted to go hunting again. I stopped cutting my hair, and a few months later I quit skiing, too. My father is an intelligent man. He never said a thing.

Drama of the
Hunting Trophies

Two years before I was born, my parents moved to the valley; they thought it was going to be a short stay. But years went by, and the family was still there. My father completely integrated into a countryside life, and at that time, hunting was the best way to prove yourself as part of the local community. I know my mother hated it. My dad would spend so many weekends in the mountains; I can still recall the unpleasant smell of his clothes

when he came home – a blend of sweat, fresh blood and adrenaline. On Sunday evening we would often have kidneys, hearts and liver for dinner. Offal is the only part of the animal the hunter can keep. My mother always had a great touch when cooking game – the meat was always soft and juicy and she would usually combine it with cranberries and apples. But there was one very strict rule – all of his hunting trophies were stored in boxes in the cellar, away from the walls of our living room where he tried to hang them. It seems to be a hunter's constitutional right, but not in our house. There were always loud discussions about it. Today, his trophies hang on the walls of Hiša Franko's dining room.

Teach Me
How to Cook Like a Fox

In Slovenian literature, there are lots of stories about foxes, in which they are mostly related to bad things. Even a woman is often compared to a fox; I like to think it's because it's a comparison to creatures that are more intelligent than men could ever dare think of. Our forest is full of foxes, and sadly, it's something that really sticks out since a fox killed my cat. Snežinka (Snowflake) was a little white cat that someone abandoned in front of the restaurant. The kitchen team adopted her, and it was only a year later that we realized Snežinka was really a boy. We kept the name, though. Snežinka was the sweetest cat on the planet, grateful but still wild. As with a lot of white cats, she eventually went blind and could also not hear very well, so we made her a little bedroom outside. And of course, her meals were always fine dining ones. She was often attacked, especially by other cats. When a cat cannot see and cannot hear, it cannot really defend itself, so I guess it was an easy job for the fox to hurt Snezinka – truly, it was brutal. I cried a lot. Sometimes I wonder if there is anything good in their nature; now, I choose to admire their cunning from afar.

Breaking the Rules

Valter, Andrej and Albin, three teenage friends, had many a fun night hunting dormice.

They cooked them on an open fire – it was a kind of boy's secret. Dormice hunting is strictly forbidden in Slovenia. My mother has her hunting secrets too. With Zdravko Likar, a local wise man and well of knowledge about the area, she would spend one day a year hunting snakes, then spend the whole night grilling and (of course) eating them. It was almost a religious ritual. There is no written trace of snake hunting in our history, though. When Valter's mother Jožica was running the kitchen of Hiša Franko, she would often receive phone calls from local hunters about the whole wild boar just shot around the corner, or the half of the little roebuck available to share, or the deer that had been the victim of a car crash. A hunters' black market, if you will. I still remember how skilled she was in putting the whole bear out of its skin. She really was a game expert. The queen of the nature.

Game was regularly on her menu, often broken down into traditional stews, goulashes and roasts. Italians loved coming over the border for the bear meat. People from the Soča Valley live alongside nature very intensely; nature dictates our lives. This is how we always know when we are allowed to break the rules, and when we simply cannot. The fox, the bear, the wolf, they all break the rules. One family.

Kaja Sajovic

To Kill a Deer

'You finally made it, I've been waiting for you for three days,' says Božo, a sweet, moustached man in full camouflage gear who greets us very enthusiastically. In the past few days, he has been scouring the hunting ground for roebuck and deer, and spent eight hours in the pouring rain picking mushrooms because he heard one of the visitors is a vegetarian. 'There you go – hunters' champagne. I've been chilling it,' he says proudly as he sets in front of us a bowl with iced water and a bottle of pear schnapps peeking out. 'Cheers!' We raise our glasses. 'Us hunters toast with left hand, because we use the right one for hugging girls,' he says jokingly.

Božo is Ana's father Bojan's best friend, and together they make for quite the comedy duo. A genuine, decades-old 'bromance' bound together by love for hunting that seems for them as much of a hobby as an escape from the four walls. They are both full of tongue-in-cheek quips like: 'When you're drinking the whole day, it's hard to stay sober.' Together they've been through everything: close encounters with a bear; pushing their luck on the dizzying ledges; gambling with their own lives hunting for chamois; antelope safaris in Namibia. We're staying at a no electricity, no showers hunting lodge on Mount Pretovč, 1,200 metres (3,900 feet) above the valley – our home for the next two days or, as Bojan puts it firmly, 'until we shoot something'. He is a no-nonsense kind of guy, and I wager a lot fitter than men half his age.

The late afternoon sun is slowly starting to glide towards the craggy mountain ridge, drenching the rocky slopes with a pink hue and throwing a long shadow on the green pastures underneath. Time to go catch ourselves dinner. 'How fit are you, Georges? Can you carry what I shoot?' Božo asks Georges Desrues, a journalist who joined us for one night. Georges gives Božo a petrified look. 'Not fit. I look fit, but I'm not. I can only carry a rabbit maybe.' Georges is writing a story about bear hunting in Slovenia, which is, for most people outside of our country, something completely exotic, and for some, such as Italians, even sacrilegious. But the fact is that the bear population is big (750 animals) and is steadily growing, so from time to time, they are repopulated in the Pyrenees or other areas – Slovenia is the largest exporter of bears in Europe. Or, we shoot them

for bear goulash. And even though you can spot a bear in these parts, the vast majority of the bear population lives in the south of Slovenia, on the border with Croatia. Some say that the bear population grew substantially during the war in Bosnia in the 90s, when even the animals were fleeing the bloody conflict. Whatever the case, the bear population is definitely on the rise – up by more than 100 percent from 1991 when we became independent. The topic of bear hunting is a controversial one, and the national forest service is constantly battling with environmentalists who would like to put an end to bear culling, while the farming communities are suffering because of more and more frequent close encounters of their stock with bears. The number of legally culled bears is small in comparison to 12,000 wild boar culled or 40,000 of deer and roebuck.

Bojan and Božo put on their olive-green shirts and backpacks, mount heavy hunting rifles on their backs and head in separate directions, each towards his own lookout where they will spend the next four hours, eyes fixated on anything that moves. We're following Bojan, constantly playing catch-up to this 72-year-old man, loaded heavily, like he was one of the soldiers fighting in these hills a century ago on the Soča frontline. We climb the old, faded wooden lookout, cramming into the tiny space. Each of us gets his own window to cover as much ground as we can. Then the waiting game begins. We are told to pay attention to any orange spots in the grass. Two hours in, Bojan suddenly picks up his binoculars. 'You see the orange spot over there?' He pauses. 'Actually never mind, it's a tree trunk.' Another hour goes by. 'You can sit here until it's pitch black, like a moron, and nothing happens. But we don't really care,' shrugs Bojan nonchalantly. Two days earlier, he had been on a hunting trip at the opposite end of the country, where the group returned to their hunting lodge at 1 a.m. 'when the last bar closed', ate liver of the deer they had caught that day at 2 a.m., went to bed and then woke up at 4 a.m. to start all over again.

We wait some more until we finally spot a roebuck on a meadow below us. Bojan picks up his binoculars, then slowly he pulls out his range finder and calculates. Contrary to popular belief, hunters don't just feverishly shoot whatever hops by. Even though there's way too many deer and wild boar in Slovenia, hunting is extremely regulated, with the exact number of each species allowed to be culled each season, on each hunting ground. Because the terrain here in the mountains above Soča is pretty challenging, the number of deer remains stable, and the hunters usually kill about 50 of them each season. It's June, so stags, killed mostly in return for trophies, are out of question, and so is deer and its offspring. The hunting season for all the aforementioned animals opens in September, and lasts until the end of year. If the hunter miscalculates the age, the consequences may be severe – not only does he pay for the animal he shot but, in the worst-case scenario, he can even lose his hunting licence. You also need to take into account your position and distance from the valley if you're actually able to carry the beast down or not. More than anything else, hunting is a tactical game. And a hobby that comes with a bunch of not-so-fun obligations such as clearing the forest trails, building mountain lodges and plumbing, making sure the feeders are stocked during the harsh winters... And beside the fact hunting is much more humane than the conditions a lot of animals raised for industrial meat production endure, it's also a necessity. Overpopulation of deer means less feeding ground for them and more health issues; the overpopulation of chamois in Slovenia is also the reason for the so-called 'chamois blindness' that affects entire herds of these animals, and the overpopulation of wild boar has a substantial negative impact on farmers and winegrowers.

Bojan is still deciding whether to shoot or not. The wind picks up slightly and he pulls out a cheat sheet with precise measurements of wind factor in shooting for any given distance. Apparently the worst thing you can do is an unclean shot, which just wounds the animal. Then you have to bring in a bloodhound, and the situation becomes much worse for all concerned. Luckily, with Bojan, apparently that's not an issue. 'My aim is one hundred percent.' The spotted roebuck disappears.

Four hours in, and Bojan seems ready to call it a day. 'You see now how boring hunting really is? Oh well, fuck it,' he says as he starts packing his gear. When we get back, Božo is looking distraught, wringing his hands restlessly. 'Bojan, a tragedy! I missed twice! The second time the deer was almost laughing at me, mistaking me for a benign tree trunk. I actually do look a little bit like a tree trunk. An old, rotten tree trunk,' rambles Božo. 'It looks like I'm finished. I might as well become a vegetarian. This is so sad I could cry.' Božo actually looks like he's about to shed a tear and it doesn't help that Georges starts calling him 'a mushroom man'. 'Bojan, tell them – in all my life I rarely missed!' Božo finds some solace in wine Ana packed for us. 'Don't write anywhere that I

missed – they might kick me out of the hunting association and I won't get a hunting funeral!' Bojan turns to me. 'Next time, tell Ana to pack us double the amount of wine.' 'Triple,' retorts Božo. A couple of hours later, at 4 a.m., it's still pitch black, but we're already on the move again, having firmly decided that we need to shoot something – and by 'we' I mean Bojan, because the rest of us were having trouble even keeping eyes open. Rays of early morning sun are starting to slowly hug the majestic landscape in front of us with warm hues of bright green. All of a sudden, Bojan spots a deer about 200 metres (656 feet) away, peeping behind a fallen tree and teasing us. 'What do you say, should I shoot?' asks Bojan, the experts that we are. The sound of the rifle going off is deafening. Bojan shakes his head. He missed. 'It was the wind. It had to be the wind, because this rifle never misses,' he says quietly. The deer is somehow still there on the meadow, taunting him. Bojan ponders on whether he should try a second shot. 'You know, the thing is, when you miss twice in a row, you get really upset and mad and you start to wonder if something's wrong with you. You just start to doubt yourself and that can be pretty dangerous...' He packs his gear and opens the door of the lookout, letting the now-bright morning sunlight flood in.

On the way back from the hut, we find some solace in early morning schnapps shot at the shepherds' hut a little higher up the mountain. It's 9 a.m., and they've been up since 4 a.m., milking the cows, so we have a mutual understanding that this is a perfectly fine time for the first toast of the day. We pour the strong, herbal liquid down our throats and head back, past the cows grazing the high mountain grass, past the World War I tunnels dug into solid rock, past the 100-year-old Austro-Hungarian chapel, hidden from the bullets of the Italian soldiers, firing fiercely from the mountain top opposite to it. We climb the nearest hill to get the 180-degree view of the stretched-out valley with the winding Soča river meandering through it. This place is called Cold Mountain, the setting of the first defence line of the troops during the big war. A cross made of two grenades reminds you of the history; the wild flowers in full bloom covering the hilltops create distance from that same history.

Back at the lodge, Valter is waiting. Ana sent him with his motorcycle, armed with six more bottles of wine. It's the last evening of hunting, the very last chance to catch something. At this point, morale was low and I would settle for a squirrel. 'Bojan, we need to shoot something. It's a must. The fact is we just don't have enough wine left for one more day. It's a matter of killing or dropping dead of thirst,' says Božo, his priorities being very straightforward. Bojan decides to try a different technique – stalking a deer. We head towards

Cold Mountain, through the nettles and along the old rusty war-era barbed wire. I spot something behind the trees bordering the pastures and silently alarm Bojan. The creature slowly disappears behind the bushes. It looked huge. Slightly greyish. A moose? Bojan smirks, the sound of a hunter definitely not impressed with his protégé. The nearest moose population is... in Sweden. It was a cow. We turn left, inland onto a super narrow footpath that takes us deep into uncharted territory. The grass is almost taller than I am and the ticks are crawling all over us like crazy. As he leads the party Bojan mumbles something about the trail being too bushy and overgrown, then grumbles, 'The last time I hunted here was 15 years ago.' After about two hours of hiking, we arrive at a dreamy clearing with a pond in the middle of it. Bojan takes a sip of cherry brandy from his flask, then puts it away suddenly and gives us a sign not to move. A roebuck. Very young, starring straight at us curiously. Bojan decides in a split second that enough is enough. He aims, he shoots, the roebuck falls flat on his side. Bojan pulls out his knife and makes a clean cut along the animal's belly, letting out the entrails. Without even flinching, he removes the heart, the liver and kidneys, but the rest is thrown behind a bush for the foxes and vultures to feast on. The last act is a ceremonial one; he walks to the nearest fir tree, plucks a branch, smears the wound with it and then carefully inserts it into roebuck's mouth. The Hunter's Blessing. Bojan then skilfully starts to tie up the roebuck into a sort of furry origami that fits into his huge backpack, but by the way he heaved it onto his back, the weight looked barely noticeable. He takes another sip of cherry brandy and starts heading towards the lodge.

The mountain is like a small village, a symbiotic community of shepherds, hunters and cattle drivers. When they heard a shot, the shepherd family from the nearby high plateau headed to our lodge to check the fallen animal and to raise a toast to the hunter. In the meantime, Valter, the designated cook for the evening, cuts the bright purple heart, liver and kidneys into dice and fries them in butter, finished with a squeeze of lemon juice.

Hunting is not a game of bloodthirsty Neanderthals here; it's like everything in these mountains, a way to remain in touch with nature, a way to keep yourself in check. For some, like Bojan, who came to this area from the other end of the country, it is a way of integrating into a close-knit community. For others, like Božo, it is a way of escaping the stresses of valley life to a place where the air is thinner, where the bonds are stronger.

The next morning we slowly head back towards the valley, Valter on his motorcycle, the rest of us in Bojan's Jeep, roebuck in the back. 'I'm sad, Bojan, I don't want to go back,' says Božo after he's done explaining the story how he attended a reception for Kim Jong Il back when he was a colonel in the Yugoslavian army. Bojan turns to him, wants to say something sarcastic, but stops. 'You know what? We'll just drop them at Hiša Franko, then we'll go grab some wine and a pack of beer, and we'll join the crew that's staying up in the highland lodge.' They leave us at the restaurant with a warm hug, then drive away, back to the mountains.

Drežnica

Ana Roš

Huljo

When a girl from Tolmin moves to Kobarid and falls in love with a local, it seems to almost be cause for the next Balkan war. The two towns are very much rivals; Tolmin may have more offices, dance schools, bars and streets, but Kobarid, 15 kilometres (9 miles) further north in the Soča Valley, boasts more restaurants, and most importantly, very special people. And the most special of these are from Drežnica. Huljo, a local hero, was one such person; good-hearted, and always there to help others. He was a builder, a very skilled hunter, best climber in town, and by far the strongest and the most fearless person in the modern history of Kobarid. Huljo was a living legend. As with a lot of locals, he loved searching and collecting military material, the remains of World War I; a battle of epic proportions took place on Mount Krn, the strangely shaped mountain right above Drežnica village. People have private collections of memorabilia, and a lot has been distributed among museums, but the villagers also use the remains of bombs, grenades and rifles as vases, or even as useful tools in the cheesemaking process. Never touch a grenade, my mother used to say. As for Huljo, he never listened to others. While trying to open one, the grenade exploded; he was gone forever. Why do I tell this story? Because most of the people of Dreznica identify themselves with Huljo. Brave, convinced, opinionated and rebellious. At whatever cost.

Goats from Drežnica are for some reason stubborn, even mean animals. Beautiful and semi-wild, the flavour of their meat is delicious, especially the goat kids. An old man once told me the legend about the only native Slovenian goat breed – *Drežniška koza*. In the 1950s, the Yugoslav authorities gave instructions to kill all the goats in the Slovenian mountain area, as they were eating too much of the forest. People from Drežnica do not like being told what to do. The goat is their gold. So, as the story goes, they decided to hide every single goat in the church in the middle of the village. There was not a single goat to be found outside. And in all the areas where farmers did kill the goats, the forest became wild and unmanageable, growing down into the valley. The goat is one of nature's caretakers.

Drežnica and the surrounding mountain villages have pastures that overlook the Gulf of Trieste. Mediterranean sea breezes change the minerality of the soil, and make all the plants taste saltier. Therefore, the animals that graze here have very distinctively flavoured meat. The goats only have one kid per year; we normally eat kid goat at Easter, before the animals are moved up to the higher pastures. Drežnica is a great example of how with Hiša Franko, we have tried to have a positive economic and social impact on the surrounding environment. For years, Valter and I knocked on the doors of the local farmers, asking them to share their products with us. 'Keep two lambs for you, but can you have four for us, too?' Step by step, year by year, the farmers began to see how much we valued their sheep, goats and rabbit, and as a result, the younger generation are beginning to see a future in traditional farming, staying put in the valley instead of searching for jobs in Ljubljana and other major cities. Today, the whole village of Drežnica is involved in this community enterprise; Emil, the butcher, will still attest to the fact that Hiša Franko is one of the most loyal customers.

Plums

There is an abundance of plum trees around Drežnica. They mostly end up in a delicious *slivovka*, which is a strong and clean-tasting plum brandy. Sometimes people would flavour it with košutnik, a root of gentian that grows high on the slopes of Krn and Krasji vrh. It is hard to find the plum in this place that's not turned into brandy; their sweet-sour taste makes it one of the best fruits in the world, to my mind. Most of this brandy is consumed during the wild rituals of the famous Drežnica carnival, which lasts for more than a month. This historically pagan event aside, all social life in the village happens around the church. One Sunday during mass, the priest gave a sermon about overconsumption of brandy. The last words were an invitation to locals to cut down all the plum trees. The devil is in a plum tree, he said. The people from Drežnica are very religious, but they never cut down the plum trees. Shortly after, the priest was sent away.

Kaja Sajovic

Where Wild Goats Roam

Emil tightens the rope and hangs the shimmering red carcass on the hook. He is Ana's butcher for kid goat and lamb and a local from Drežnica, a village 15 minutes from Hiša Franko. Drežnica is a very special place, one that strikes you with its fairytale setting on the foothills of the mountains, and, because of its geographical position, it is also the only place in the valley with a Mediterranean climate. As it's so secluded and disconnected from the outside world, the people of Drežnica have a particular reputation. They claim they are descendants of Celts, but the rest of the valley just call them wild, untamed and 'special'. Emil, who comes from a family of goat breeders, became a butcher right after finishing school; he worked at butchers' shops around the valley before starting his own business. A few years ago, Ana called Emil saying she needed a regular supply of kid goat, and ever since that call, he has worked with Hiša Franko. But because bureaucracy in Slovenia can be quite strict, and Ana was too big a customer was for his business to continue in the same vein, Emil and the local butchers and goat breeders organized themselves, got all the necessary papers, and started a co-op. Now, they are about to open a proper butchery and a grill house on the premises of an old, long shut down village shop.

They raise a lot of lamb in Drežnica, but the star product is definitely Drežnica goat, the only autochthonous breed in Slovenia. It's horned, temperamental and a little bit mean in spirit, with black fur, and spends part of the year on the mountains, grazing on the rich meadow grass. The meat is leaner and with a specific goaty taste that Emil compares to cheese from the alpine pastures – which, coincidentally, used to be made with the rennet sourced from goat's stomachs. 'It's not for everyone, for sure – it's an acquired taste – but I'm a firm believer that a goat needs to taste like a goat and a sheep like a sheep,' says Emil. There's almost 300 goats in Drežnica now (one for every two villagers). But before and during World War II, this number was much higher; people in Drežnica lived off the goats. Only the rich had cows, the rest had semi-wild goats that they first caught on the mountain and tamed the best they could. Every morning, people would then drive them back to that very same mountain to graze within the parameters of a rusty barbed wire fence. Drežnica's goat was so famous, the Italians used to come here in hordes, buying up the meat and skin – both were highly praised in the border towns of Trieste and Gorizia. Although the breeding of goats has been an issue since the 18th century, when Austro-Hungarian rulers tried to limit goat breeding because of the damage they caused to the grazing lands, it was in the 1950s under Yugoslavian rule that Drežnica's goats really became a target and almost became extinct. The argument for the decree to kill off all goats in the area was that they were causing too much damage. That was the official reason. Unofficially, it was a lot more nefarious and damning for this rural area that so depended on farming. During the period of heavy industrialization, the socialist authorities tried to force people from the fields to the factories because there was not a big enough workforce. And in Drežnica, that meant getting rid of all the goats. Every goat breeder had to either sell his animals, butcher them – or face the consequences. The foresters were ordered to clear every corner of Drežnica and the surrounding pastures, and kill every single goat. For the villagers, this was almost like a death sentence, so many of them escaped across the border to Italy. As for the rest of the farmers, they either gave in, or they tried to hide their goats in the most hard-to-get, precipitous, almost inaccessible parts of the mountains. A while back, Ana told me a local legend; she said that Drežnica's goats survived because the locals locked them inside the church. Well, like most of the local legends, this one turned out to not be *exactly* true. In actual fact, one of the places the locals were hiding their goats was a popular waterfall, Kozjak; the name could be loosely translated as 'Goat's Falls'. Before this, though, Kozjak used to be called Church Falls, before the socialist authorities forbade the name. Drežnica breeders hid goats behind the falls. Mystery solved!

Even though most Slovenians have never visited Drežnica, everyone has heard of it because the village and its goats were popularized through a traditional folk song:

'Ring ring ring, Drežnica, where are the goats? Up on the mountain where there's no stream...'

As children we sang this, unknowingly and joyously referencing the dark period in Drežnica's history. The goat culling lasted for about ten years, and somehow the feisty creature managed to survive, either in these hidden parts known only to locals, or way up in the mountains where they were almost completely absorbed into the mountain goat population. You can still see some Drežnica goats running wild above the tree line. The future of this breed is now safe, though, thanks to a clinic that preserves Drežnica's goat gene samples.

Since we are talking about an endangered species, there's only so much kid goat available every year, and their fertility varies, so at the start of the season Emil gives Ana an estimate of how many will be available. Roughly 50 end up in Hiša Franko, their biggest consumer. Unlike most of Emil's customers, Ana takes the whole goat and also uses the offal, which features heavily on the menu. Whenever Drežnica runs out of kid goat, Ana switches to lamb. The sheep herd in Drežnica is roughly the same as the population – 600 – and, just like the goats, Hiša Franko is the main customer. The people here are meat-and-potatoes kind of eaters, and not regular guests of Hiša Franko. They don't really understand the kind of haute cuisine Ana is serving, but they do speak of her with respect and pride for what she has achieved and how she has managed to introduce Drežnica to the world.

One such supporter is Mirko, the elderly owner of a small but priceless collection of World War I memorabilia he keeps in the attic of his house. 'She did good,' he nods. 'Open every day, all day long, when we're home', reads a wooden sign hanging outside of Mirko's house. He started collecting the war artifacts scattered throughout these mountains as a boy, and now you can find everything ranging from faded Mussolini photos and hand grenades to old coins and ampoules of morphine in his attic. We first meet Mirko inside the old tavern, next to the gigantic, oversized church that dominates the entire village. It's 11 a.m. on Sunday morning, and the parliamentary election day in Slovenia. In Drežnica, it's customary that after the church service, men go for a pre-noon drink. The tavern was so badly damaged during one of the earthquakes in 2004 that the house needed to be evacuated and marked with a large red dot on the front, which means it's supposed to be demolished. Fourteen years later, the house still stands, but the tavern only opens for that 'one drink' after service.

Drežnica, perhaps surprisingly, also used to have a well-known nightclub called Pletrje. Everyone in the valley knew of it because the music would blast out until the early hours of the morning, and on Saturday nights it was packed with young people coming from as far away as Tolmin. After the final notes of Gloria Gaynor's *I Will Survive* faded into the morning sun, the local boys would head directly to church, which really served more as a pretext for that 'one drink' at the tavern, where they talked about the events of the previous night. That drink was usually a shot of gentian, strong herbal bitters, that turned into three gentians and three beers – and another day of drinking. Pletrje's building still stands, but that Sunday, it was reimagined as a polling station.

I walk into the tavern, a den of grey-haired men, everyone clinging to his beer, wine spritzer or something stronger. One side of the tavern is covered with trophies, and on the other wall hangs an old, sepia-toned photo of Mount Krn, and a painting of farmer on his cart. The men turn their heads and fixate their eyes on me with incredulity. The only other woman here is behind the counter, serving the drinks. 'Err. . . where are all the women?' I ask Mirko when I locate him. 'They are in another tavern. Plus, they have to cook.'

Oh, Drežnica is *that* kind of place. As Mirko explained, here it's still expected that at noon, after the church bell rings *Ave Maria*, the housewife brings lunch to the table, otherwise she's considered sloppy. And if a boy is not home after the second ringing of *Ave Maria* in the evening, anyone is allowed to pour a bucket of water over him. They like to keep their traditions alive here. And one of the most important ones in Drežnica is their Mardi Gras carnival. At this point, it's no surprise for me to learn that only boys are allowed to wear masks, specifically boys who have turned eighteen. They make their own masks that separate themselves into 'pretty ones' and 'ugly ones'. The boys with ugly masks chase the children and scare them, whereas the pretty ones go around the village and collect gifts. In Drežnica, Mardi Gras plays such a large role in community life that even the villagers who moved abroad return home just to participate. There is one catch, though – you're only allowed to wear a mask until you marry.

Someone knocks on Mirko's door, visitors. A young family of four, the husband was obviously born and raised in Drežnica. 'You two can join the women in the kitchen if you're bored,' says Mirko. 'Better they don't, you know how they say it will rain if you have four women together,' points out the visitor. It rained anyway.

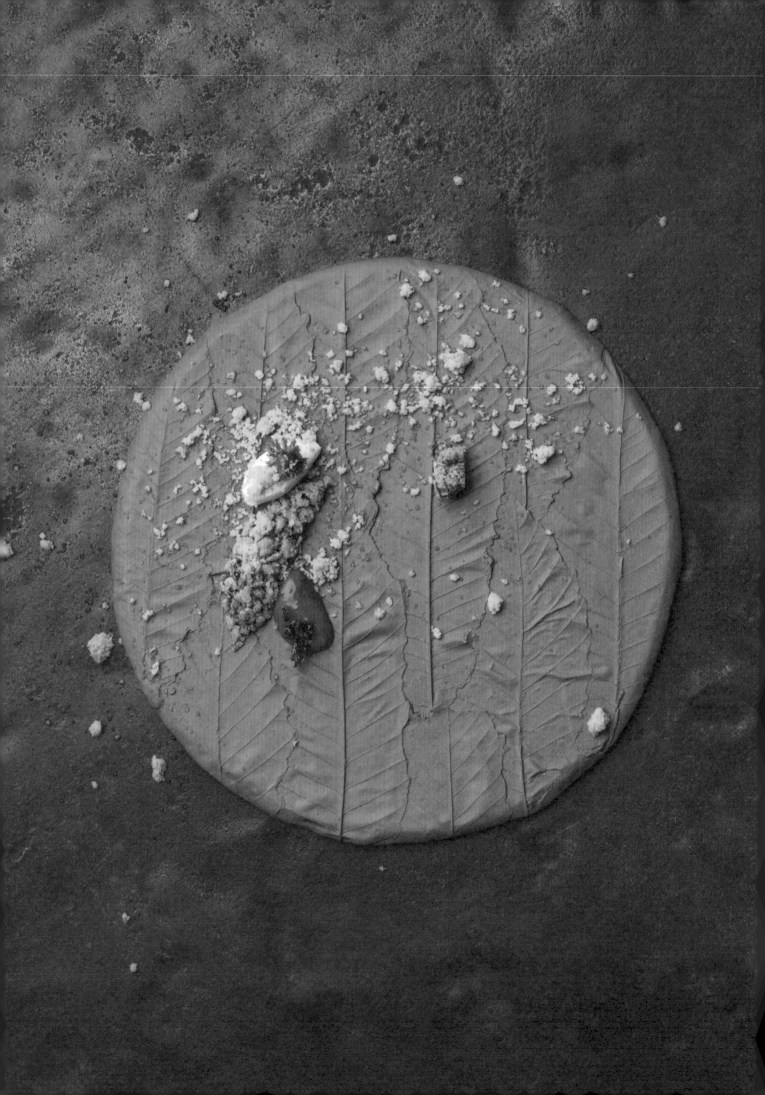

Mediterranean Terrace

Ana Roš

Chef's Table
Opening Scenes

The Netflix team spent almost three weeks with us. There were 20 of them, shooting twelve hours per day, six days a week, but a few hours before wrapping, there were murmurs of something being 'missing'. 'We need a place that could connect the whole story together.'

That last evening, just before dark, I brought them to Kolovrat. It is not the kind of mountain that books usually talk about. Kolovrat is a place for people who can see. In the first scenes of my *Chef's Table* episode, the lush green hill I climb, and upon reaching the top, tuck my curly blonde hair behind my ear, and stare towards the lowlands and towards the sea, that is Kolovrat.

The Mediterranean Terrace
without Aperitivo

When you stand on the top of that mountain, you understand exactly why I cook the way I cook. You can see where I source my ingredients from, you can grasp why our culture is such a melting pot, you can hear the Slovenian language with the Italian intonation going into the Italian language with the Slovenian intonation, you can taste why the food of the Soča Valley has little to do with traditional Slovenian cuisine, but is so close to that of Valli del Natisone (Nadiške doline), Benečija (Slavia Veneta) and Friuli. Kolovrat is like a huge natural lighthouse overlooking the bay of Trieste. If you look, you can see it all; from the lagoon, Grado, Trieste, Koper and Izola straight to the peninsula of Savudrija in Croatia. On a bright day, if you are lucky, you can see Venice. At Kolovrat's peak, it is so easy to understand why spices are a part of our traditional cuisine, and why I use them so often. You can see how close Venice really is. And since we are on the spice routes between Venice and Vienna, Venetians have been leaving traces on their route, paying people in spices. In old-fashioned recipes there are cinnamon, cardamom, cloves and peppercorns, for instance. If you turn around and face north, you can spot the snowy peaks of Slovenian and Austrian mountains. You may sense Villach, Klagenfurt and further on Salzburg and Vienna, and get a sense of the scale of the Austro-Hungarian empire. Župa-Juha-Rind-

suppe. And of course, down in the valley there are rivers, lakes and forests. Behind the meadows of Pretovč and Sleme, you can see all the villages of the Krn mountain chain, and Drežnica, with its majestic church, and even more majestic history.

Buon Giorno,
Dober Dan

Kolovrat is also one of those border mountains where people have always spoken two languages. In the times of Yugoslavia, when the borders were hermetically closed, the locals from both sides were still meeting on the top.

'Dober dan, buon giorno!'
'Come va? Dobro, hvala.'

That border has always been political alone; wanted by people from the outside world.

It was supposed to divide families, the culture, the language and the table. But the people who wanted the borders never understood quite how stubborn mountain people are. Maria alla Posta and Teresa di Sale e Pepe are two beautiful souls, two great female chefs with Italian passports and nationality, but with Slovenian hearts. They both speak that broken Slovenian Italian or Italian Slovenian, as you want to call it, and they both prove that the kitchen knows no borders at all. Their food is almost an anthropological interpretation of our culture, past, present and future.

Raspberries Do Not Speak
Slovenian or Italian

In these hot days of summer 2018, when I am writing the final chapters of my book, hidden in our Istrian house, Valter's crazy uncle Marko is on Kolovrat foraging wild raspberries and green juniper berries. Sometimes he picks on the Slovenian side, other times on the Italian side. Raspberries do not speak two languages. The only language they know is the language of nature. Kolovrat is the storyteller of my (food) philosophy.

Kaja Sajovic

A Crossroads

It was one of the shots that made viewers fall in love with Hiša Franko – Ana with her hair blowing in the wind, cheeks rosy after hiking up the Kolovrat mountain ridge above her parents' house in Livek with her dog, Prince. Kolovrat was definitely the right backdrop to set off the *Chef's Table* episode, filled with emotions, family drama and mesmerizing scenery. The views, weather conditions and especially history here are all dramatic – especially if you come up here on one of those cold, wintery days when the atmosphere in the valley is almost depressive. This high mountain plateau was the setting for one of the key battles in World War I, the Battle of Caporetto (Kobarid). It's where young Erwin Rommel, 'the Desert Fox', fought – and won. It's where the impenetrable border stations with Italy were set. And now it's an open air museum, its grassy terrain completely studded with tunnels, trenches and caverns. But all the history aside, it's also a place that perfectly explains Ana's signature move of combining seafood with meat. '*Mare e monti*'. Sea and mountains.

There's a logic behind it that goes beyond Ana's personal taste – if you hike Kolovrat or some other local mountains where the sheep, goats and cattle graze, where the wild boars (and sometimes bears) roam, you can actually see the lagoon in Italy where Ana gets her seafood.

On a clear day, your view stretches almost all the way to Venice, where most of the fish from the lagoon end up in the Rialto fish market, and to Ruga dei Spezieri, the 'street of the spice merchants' where back in the day, the spices from Africa and Middle East were sold. The spice route from Venice to Vienna went through Kobarid. From up here, on top of Kolovrat, you can see the Adriatic Sea, you can smell it, you can taste the salt when the wind blows the right way. So, this is Kolovrat. A battlefield. A border ridge. A crossroads. A viewpoint. A magical place.

Ana Roš

Ana Meets Jo

It was the hottest possible day in August, a couple of years ago, when my daughter Eva Klara reluctantly agreed to join me on a short trip to Austria to check a place for the upcoming wedding of Nico, one of Hiša Franko's most loyal guests. On our way back, we went for lunch at Ilija, the restaurant at a golf course in Tarvisio, Italy that served incredible seafood in a stunning mountain location. The restaurant was full, and we were squeezed in between tables of loud Italian golf players. 'Hey, where do you come from?' A reddish-haired, very self-confident guy asked us in English. It was obvious he was a golf teacher. 'Slovenia,' I replied. 'Well, Slovenia is big. I had girlfriends in Bled, Portorož and Ljubljana'. He talks only to Eva Klara. I do not exist. 'Well, we live in Kobarid,' she says. 'Really? There is a famous restaurant in Kobarid. Hiša Franko. Have you ever heard of it?' She looks at him: 'Yes, Hiša Franko is our house.' I feel amused. This game looks promising, and Eva Klara speaks excellent English for her age. 'No, my sweet girl, you don't understand, I speak about the famous restaurant with a famous female chef, a bit outside of Kobarid.' Eva Klara gets upset. 'Franko is my grandfather and Hiša Franko is my home.' He sighs. 'And who is the nice lady with you? Your mother?' She retorts, 'Yes, she is my mother, and she is the chef you are talking about.' There was a silence. 'She cannot be a cook. She looks too blonde, too pretty, too feminine, too much a mother, too much as a woman. . .' Jesus, I thought, I have lost count of the times that I was in a similar situation to this. 'Well, you are wrong. My mum is the chef of Hiša Franko.' The following day, Jo(nathan) dropped into Hiša Franko. He quickly became one of the most regular – and it must be said, critical – customers, and one of the best friends I've ever had.

Jo Introduces me to Achille

Jonathan, or Jo, as we call him, is from Piemonte in Italy, but today he works as a golf instructor in Lignano Sabbiadoro. He is a true food lover – very discerning, to the point of sometimes being too honest at the table. After one dinner in Hiša Franko, he told me that he thought the quality of the fish I was working with was not good enough. Despite his direct nature, Jo is a very pragmatic person who always looks for a solution to a problem. A few evenings later, he introduced me to Achille, who spoke a rare dialect that was a mix of Friulano and Veneziano, known as 'la laguna'. Achille is the man from the lagoon, a fisherman, and a president of the Cooperation of Shellfish Hunters, a huge fishing reserve that stretches from Grado to Venice. And, by sheer coincidence, this is precisely the part of the sea that we can see from our mountains. The sea that spices up the cool salty breeze, which affects the minerality of our mountain soil, changes the taste of the plants, and therefore the flavour of our animals.

That night, Achille fell in love with my food, and this was how one of the most important parts of our supply chain was found.

The following day I contacted Claudio, who every day at 2 p.m. attends the fish auction in the heart of the lagoon village of Marano Lagunare to buy fish for us: sweet clams, the sweetest imaginable squid, sea snails, canocce, sole and turbot of all sizes, sea bream. The lagoon is 50 kilometres (31 miles) as the crow flies from the Soča Valley. It is one of the most silent places I have ever been.

A Day in the Lagoon

People tend to not appreciate what's right in front of them. We know they exist, but we somehow think we have our lifetime to visit them. This is why I never really visited the lagoon. That's what's been so great about writing this book – it forced me to open my eyes and see places, people and things around me.

During my first evening in the lagoon, there was a huge thunderstorm on the sea.

Roby and Achille had just arrived from their fishing trip, where they were trying to catch dinner for us; Roby's wife Joy had set a beautiful table with crystal glasses and silver tableware. Since razor clam hunting is officially closed in July, Achille had to give a kind of silent permission to Roby to fish some for us. They were still alive, and jumped as they hit the heat of the grill, where we were carefully placing them. 'Could you please move to the table. I would like to serve your food in a proper, elegant way,' Joy said, pointing to a pile of white porcelain plates. But she could not stop our greedy hands eating directly from the grill – the clams were so juicy, sweet and salty. Just fished, raw, no lemon or olive oil – exactly as I ate them in my childhood. In Marano Lagunare, they never use olive oil to season the seafood, not even when the seafood is raw – it's just too fresh for it.

The morning after that dinner, we left for the sea at 5 a.m. The early sun was a shimmering gold against the lagoon, and there was absolute silence – even the birds were still asleep. We passed the channel of Lignano Sabbiadoro and entered the open sea where Achille and Roby, together with my sous chef Leonardo, dropped the nets at 1 a.m. 'When do you sleep, Roby?' I asked. 'I sleep when there is time to sleep, Ana. I even have time to make babies,' he replies, gazing over at his wife with a smile. There were ten fish and a lot of (apparently) useless crabs. 'Wait,' I called when he tried to break their legs and turn them back to the water. 'Let's try to cook them,' I pleaded.

'We do not eat them. It is just crab.' Ah, people from the sea. They can still afford to say no to the things they do not know well enough or that were never explained to them. After fishing we stopped in one of the beautiful fisherman houses, built with straw of the lagoon plants, right in the mouth of the river Stella, to grill tiny sea bream and cook some clams with garlic and white wine. Sitting on the wooden deck, overlooking low bushes of the lagoon with a glass of wine for the road, I felt really happy.

That early morning Roby and Achille gave me a very good life lesson. Happiness is not in the number (of fish); happiness is in knowing exactly what you are doing, and that as a result of teaching yourself that skill, you will be able to do that thing for the rest of your life.

Kaja Sajovic

A Day in the Lagoon

Marano Lagunare. Marano on the Lagoon. The name rolls off your tongue like the gentle waves we cut through with our fishing boat at 5.30 a.m. It's still dark when we set out, sea posts each with a seagull sitting on top like a feathery statue, just barely visible in the pink-hued dawn. 'Venezia', points the signpost towards the west. 'Lignano', points the signpost towards the east. The swans are bathing in the dim light, elegant silhouettes on the calm water. We headed towards Marano the previous afternoon, after the lunch service, squeezing into Ana's car, plus crates of wine and packages of cheese for the fishermen. Tracy Chapman's *Fast Car* was playing as we speeded down A23 towards the Italian sea, a mere hour's drive from Hiša.

Roby and Achille were already there, greeting us with a warm *ciao* and a *bacio* on the cheek. They are Ana's go-to-fishermen, with Achille as some sort of *capo di banda* among his peers here in the northern Adriatic. In Friuli-Venezia Giulia, he decides what to fish and when. He manages the 'Cooperativa Marano', or fishing co-op, comprising around 200 fishermen. It used to be a lot more, Marano being a strong fishing community going all the way back to the times of the Venetian Republic, when the livelihoods of the locals depended almost solely on fishing. The lagoon of Marano is the largest lagoon in Friuli-Venezia Giulia, and at the same time the northernmost part of the entire Mediterranean sea. Marano Lagunare is the only settlement along the lagoon coast, and still boasts the largest fishing fleet and the largest fish market in Friuli. Our plan was to hit the open sea that evening, but the dark, ominous clouds predicted a storm coming, so we mutually decided an Aperol-Spritz or two on the main square would be a wiser decision – an aperitivo before the dinner at Roby's house, a feast of clams, mussels and razor clams: catch of the day, as fresh as they come. The long, finger-like shells squirm like worms when the heat hits them. We start eating them straight from the grates. With the sweet clams we don't even wait as long, we just eat them raw. By the time we finish, it's midnight, and Roby and Achille are off to have a power nap before throwing the nets in the water at 2 a.m. – we are joining them a couple of hours later. All the clouds from the previous evening have dispersed, and the early morning sun is shining bright on the nets that Roby and Achille are pulling from the lagoon. Hundreds of metres of nets, most of it depressingly empty. 'It's a disastrous fishing season. There's no fish whatsoever this year. And with squid, it's even worse,' says Roby as he shakes his head, giving me an answer as to why Ana doesn't have squid on the menu this summer. A lone sea snail is twisted somewhere in there, next to a seaweed. A mantis shrimp makes Ana jump with joy, but Roby and Achille continue to shake their heads. Finally, halfway through, some real fish are slowly starting to show up in the net – a sole, a bass, a bream. 'These days, I don't catch more than 20 fish in three hours. You do the maths. I get ten Euros (£8/$12) for 1 kilo (2 lb) of fish. I would need to catch 10 kilos (22 lb) to get 100 Euros (£80/$120) – and we've probably just used most of that money for fuel,' says Roby.

Almost one-seventh of the lagoon consists of nature reserves to protect the local flora and fauna, so they never overfished in this area because the fishing is extremely regulated. And yet, for some reason there are no fish. And it's been this way for two or three seasons now. Shellfish aren't doing much better. Ironically, the problem with shellfish is not the pollution, but the lack of it. The greener we've gone with the waste management, the sewage systems, the detergents, the more the shellfish population has dwindled. Seashells are water filters, so they basically feed on dirt, and clean sea means the death of them. 'There are no clams, no razor clams. . . I've always been an optimist by nature, but I'm running out of hope now. The environment has changed, their habitat has changed. There's nothing. The sea floor is overgrown with plants and seaweed because the water is too clean and the sun peers through, so the photosynthesis works in overdrive and the seaweed is booming and smothering all other life along the way,' says a resigned Roby.

Then and there, Ana decides it's time to do a vegetarian menu with seaweed plates. A couple of weeks later, she puts out her version of lagoon street food – fried pickerels with a side salad made of three kinds of algae and seaweed with a kombu-soy sauce dressing. Mid-sea, we switch the boats and hop on a squilla mantis boat. Unlike with the fish, there's no shortage of mantis here. These cheap prawns (shrimp) with watery but tasty meat sell for a mere 6 Euros (£5/$7) a kilo, so Ana immediately starts to brainstorm how she can use them. A broth? A fish soup? The Italian sea is abundant with mantis, and Marano Lagunare fishermen have stiff competition from Veneto and Venice in particular. The two guys on board the boat offer us some freshly caught mantis. We suck the tender, sweet and salty meat out, savouring the taste of the sea. The two fishermen look a lot less excited about their catch than we do. 'I don't even eat them cooked, let alone raw,' one of them says, pulling a face. 'Honestly, I don't like fish in general.' There you go. His older, grumpier colleague gestures us to stay put on the stern of the ship as he starts pulling out the new set of crates and emptying them in two fast, routine moves. He fills the empty ones with defrosted sardines – bait for mantis – and piles them up on the ship.

Achille and Roby return and we change boats again, heading to Lignano for breakfast. We breeze towards the town that looks almost like it floats on water, the morning light making even the souless, uniform apartment buildings look like diamonds on top of the shimmery blue sea. Croissants, espresso, the sea air and the melodic sound of chattering in Italian from the neighbouring tables is a really fine start to a day. We pick up Roby's wife Joy and eight-year old daughter Vanessa, a full picnic basket and a crate of wine in Marano, then we head out to the lagoon, to the area where the Stella river flows into the Adriatic. We make our way past the swans and tall marshy grass towards the small, hay-covered safari-style huts. It's 10 a.m. and we take in the dream-like scenery with glasses of sparkling in our hands. Suddenly, the fish start to jump out of the water all around us, with one landing right on the deck of the boat, squirming and jumping on the wet floor, prompting us to almost drop our sparkling. 'Have you ever seen the catch actually jumping on its own to your boat?' laughs Roby, incredulously. 'In recent years, I have never seen so many fish! You must have brought us good luck.' We pass a sand dune with a couple of tiny safari huts and pull in at a larger one with its own pier, blooming pink oleanders in front of it and a surprisingly large alcohol stock inside. We make ourselves at home in this lagoon paradise, the women setting up the table, the men starting the grill. Ana pours the hosts some Slovenian wine and cuts the aged Tolminc cheese. We feast on grilled fish and wine – so simple, but delicious.

Back in sleepy Marano, the villagers enjoy their slow Mediterranean pace, shifting from their first Aperol Spritz and a second espresso on the town square to lingering in front of the obituaries plastered on the panels, like it's their favourite pastime. We catch the daily fish auction at 2 p.m., where only buyers, accredited by the co-op, can buy fish, crab, mussels and prawns that sell for ridiculous prices. Mantis shrimp for three Euros (£2.50/$350) a kilo, red mullet for five Euros (£4/$6), Adriatic squid for 12 Euros (£10/$13), scallops for 10 Euros (£9/$11) – in Lignano's restaurants, they sell those same scallops for six Euros (£5/$7) a piece. Competition – be it from Veneto, be it from Thailand, Patagonia or Vietnam – is brutal. Do we care enough whether we eat previously frozen seafood? Do we care whether it comes from the Indian Ocean or from the lagoon, so close you can see it from Ana's mountainous back garden? Can we even tell the difference between a farmed sea bass and a wild one? And do we have a plan B when the sea no longer yields fish? Achille and Roby do. If worst comes to worst, they plan to eventually switch to tourism, driving visitors around the lagoon like they did with us, leaving the centuries-old fishing history of Marano Lagunare to become just that – history.

Istria

Ana Roš

Smuggling Cigarettes

My parents are children of the sixties. Whenever I listen to their crazy stories, I have nothing to compare.

My father and my mother met as students in Ljubljana. She was a beautiful, always golden blonde girl. Her life was all about the sea. He was a handsome, very ambitious and very sporty guy. And apparently they both knew how to party. For years they would earn their pocket money working as stewards on a speedboat that ran between different coastal towns in Istria and Venice. But they made their real money on those boat trips by bringing cigarettes called *Le Bionde* – a nickname for Marlboro lights. In Yugoslavia, the cigarettes never cost a lot, and reselling them in Venice for a higher price was profitable enough for my parents to buy a property in the Istrian countryside with an old stone house and a fig tree in the courtyard.

Katja and Bojan were eventually fined, and the next day the local Venice newspaper the day after reported about the 'blondes' swimming in the gulf of Venice. But the house is still exactly the same as the day my 24-year-old parents put the last brick in the building. Not a single stone has been moved or removed since that summer of 1970. This chapter is about my love story with Istria.

The President

20 kg ripe tomatoes
50 g basil
300 g celery
500 g golden onion
100 g garlic
30 g salt

Boil the tomatoes quickly, then peel them. Assemble all the ingredients in a big pot and cook for 30 minutes. Separate the water and reserve (for recipes with tomato water). Pass the solids and conserve.

A few years ago, the Slovenian president escorted by members of his Cabinet came to Hiša Franko. When they first called we told them the restaurant was full. But on second thought, how could we say no to the President?

We moved one of the reservations to the fireplace and gave him the nicest table in the house. We had just changed some dishes on the menu, and I was looking forward to seeing if he enjoyed them. The whole dining room and the kitchen team was excited – this was definitely not an everyday occurrence. A few minutes after their arrival, Valter came to the kitchen with a weird expression on his face. 'Ana,' he whispered, 'the President wants pasta with tomato sauce.' There was an overall silence. 'No. No way, Valter.' Valter struggled, 'But how can I say no to the President?'

After some pan flying moments, as I call them, I finally gave up and cooked the President pasta with tomato sauce. Pasta with our Istrian tomato sauce. Every August, my father with his two brothers would occupy the little stone Istrian house and break down 800 kilos (1,700 lb) of the sweetest tomatoes in the world into an exquisite sauce. When the President was leaving the restaurant, I at first refused to see him. I was angry. But how can you say no to the President?

We were standing at the door and he was praising the quality and flavour of our tomato sauce.

The sauce seemed to be simply unforgettable. A few months later he awarded me the Golden Apple, an award given to young people in Slovenia who are a good example and provide motivation for others. Ah, at the end it was all about the humble tomato.

The Best Restaurant in the World

If I you asked me what my dream restaurant would be, I could tell you instantly – a place with only local and seasonal cooking, no compromises, set in Istria. Not a lot of people know that Istrian traditional cuisine, despite being on the coast, isn't particularly fish or seafood-focussed. It's a diet of wild boar, wild birds, eggs, local cuttle Boškarinac, pork, goat, vegetables, *bobići* (corn), handmade pasta *fuži*, a lot of chicken and plenty of tomato. Istrian prosciutto, too, is very popular, but due to the hot weather, it's much saltier than its counterparts.

I was 15 when I tried my first white truffles. My father let me come to a truffle-tasting dinner that he was hosting by way of thanks to some people from the village for taking care of our Istrian stone house while we were

away. We were all truffle virgins. It was so interesting to see locals discovering a fruit of their land, and the look of surprise on their faces when they tasted it. There is an important truffle hunting area right by our house, but it's become a very well kept secret, mostly thanks to the neighbouring Italians.

People in Istria have gardens the whole year around. There is no need for greenhouses as there is never a winter frost. Foraging is of much less importance here; there's not the same need for it as there is in the mountains. But every time I put my running shoes on, I feel blessed to understand the wealth of wild food that is hidden in the low, dense bushes. Wild asparagus in spring, wild hops, rock samphire, wild fennel, wild dill, wild cherries. . . There are the sweetest figs in the world, barely discovered, and there is little interest for wild blackberries or tiny pink wine peaches. Every house in the Istrian countryside has a stone cellar for wine and olive oil storage. The olive oil especially is incredibly good quality, and it's starting to get a lot of attention, which is having a profound effect on the price of the land. Olive trees today seem to be the tomato plants of yesterday.

My Istrian Summers

My parents owned a little red boat with shiny white leather seats that was named after my sister Maja. That boat was my door to (food) paradise. The boat was always ready for great meals; there were bottles of wine on board, earthy-flavoured, ripe tomatoes, freshly picked cucumbers, olive oil and basil. Every August day of my childhood 'Maja' was on another expedition.

We would usually wait for the first morning fisherman's boats to come back to the port of Novigrad. Our shopping was always about sweet small scallops, sardines, anchovies or other types of blue fish. A splash of seawater with some olive oil and basil was the natural dressing for tomatoes and chargrilled sardines. And our lunchtime meal lasted the whole day. There was never a table, nor knives and forks. I would always eat tomatoes like apples, and the anchovies I would devour whole, including bones and heads. The sea in front of Novigrad is very shallow and the risk of the boats hitting the underwater rocks is very big. It was known as Čeri, and it was our favourite spot for swimming and diving. My mother was an oyster queen; I would count the minutes for her to come back on the boat, the yellow net around her waist full of shells; a few moments later I was in oyster heaven. *Kamenica*, meaning 'the stone', is a wild oyster with a particularly irony, mineral flavour. My love of raw seafood at a young age, without any condiment, not even lemon, always surprised people. My father was a master

of clam scavenging – you could hear exactly where he was by a tiny 'tick tick' – the noise of the hammer on the rock, and the tweezers trying to get a hold of the clam without crushing it. Today, it is strictly forbidden to pick them. The bottom of the sea needs time to recover.

I spent hours and hours diving, discovering old shipwrecks and amazing, sometimes untouched wine and olive oil amphoras that had sunk centuries before with their mother boats. How can you forget such an intense childhood food memory? In the mountains around the Mirna river, the magical place where the fresh waters meet the salty ones, my parents found a perfect spot to pick river clams. The rule was to enter the water completely naked and then crawl in the mud, risking cuts from the sharp edges of broken shells. An hour later, those clams had been turned into delicious *spaghetti alle vongole*. Every evening, we would bring the freshly picked seafood to our little stone house and cook it down to *brodetto*, *buzara* or fish soups and salads. There were always friends, loud music, wine and a lot of good feeling. Once, one of these August days, I found a beautiful pearl in one of the mussels. How many times in your life do you find a pearl?

Sunce Sije, Sonce Sije; We Need a Lot of Sun for Good Tomatoes

On the day that our August holiday was over, we needed to pack our suitcases, and the tomato sauce we had cooked, into a little Cabrio car named Diana. There was usually very little place for my sister and me. We would have to sit on the boxes full of tomatoes with our heads up to the open sky. When we reached the Dragonja river, the border river between Croatia and Slovenia, we would start singing 'the sun is shining' in both languages. With all that wind, loud music and the aroma of ripe tomatoes, we perhaps never felt so happy and free.

But back to the tomatoes – another tradition was my father insisting that my sister and I help the farmers harvest them. The sun was blazing hot, and there was something mystical about the enticing flavour of *bevanda* – a blend of oxidized Malvasia grapes and water – and the colourful tomato fields. The tomato leaves turned the skin of my hands green, and covered my fingers in little scratches. When we felt hungry, we would take a tomato. When we felt thirsty, we would take a tomato. Today, most of those endless fields in Istria are abandoned. The main cause is globalization; even if they were green and tasteless, people were lured by cheaper alternatives. The farmers were never able to compete with the price, or learn the rules of the game of capitalism.

Nino and Damir

When we first started photographing the Istria chapter for this book, I wanted to bring our photographer Suzan on a fishing trip – all my memories of Istria are connected to the seafood. And so on a hot July evening, in a big white boat, we sailed to the middle of the bay of Dajla to drop our fishing nets. The place looked promising, and the fishermen seemed confident as we headed back to shore. Twelve hours later, we left for the sea again to investigate our catch, and expectations were high. But when we pulled up the nets, there were only three small fish in the whole thing.

Where were the fish? Wild, greedy and unregulated practices have, in less than 20 years, almost emptied the northern Adriatic Sea. And the fish that are caught off the coast of Istria are usually sold around the world, and not back to the locals. It's a similar story with the famous langoustine from Kvarner-kvarnerski škamp, which is the sweetest and the firmest langoustine I have ever tasted. The market demand was too big for what the sea had to offer, and the price went sky high.

A year ago I had a chat with a local fisherman who had just come off the boat from the sea. 'So, are you happy with your catch of the day?' He smiled. 'Today was a great day. I have 5 kilos (11 lb) of langoustines.' With my eyes, I measured the size of the boat and then a little box of scampi. 'Did you mean *50* kilos (110 lb)?' He started laughing in a sad way. 'My little blonde Slovenian friend, ten years ago we would complain when the night gave us 100 kilos (220 lb) of them. Today, we are happy when the night gives us five. All of my fishing friends sold their boats already.' That said, there are still a few restaurants in Istria where you can eat local fish. Nino from Asterea and Damir from Damir e Ornela meet their own fisherman every day very early in the morning. They never wanted to share their supplier details with me.

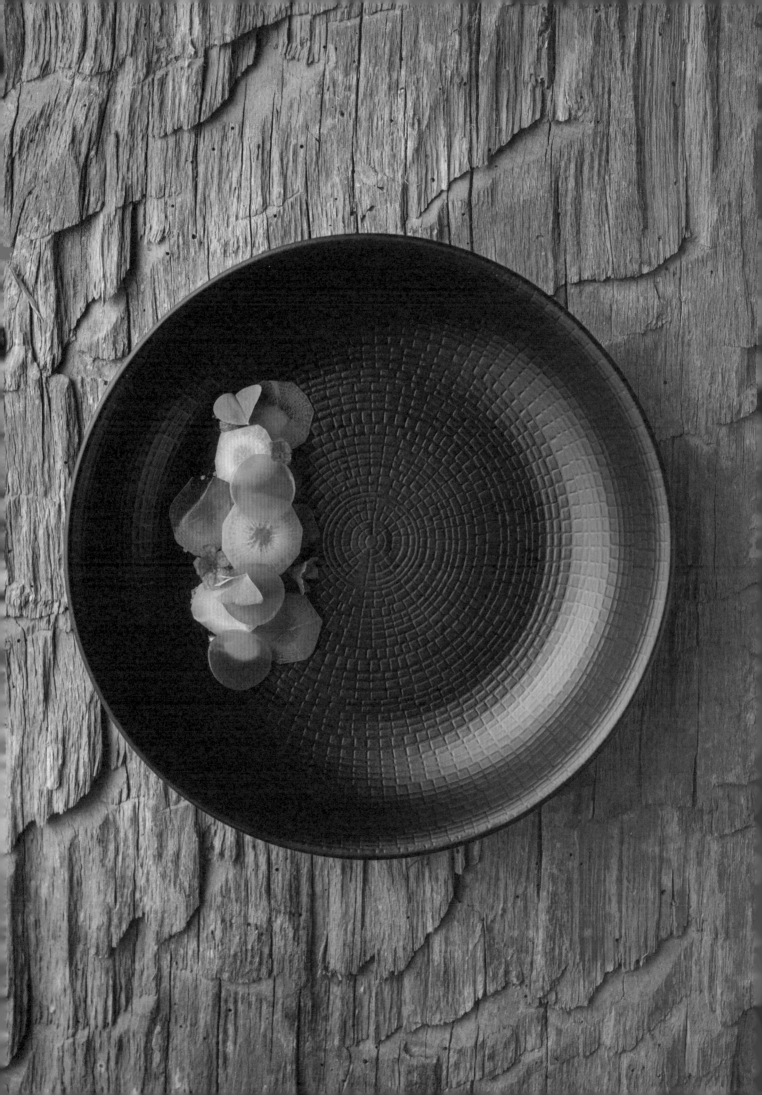

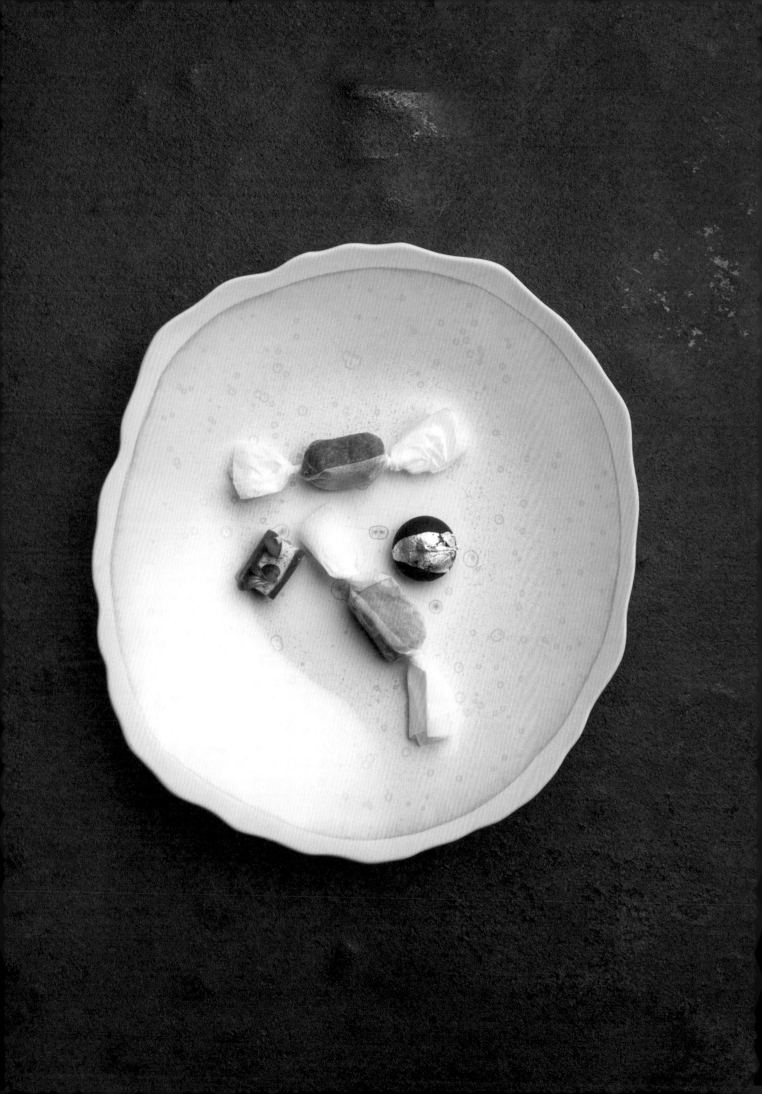

Kaja Sajovic

Rise and Shine, Smell the Tomatoes

'Bananarama!' enthusiastically proclaims over-enthusiastic Smiljan, the youngest of the three Roš brothers. The oldest, Bojan, Ana's father, sways his hips back and forth and hums, 'She's got it, yeah, baby, she's got it, I'm your Venus, I'm your fire. . .' They made pretty monotonous tomato sauce making look almost fun. Once a year, for five days, Smiljan, Dušan and Bojan Roš bond over cutting, cooking and bottling the red-ripe Istrian plum tomato.

Ana's summerhouse in Croatia is no luxurious seaside hacienda – it's Robinson Crusoe-style, a 100-year-old, refurbished wheat storage barn in the middle of nowhere. Bojan and Katja first leased the house as students, in 1968. They took the bus to the nearby village of Brtonigla, then walked, loaded with luggage, to the tiny settlement of Nova Vas. When they first started going there, there was nothing – no electricity, no supermarket, no bars, no shade, and the back garden was frequented by the rats from the nearby rubbish dump. And yet, that was Istria as it once was – wild, rugged, and all the more charming for it. Maybe it's the air, mixed with salt from the nearby Adriatic, maybe it's the soil, red as brick, maybe it's the scent of fig leaves that fills the dilapidated stone alleys and sun-drenched village squares. For Slovenians, Istria was our closest sea getaway, so we often took it for granted. Almost everyone spent the summers here on the coast, usually staying in the old Adria caravans that ex-Yugoslavia was overrun with. They were all the same – white and blue, the colours of the Adriatic, with basic equipment and a canopy that took us forever to set. Our summers were modest, with just the bare minimum, a tacky fun fair at the nearest resort town serving as the biggest source of entertainment – but none of us would trade those summers for the world. We went swimming in the morning, then we scoured the rocks for mussels and oysters that we then feasted on for dinner, along with sardines from the local fish market, tomatoes we picked up at the road-side stands, and bottles of bright lemony malvasia from the nearby farmer. Twenty years later, Istria isn't the same place any more. Its campgrounds have been largely sold off to huge international companies, its seaside villages overrun with cheap apartment buildings, its roadside stands replaced by supermarket chains. The attributes that made Istria such a special place – juicy tomatoes, exquisite olive oil, truffles, wine and fish – got a little lost somewhere, buried underneath a pile of cheap imports. They are still there, though; you just have to look for them.

In Nova Vas, back in the day, practically everyone made a living from growing tomatoes and onions. Today, one single producer is left – Germano. All the rest quit, turning their hands to tourism instead. It doesn't pay to grow tomatoes any more. And the supermarket competition is too steep. But Germano and his wife are soldiering on, even though they had to let go of all the helpers. In their sun-scorched fields next to the Mirna river they grow endless garlic, onions, watermelons and melons. But the star product is the plum tomato. Blood red, juicy, full of flavour. Eleven thousand of them a season, like wild weeds. People used to go crazy for them, but nowadays, Germano struggles. International chains are killing the small farmers. Their buying price is so ridiculously low that the farmers just don't bother. There is no way of competing with them. 'Today it's far easier to get the produce from a major chain. It's cheaper and faster. That's the saddest part,' one of the more socially conscious Istrian restaurateurs said to me.

It's 7 a.m., and the smell of cooked-down tomatoes, onions and basil sneaks through the windows to bedrooms upstairs. The brothers Roš are already in full working mode. Germano brought them a truckload of cases of plum tomatoes that they are now hosing down and chopping under the shade of the large fig tree in the garden. Smiljan, apparently the least disciplined of the brothers, grunts something about Bojan, 'the drill sergeant', waking him up 'very violently' at 6 a.m., but after some bantering, they let it go. Behind them, a row of chickens potter through the olive grove. In the background, Nino, their half-blind, but stubbornly active neighbour, is steering his tractor, shirt off, with the proud, upright position worthy of a king. On the small transistor radio, Bananarama has been replaced by The Clash. Bojan whistles along to 'London Calling' as he pounds the tomatoes in a large cauldron over the fire. He removes the tomato water with the ladle and pours it into jars, ready to be pasteurized. They used to throw it away, but three years ago Ana started using it, so now they are

Golden Mackerel → p. 246

bottling it. Tomato water jelly on sardines, beef tongue in tomato water, sourdough starter with tomato water.

When you take a look at the fine dining plates Ana serves, you would never associate them with this rural Istrian setting – a chicken coop on one side, a crumbling garage/kitchen/storage room on the other, tomato salsa that was once served to the President, simmering in a rusty old cauldron originally used for spirit distilling. And yet, the result is phenomenal. Unlike the locals, who use just tomatoes and basil, Bojan adds onions, garlic, celery, herbs and salt. It's a recipe passed on to Katja Roš by her mother, born on the Slovenian side of Istria. When the tomatoes are simmered down, Bojan runs them through an unsophisticated looking machine that resembles an old meat grinder. 'Katja used to mock me endlessly for this machine that I bought for peeling the tomatoes. But then I organized a blind tasting of salsas in Hiša Franko,' brags Bojan, as a smile spreads across his face. In order to prove his equally strong-headed wife wrong, he bought ten salsas in Italy, ranging from super cheap to unnecessarily pricey. The eleventh one was his. You can guess whose salsa won. 'Hands down. The most expensive sauce came second. And after that Katja stopped irking me!' declares a triumphant Bojan.

Bojan's bright white, form-fitting white Emporio Armani T-shirt is now sprayed with red stains, Dexter-style, as he vehemently stuffs the machine with cooked tomatoes. He is braving the midday heat with a safari cap shielding his neck. At a certain point one of the neighbours comes to check if the trio of masochistic Slovenian brothers aren't sunstruck yet. There's no real danger of that – Bojan is built like a machine, and Smiljan and Dušan are riding out the heat by drinking beer under the fig tree. 'Mobee', they call it. 'Morning beer'. 'Afbee' is the afternoon version of it, and they don't exactly hold back. 'We used to bottle the sauce in our empty beer bottles. So, whenever we ran out of bottles, we would quickly drink ten beers to get the containers,' smiles Smiljan. At midday, they sit down for a lunch of soft, white pillowy bread, aged Tolminc cheese from Valter's cellar, and Bojan's homemade pork salami. Then they are back at work. 600 kilos (1,300 lb) of tomatoes in a couple of days, most of it for Hiša Franko, and the rest split evenly between the brothers.

In the evening we eat at the nearby Konoba Astarea, a rare authentic Istrian konobas (taverns) that use local ingredients to whip up simple, but delicious dishes. Grilled fish, veal shank under the iron lid, Mediterranean salad of octopus and potatoes, marinated anchovies, fresh raw prawns drizzled with thick, spicy olive oil. 'Have you taken your cholesterol and your high pressure pills yet?' Bojan asks his younger brother, his doctor profession kicking in. 'I haven't. I'll take it in the morning, that's

ok, right?' asks Smiljan, and takes another sip of malvasia. He has clearly adapted the leisurely Istrian attitude.

The next day I head to San Rocco, one of the first boutique hotels in Istria that its owner Tullio Fernetich, a visionary and a former two-term mayor of Brtonigla, built on the outskirts of the village. Tullio is a no-nonsense kind of man, with his feet firmly on the ground. In the 1990s, after the Balkan war, he was at the forefront of tourism development of Istria, and now, he is the loudest critic of it. 'Aaaah, what to say about it? About the whole Istrian tourism story?' he smirks as he takes a sip of local sparkling wine. 'In Yugoslavia, we used to live better than they did inland, because of the Italians who were coming here for lunch. Back then, Istria was the leading gastronomic region,' declares Tullio. Unlike the rest of Croatia, Istria managed to stay clear of the war-induced chaos of the 1990s, but it was after the Balkan war that the real Istrian renaissance began. People opened up to the world, they started travelling... Those in the hospitality and wine business who were most receptive to those influences and ideas were the ones who set the tone of what Istria could become: a boutique destination in every sense of the word, not just a cliché that tourist boards use. 'I'm not throwing out empty platitudes – the diversification of plants and animals we have here in the radius of 50 kilometres (30 miles), you can't find elsewhere in a 1,000 kilometre (600 mile) radius! Our fish, our plum tomatoes, our olive oil are top notch – we shouldn't spoil what nature gifted us with so generously. We need romantics like Ana, people who have put all this before the big buck,' insists Tullio.

He previously worked as a sommelier in Tuscany where tourism flourished even though the sea – a big commercial draw – was miles away. He thought he could do the same for Istria's inland, for a long time perceived as the Croatian seaside's ugly, neglected duckling. 'The decision was gutsy, but the right one to make,' remembers Tullio. 'As a result, a couple of top-end restaurants and serious winemakers emerged, and that's how everything started.' He leans back in his chair. 'Now, have we managed to retain this upward swing? A lot of people think we haven't, that we've lost the drive that we had in those years. I would put it this way: with time, you get real, and you have to face the market. You can certainly be romantic, but the reality is you have to have the financial results to back that up.'

And the fact is, as Tullio puts it, the 350,000 guests that stay in Istria daily don't appreciate the upscale romanticism that San Rocco (or Hiša Franko) offers: homegrown produce from the backyard garden, homemade olive oil from the 1,200 olive trees, homemade wine vinegar, and Istrian seafood delivered by fishermen.

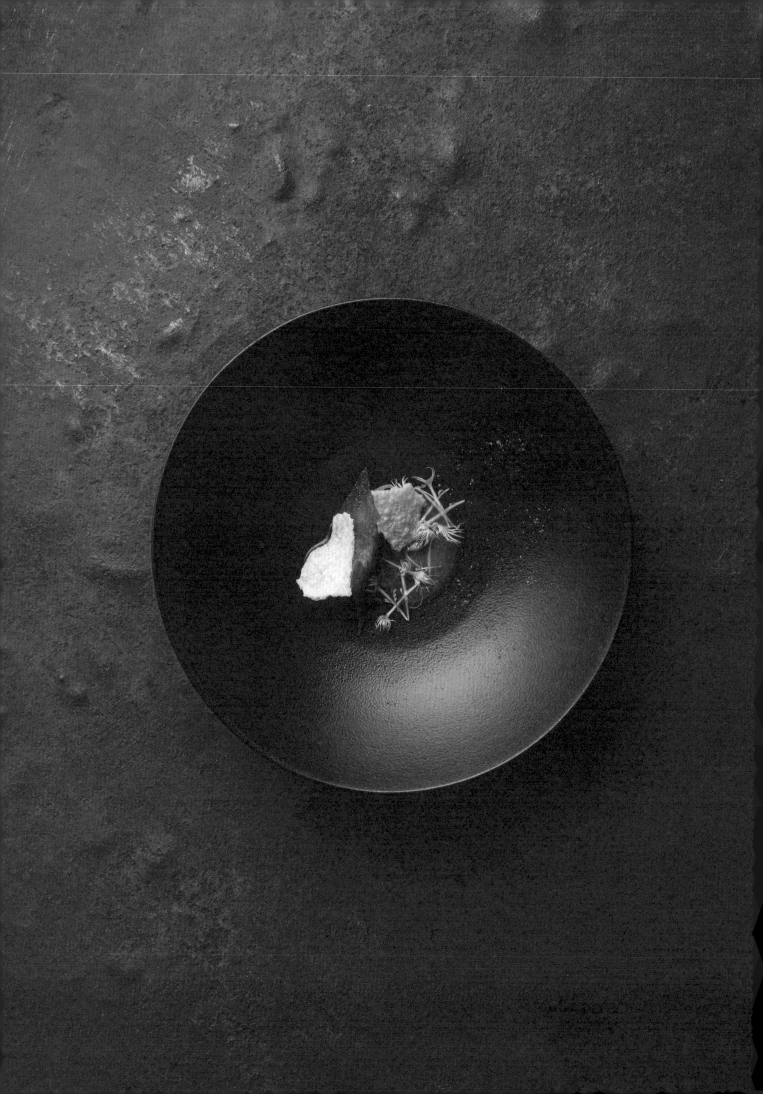

Big
World

Ana Roš

The Influence of Travelling

In a lot of interviews, I'm asked what I believe makes my kitchen so different from others. In my eyes, the kitchen is a symbiosis of three elements: the territory, the season and the personality of the chef. And that personality is not only something you inherit; rather, it's a collage, a patchwork of all our life experiences. Travelling, childhood memories, parents, grandparents, birth, death, love, religion, teachers, friends, schoolmates... they are all part of it.

From the age of 16, I've been on the road. I started travelling with my parents, I continued travelling as a student and later with Valter. We had a silent agreement that we would always travel, regardless of our financial situation. And we did. Low budget, sometimes practically no budget, backpacking with our now almost-grown children as babies – we never gave up discovering the world. But I have never travelled more than I do today. It is mostly for work; sometimes I get back home exhausted, but always richer in my soul. I often take my children on my working trips. Discovering other cultures – and food – and understanding diversity is the biggest gift you can give to a child.

Exploring Africa

I was born in Yugoslavia in the kingdom of Tito, a bon vivant, a dictator and a dreamer. Surrounded by the most beautiful women on the planet in his white suits and with a cigar in his right hand, he was ruling one of the most controversial countries in the world. It was sold as a place where everyone had a job, a right to schooling, medical care, a forty-hour working week and a month of holidays. The intellectual, the lawyer, the doctor, the teacher, the hairdresser, the chef and the simple industry worker all had equal rights and similar money. I never understood that drinking bitter chicory infusion instead of flavourful Arabica coffee was not democracy.

I never considered travelling, because no one was travelling. And I did not dream of bananas, because I thought they belonged to the world of books and faraway places. Sometimes our minds trick us into not wishing for what we can't have. When I was 14, the family of my best friend, Tina, decided to move to Africa. We

were all people of the valley, mentally entrenched in our surroundings, and unaware of the vastness of the outside world. The three of us, Tina, Maja and I, were sitting in Tina's room with a globe on the table. 'There,' she said. 'Tanzania is there.' It looked so so far away – I needed to turn the globe upside down to spot it.

I could not imagine how many hours, days of flying you need to reach Africa. A year later, in 1989, my parents bought tickets to Tanzania for the whole family. We took a train to Trieste Centrale to catch another train, which would lead to an Ethiopian airlines flight from Rome. We stopped in Cairo, Addis Ababa and Rwanda before reaching Dar es Salaam almost two days later. In those two beautiful months in Africa, I learnt all about spices, papayas, mangoes and yes, thousands of different varieties of bananas. I knew how to barter with fishermen, and how to recognize the freshest cashew nuts. Jerry, the family driver, took us to daily markets and evening parties. The trip was slightly marred when I was violently robbed on the Dar es Salaam main 'oyster beach' while flirting with a young Austrian boy, but the experience taught me how to forgive. I got back home a different Ana. I had fallen in love with Africa, and I swore to myself that I would never stop discovering the world. That trip was one of the reasons I decided to study diplomatic science.

Cape Verde

Eva Klara was barely five months old and Svit had just turned two when we accepted the invitation of a good friend of ours to visit him in Cape Verde. Both children were still in nappies, and backpacking with them seemed like a big challenge, but we accepted it. Boa Vista is one of the twelve islands lost in the sea between Senegal and Brazil. There, our friend Gorazd had found his own paradise; he exchanged a stressful city life in Ljubljana for a white and blue Portuguese colonial house on the never-ending beach that was beyond the knowledge of tourists, and had great wind for surfing. There was a community of 3,000 people living on the island, eating from what Jacques Cousteau declared as the richest sea in the world. Those were happy days; we spent our days and nights dancing with the locals, drinking punch and eating what the sea gave us that day with a bowl of rice. Do you think you need more to survive? Do you think you need more to be happy? We go back to that remote island every year, and sometimes we spend two months together, enjoying the barefoot life in a house without water and electricity. We fish, while Svit and Eva Klara go surfing with the local children. I read in the sunshine, and cook what Valter has brought home from the sea. I sometimes invite local people to join us for dinner; I have been amused by their surprise when tasting my flavour combinations, until I understood they did not really like it. Food, just like the rest of life, was simple, as true to its natural state as possible. As it should be.

On the Train
through Madagascar

I am also often asked about my favourite eating experience. Well, first off, it is not a restaurant. It is a train ride between Fianarantsoa and Manakara in central Madagascar. An old Swiss train from the 19th century with wooden benches, it's full of local people, loud singing, tonnes of bananas, lychees, mangoes, pineapples, homegrown vegetables, medicines, fuel and water, all mixed up together. This train is the only connection between Fianarantsoa and the east coast, and supplies to the villages come from this. It is a real misery when the train breaks down. And it happens very often. The train takes between 14 and 34 hours to reach its final destination, barely 120 kilometres (75 miles) away. But the hours I spent on that were the most magical hours of my life.

The train stops at every station to load and unload what people need, plus what people need to buy and sell. There was a young French teacher sitting on a bench close to us. He had lived in Madagascar for years, and it was his second trip to Manakara. His stories opened our minds and hearts, and fuelled our appetite for that train ride. All the windows were wide open the whole time, and the train was so slow you could have run alongside it. At every station, there were thousands of hands shooting out, offering us the most delicious food you could dream of. And at every station, it was different. Raw crayfish with fruity dressings, crispy chicken feet, sweet and juicy pork ribs, fish fillets in French-style sauces, rice balls, steamed and charcoal grilled corn, lychees in chilli salt, slices of caramelized banana, cold sugary pineapple pieces. . . It was 24 hours of eating, partying, laughing, dancing, eating again and eating again, until finally we started filling up our pockets, thinking of supplies for when the journey ended. During the train ride, a strong monsoon rain came across us, making the train stop and everyone dodge the splashes of rain – but we did not close the windows. At one of the final stations, a huge group of children was waiting for the train to come. It stopped in that village every third day, and it was one of the big moments in the local life. Our friend from that journey, the young French teacher, was standing on the steps of the train and made all those children start singing and dancing the *Macarena*. Svit and Eva Klara needed some time to overcome their shyness, but they finally joined them, wondering how children in a place without electricity, radio or television could know how to sing and dance along to that song. That picture is one of the most beautiful postcards of my life. Dancing children, happy children.

Whenever Eva Klara
Thinks of Vietnam,
She Thinks of Fish Sauce

My children have been lucky enough to travel around a large part of the world already. Mostly backpacking, and always eating strictly local, often street food. Eva Klara was two years old when we left for our forty-day trip around Vietnam. It was 2006, and we met just a handful of other backpackers on the whole journey. There was almost no tourism in Vietnam at that point.

The whole 'NO! NO!' story started on our first evening; we tried so many soups, fish, vegetables, rice paper rolls and noodles, but Eva Klara was not enjoying the experience at all.

My children have always been very open to food, but when they said 'NO!' to something, I was never difficult about it. But Eva Klara did not touch any of that food at all. Not that evening. And not the following ones. *'Hanoi je gnoj'* (Hanoi has a weird smell). 'Eva Klara?!'

For the following weeks, she only ate steamed rice. I was tempted to take her to an Italian pizzeria, in Hue, but I resisted. 'We are not going to eat pizza and pasta in Vietnam,' I declared. In Mui Ne, a little fishing village in southern Vietnam (I guess it is not that small and tourist-free any more), I finally understood what was bothering my little girl so much. The whole coast was covered with fermented fish, drying in the hot sun, getting ready to end up in nham pla, the famous Vietnamese fish sauce. The pungent fishy smell was persistent, spicy and strong. 'Hanoi je gnoj.' That evening, I asked the old food vendor to avoid putting fish sauce in Eva Klara's rice paper rolls. Success! My little girl was hungry again.

Life is Too Short
for a Shitty Caipirinha

I love a gin and tonic, and I love a caipirinha. I feel blessed when I have a glass of it on the beach in Cape Verde, trying to imagine Brazil on the other side of the Atlantic Ocean with a good book in my hands. In October 2017, I was cooking a dinner with Rafa Costa de Silva in the heart of Rio de Janeiro. This was the first time I met Alexandra Forbes, a Canadian-Brazilian food journalist. She came to our lunch with her future husband and Jock Zonfrillo, one of my favourite chefs and a good friend. After lunch, Alex invited me to Urka for the best caipirinha in town. We were sitting on a little stone wall overlooking the sea, snacking on pastels with plenty of chilli oil on the top, ordering one after the other of the sugar-coated glasses full of that inviting, powerful drink. The chef of the bar came around and she recognized us. She called the owner, and that was the beginning of more drinks, more pastels, more chilli oil. 'Everything is on the house!' the owner declared, apparently enjoying our good mood and our company. The waiter came over with another round of drinks. I see Alexandra taking a glass, calling back the boy and ordering him to take all the drinks back and make fresh ones. 'Alex, what's wrong?' I asked. 'Too much sugar, Ana,' she replied. 'But Alex, we've been offered all of these drinks for free.' She smiled. 'I understand, Ana, but life is in the detail, and the detail here is that gram of sugar. It is too short to drink shitty caipirinhas.' Whenever I eat and cook, I think of that phrase. Life is too short for shitty caipirinhas. The happiness is in that little gram of sugar.

Failure is the Engine of Success

Ana Roš

An Exotic Animal

I was in Mougins, a romantic little French town on the Côte d'Azur just outside of Cannes. There was a food festival with a lot of chefs from all around the world. I was not someone new any more. During the opening cocktail party, I met David Higgs, the celebrity chef from South Africa. After an hour of chatting, I realized that he thought I was a Dutch journalist. 'No, chef, I am also a chef, and from Slovenia.' He seemed amused and annoyed at the same time. 'Really?' he said. It was a kind of Kruger Park safari situation; a polymath European tourist just spotted an example of the rarest amur leopard. I forgot to tell David I was also completely self-taught, and pretty old when I began, too.

Andrea

I first met Andrea Petrini in San Patrignano; I had heard a lot about him already, mostly through our common friend, the Italian food journalist Anna Morelli.

I was cooking a simple, hand-rolled pasta with fresh elder blossoms melted in butter and Parmesan when a guy with strange glasses stood up and asked me why, in fine dining restaurants, did we rarely taste such intense and distinctive flavours. With my usual do-not-disturb-me-while-I-am-cooking tone, I told him that the problem was with food critics, who usually measure the quality of the food by the skill of the chef to transform the main ingredient into something as far away from its original state as possible. After the conference he introduced himself in person. No prizes for guessing who it was. Afterwards, I just thought 'I guess I fucked up again.' But that's not what Petrini thought.

The following day he phoned and invited me to Le Grand Fooding in New York. Six months later, I was the first female chef to be invited to the original version of Cook it Raw, an environmental movement created by the best chefs of the world. I was so looking forward to it, but I was also so scared to fail. In those five days in the countryside of Poland, days full of doubts and low self-esteem, days full of moments I wanted to give up, I finally turned from thoughts of abject failure to total confidence – 'I can do it.'

But this initial 'Bridget Jones syndrome' started when I missed my flight to Warsaw. I was so tired that I didn't hear my alarm clock. You can imagine my embarrassment when I walked into the Atelier Amaro restaurant in the centre of Warsaw, 12 hours late with 20 men staring at me with obvious 'who the fuck is this' expressions on their faces. A day later, I managed to capsize a wooden canoe full of vodka bottles and food; I was swimming in the middle of the river, fully dressed, in front of most influential food journalists on the planet. So much for my wild water kayak expertise. A few hours later, I was seriously bitten by a huge dog, and the following day, I had my first allergic reaction to a bee sting in my life, needing a doctor and an antihistamine shot. But at the final dinner, when every one of us needed to cook a dish that would reassume his understanding of Polish culture, I proved I could cook. I risked failure by avoiding playing it safe. I told myself that if I could leave my comfort zone, I had made it. If the journalists at first thought my presence at Cook it Raw in Poland was a political move on the part of the organizers to shut down questions from the world's media about the absence of female chefs, then after dinner, they had second thoughts, and understood why Andrea Petrini believed I stood out.

The Cake for Mr. Napolitano, the Italian President

It was Spring 2011, a few weeks before the celebrations of Slovenia's 20th anniversary of independence, when I got a phone call from the Cabinet of Danilo Turk, the President of Slovenia. He was a regular summer visitor to Nebesa, and he loved coming to Hiša Franko for a dinner or two. He was one of our most curious guests, he was always writing down comments and interrogating me after his meal about every single detail that he found interesting. The President wanted me to cook lunch for a hundred VIP guests that he had invited to celebrate Slovenian independence. The list included Austrian, Hungarian, Croatian and Italian presidents, plenty of prime ministers and ministers, the mayor of Ljubljana, and a few ambassadors. Once again – how can you say no to a President?

The Italian President, Napolitano, was celebrating his 80th birthday on that same day. A 100-serving cake was requested to surprise him. Not too creamy, if possible. 'Could an apricot-ginger one work?' I had never baked cakes in my life, and I had never tried an apricot and ginger one. I didn't think too much about it, and just imagined that whatever we made would be exactly what President Napolitano would like to eat. At 6 a.m. on the day of the lunch, I entered the restaurant to pack the food and leave for Ljubljana. My pastry chefs were still in the kitchen. I walked in. The apricot ginger cake was melting and falling apart, and everyone was crying. It was five hours to one of the most important diplomatic lunches in Slovenian history and I had no birthday cake. I called Matej Tomažič, one of my chef friends who always finds a solution to a problem. 'Drive to Ljubljana, girl. And do not cry. I will figure out something.'

It was midday, the expectations and the temperature were high, and the famous lunch was about to start, when Matej entered the kitchen of Ljubljana castle and murmured, 'Do not worry.' He had a huge package in his hands. The cake looked perfect; there were even five colourful butterflies on the dark chocolate glaze. At the end of the service, the President called me to the table to make my official presentation. When I bent down to whisper Happy Birthday to Mr. Napoletano, the Italian president said: 'It was an amazing lunch, thank you so much. But the best part of this experience was the cake. It was simply wonderful.' I was standing there, at the table of five presidents, surrounded by many prime ministers and ministers, and I was speechless. I was tempted to tell the truth and to admit my failure. But sometimes, it is better not to. Ah. . . and about the cake mystery. Matej called the pastry shop, Saint Honore, in Trieste, and told them his friend needs a cake for the Italian president. It took an hour to convince them he was not lying. There was a huge 'not creamy' cake on order for a customer that morning, and they simply informed the client to come and pick up their cake a few hours later. And the butterflies? Saint Honore's pastry chef added one for each president.

Facing Failure

I am very similar to my son Svit. I like walking on the edge, I like taking risks, and I am open to accepting the consequences for my failure. I hate comfort zones, I find them the killers of evolution. This is why my food is different and unique. This is why people either like it or don't like it at all. There is nothing in between. When I disappoint people, I am ready to face it. There are not a lot of compromises in my food; I rarely play it safe. But I always listen to the critic.

I prefer constructive criticism to glowing praise. Many years ago, a famous Slovenian food critic, Tomaž Sršen, came for dinner – and he didn't like it. For weeks, I could not read his review. But one morning, I forced myself to open the newspaper and face my reality. And a lot of what he said was right. I read that story a lot of times. I almost learnt the text by heart. On my way to the top, I've always listened to what my guests had to say. They may be wrong. They may not understand me sometimes. But I listen to them, and I memorize.

Kitchen Legends, Beauties & Tattoos

Ana Roš

Ana Roš

Faces of Hiša Franko—The Team

'Don't look ahead, there's stormy weather.
Another roadblock in our way.
But if we go, we go together
Our hands are tied here if we stay'.
– Santigold, *Disparate Youth*

Strong

Quando ti vedono come una donna forte, pensano che tu non abbia bisogno di niente o di nessuno, che possa sopportare tutto e superare tutto quello che ti accade. Che non ti dispiaccia non essere ascoltata, curata o amata.

Quando ti vedono come una donna forte, ti cercano perché li aiuti a portare le loro croci. Ti parlano e pensano che tu non abbia il bisogno di essere ascoltata.

Non si chiede ad una donna forte se è stanca, soffre o se è caduta, se ha ansia o paura. L'importante è che sia sempre li: un faro nella nebbia o una roccia in mezzo al mare.

La donna forte non viene mai perdonata. Se perde il controllo, dicono che sia debole o isterica.

Quando la donna forte scompare per un minuto, tutti se ne accorgono ma quando c'è, la sua presenza è abituale.

Ma da dove lei prenda la forza necessaria ogni giorno per essere quel tipo di donna non ha importanza per nessuno.

Power and Respect

In a war of tattoos and pretty kitchen girls, who is the winner? I honestly do not know.

But my bet is on the girls.

Yvonne, Ines, Maša, Nataša, Marta, Duan, Kristina, Teja, Ivana, Francesca… all such beautiful women, breaking down rabbits, lamb and goats, handling knives, baking the best bread on earth, skipping breaks when everyone else is smoking their cigarette or taking a nap. Girls that dare to wear red lipstick instead of tattoos, articulated, educated, intelligent, humble and opinionated.

Yvonne is my American sous chef, so focused in the kitchen and so open and honest in her private life.

A girl who worked in the Hollywood film industry, she ended up living in a mountain village surrounded by forest and wildlife. Her references were incredible; sous chef of chef Tusk in Oregon and Californian three-Michelin-starred Quince, she decided to travel the world to work with me. Thank you, girl. Just avoid crushing more cars, please.

Ines joined Hiša Franko after her long stage in Mugaritz. She is a stunning Portuguese woman, an amazing chef and always caring for others.

Maša. My pastry chef in Kobarid with a PhD in Croatian literature. So Mediterranean, so beautiful, always determined, and forever curious.

Nataša Djuric, my bread queen. She already had her sourdough book published when she started working with me, and her reputation in the world of bread far exceeds my fame. She took over bread when Francesca left, and made the best loaf I had ever tasted in any restaurant around the world. So much for my humbleness. Nataša is very similar to me: vulnerable, sensible and always looking to be better. At the time of writing, Nataša is the only Slovenian chef working in the kitchen.

Marta is Italian; she works with the live fire, catching and killing trout, breaking down whatever we are cooking in that particular moment.

The golden hands of my dishwasher Duan, a tiny Thai woman who married my friend Peter, ensure that the kitchen of Hiša Franko is not only clean, but also makes us see how much respect is owed to her line of work, and her personal dedication. Chapeau.

Kristina is 53 at the time of this writing. She has been a part of Hiša Franko for more than 10 years. Kristina works as long and hard as everyone else, and she doesn't want mercy because of her age or gender. I only hope she can see my gratitude.

One day, Leo, my head chef, decided the girls in the kitchen needed flowers. He asked Piko, our gardener, to bring them every week as a mark of love and respect. Colourful bouquets are dotted all around the pass of the cold and dessert sections.

But before Leonardo there was Emily. Emily was my sous chef at Hiša Franko for two years. Emily helped the restaurant in its transition from a family-run to a professional restaurant. She is a small, powerful and heavily

tattooed Korean-American girl. She was my best friend and my best working partner in those two years. When there is too much love, there is never a happy end. I still miss her.

Leonardo, Michael, Illias, Sebastian, Matteo, Bernard, Sadmir… my *malakas*!! Thank you for coming from all around the world to cook with me, accepting unconditionally my (female) authority; the most loyal team of young men one could dream of.

Leonardo, my Colombian head chef, has taught me lessons about humble authority and hard work without complaining. Leo showed me the power of being loyal, respectful but demanding. He made me plate again, season the meat and taste my food. Leonardo made me understand how much he needs 'Ana the chef,' and how much my team needs me.

Michael, my South African sous chef, is the walking encyclopedia of Hiša Franko. Michael gave me a lesson about the importance of listening to your team and believing in the genius of every single person you work with.

Ah, Illias and Sebastian. When I met our Greek chef Illias and asked him about his name, he suggested I call him *malaka*. Only months later, after having done an interview with Greek journalist Dimitris Antonopoulos, in which I called Illias 'my Greek malaka', I gently asked him for a better explanation what malaka really means. 'Well, asshole chef.' Silence. Horror. 'But don't worry, chef, in Greece it's a friendly term.' Sebastian and Illias, always in a good mood, always pushing, always hardworking. Once we came from an event in Ljubljana at 2.30 a.m., all tired and in need of sleep. The following night during the service debriefing, I heard that my malakas came to work at 5 a.m. that day. I looked at the time and it was late, again – 1.30 a.m of the following day. 'Illias, what the hell are you doing here?' I shouted. 'Working, chef.' I frowned. 'You have 10 seconds to leave the kitchen, Illias!' He laughed. 'No, chef. I still have a little work to do.' My Greek malaka.

So many times, I have been asked to state my preference for a woman or a man in my kitchen. After many years of looking for the right answer, I can honestly say it's this: gender (hormonal) balance. We of course see love and hearts on the walls, we see flirting, we experience fights and tears. But this is life. And if nothing else, the kitchen is life.

Alen and Matjaž

Two icons of Hiša Franko. I first met Matjaz when he was working as a cashier at the local supermarket Planika. I was pregnant, and he always insisted on helping me bring my shopping bags to the car. He was actually one of the only people to see me as a pregnant woman, not a chef, not a business owner. One day, I asked him to join our team. His answer still makes me laugh: 'Well, Chef Roš, I really do not think so. I have to take care of my social and economic security.' But in the end, he was willing to try. And he has been trying and testing us for some years now. Matjaž has been THE face of the house; he has a talent of remembering faces and food preferences, he can spot a circumstance that requires disgression a mile off, and he was the first in the house to go on his knees while talking to the people at the table. Today, Matjaž is our breakfast chef.

Alen is. . . Alen. One of the most talented sommeliers I have ever met, and so much in love with Valter and his wine stories. He left his friends, his lovers and his life to come and work with us. He refilled Valter's wine cellar, he put down service rules and he is the one who makes the younger generation fall in love with his work. Alen was one of the most important people in the transition period of Hiša Franko. I wish I could triplicate him.

Dejan and Manca

Every house needs 'a Dejan'. Papers, numbers, staff visas, housing, controlling Alen's wine shopping, fixing Yvonne's car adventures. Dejan is a father figure at Hiša Franko. There are moments he is sick of our countless demands – then papers start flying and chairs begin moving, and we all know it is time to hide in a corner. After his calming-down cigarette in the sun, he comes back in and starts again.

Manca is my assistant, my counsellor, a psychotherapist to everyone and the wise (wo)man of Hiša Franko. Manca is the architect of success of Hiša Franko. Manca knows how to network, she knows when to hand a business card or handle a management crisis. *Manca, hvala lepa.*

Tomorrow

Andrea Petrini

Post-pastoralia:
and the Dream Will Keep Rolling

Once upon a time there was a little girl. Much better: once upon a time there was a clever little girl in a green coat. One day, Little Green Riding Hood – green, of course, as the colour of her beloved country – went into the woods. Alone. Unlike Hans, unlike Gretel, she didn't have a clue, a hint of what to do or a trail of stones to return to. But she made it all by herself, no help needed. And, despite all odds, came back a woman. Everybody then rushed to her place down in the valley to greet her back home with presents and good will. Of course, she never was the same again. Once you manage to see the world, you change forever. She had been dating and hanging out with the Wolf and, as the truly foxy person she was, she nailed the old fucker once and for all. A happy end of the story to be continued – in a fairytale, you might think this was the conclusion – but it was only the beginning of a brand new one.

Like the most universal fairytales, this Slovenian one comes with a complimentary bonus or, if you behave, even two. You have to go with the flow, though, and abandon all you already know. Our present fairytale might sound like a most convenient resumé. A public recap of general interest that fits all sizes and needs, a *Reader's Digest* meant to help the slow ones to carefully insert, step by step, the right pieces into the puzzle. Oh, but beware, dear reader, when you enter our beautiful realm. Ana Roš is, for sure, our cherished Slovenian Queenie. She might knit for us all the most dexterous, the most plausible storytelling one could stumble into these days, but Hiša Franko in truth is no fancy fairytale. Her life and times are a much more complex, rewarding narrative. When it comes to cooking, to devoting your life to the stove, to representing your country and pushing things through, no one has taken this as literally as Ana did. The long and winding road sports many narrow bends, sudden cul de sacs, uncountable parallel paths and a profuseness of hidden ways. To circle down and get closer to the spotted truth. Each fellow traveller that sets down on his way to Kobarid should take time to breathe, to enjoy the wanderlust. The future lies ahead, but so does the past. And nowhere more than at Ana and Valter's Hiša Franko does it go round and around.

Do you remember Vincente Minnelli's *Brigadoon*? It was the beautiful musical with Cyd Charisse and Gene Kelly, shot in the mid-fifties in a Technicolor as vivid as an acid trip. The story of that couple of smart city kids from New York who went hunting and got lost in the Scottish Highlands, hidden behind the thickest mist, in a spellbinding country village that was almost cartoon-like (it's the economics of a MGM studio movie, you stupid!), cast away from the real world. A village that would magically come back to life only one day per year. You couldn't help falling in love with all those folksy folks, singing by the fountain and dancing on the bridge across the whispers of a flowing river. You couldn't help taking for granted that such a magical place really exists – and truly, this is Kobarid, where the sea and the mountains frame well-preserved nature, and the down-to-earth business of high-quality agriculture stands as a symbolic relic of pre-capitalism. At the crossroads of overlapping cultures where Eastern European, Balkan, northern Italian and Austro-Hungarian identities engage with and morph into one another. That's Slovenia, baby. It is also Ana's lab, where the old has to coexist with the new. And the new has to fully understand all the experiences, all the layerings of traditions, and legacies of culture that have continued through the ages, unless you let amnesia to take over your mind and limbs.

Fellow Traveller, there is no better place nowadays, and there won't be for sure a better one for years and years, than the magic kingdom of Slovenia, if you really care to cast a glimpse to the world the way it is and eventually the way it should be. Surrender, unless you have already done so, to that irresistible *Brigadoon* feel. Step in, buy yourself a good seat, get a snack and a dry cocktail or two or, if that's your wish, a glass of orange wine (don't be shy, call Valter, it's the speciality of the house) to sip through the show. Enjoy all that singing, all that dancing around. All that community feeling 'in da house'. But should you feel startled by all the never-ending activity, please remember this: unconditional love for this place, and love at first sight, comes in many guises. But before the flirting, before the prepping, comes all the props; the ad hoc scenography; the choreography of a rather unique storyline with a dramaturgy that wouldn't seem so real, so unique, without what in literature is referred to, particularly in the relation between the reader and the text, as 'the suspension of disbelief'. You have indeed to believe what you see, to make Slovenia your own. You have to become Slovenia. You have to be part of the show. Go shyless, step behind the scene(s), and get acquainted backstage with all the staff.

Hiša Franko's cast is top-notch, a truly international dream team made real. A safe h(e)aven, a living political warning against all the wrongness sadly going on around us. Hiša Franko is a talent-seeking, experience-forming, creative pool with open doors; bordering countries are sadly closing theirs, spreading shadows of fear. The witch hunt, the tracking of the Other, is happening everywhere, including past the Slovenian border. We don't believe, and Ana Roš and Valter neither, in the happy island cut off from the rest of the world. That non-sense never existed – no one is an island, everyone is connected, everything is illuminated.

Before asking Ana herself, speak to her staff in the kitchen, at reception and in the rooms: 'How does it feel to be working and living in Slovenia in this second half of the year 2018?' They will all tell you their stories of pots and pans and broken hearts. And finally, of ending up in Kobarid, where everything seems to fit together. It might look like a Neverland, or a tiny spot lost at the other end of the world. Nevertheless Hiša Franko is where, in the end, all these different stories, all these fragments of life, come together and make sense. A place in time, something real, that has its own story, that collects narratives and works on a newly found and reshaped tradition. A creative space with a strong purpose, a household on a mission. Making bonds, creating ties, linking lives. Setting the conditions for a big change.

Everybody should get through the official celebratory picture: Hiša Franko is much more than just another destination restaurant to tick off on your travel bucket list. And damn all that Instagram frenzy – Ana Roš deserves a whole lotta love, better than the gendered dialogues and predictable honours of the 'It Girl' of the moment. You might have been there yourself by now. If not, you have at least been browsing through this book, and just briefly paused on this latter chapter, an afterword that's meant more as a continuation, to keep the history going, to set a scene for a possible future, to gather pace once the reading is over. What's next? What's going to happen now? Those are the questions that everybody keeps asking.

Temptations are meant to be indulged – or so said Oscar Wilde (at least, he said something like that). But temptations can also be misleading. And it is quite tempting to try to figure out what's supposed to come next in the wake of the old linear way of thinking. A step by step, always moving forward, never looking back

state of mind. It's too predictable and passé. Too stuck in the illusory, a blind faith in progress that has haunted us for centuries. Never trust the appearances: there's a double dose of irony in Ana Roš' approach to this book. She is just 40, and already, she has been compelled to deliver the definitive introduction to her work, a collection of 90 of the most emblematic that were developed in a creative thunderstorm under Hiša Franko's roof.

They are all mostly brand new, spanning the last two or three seasons at the restaurant. You might regret the ontological lack of some of the milestone dishes from her early days. Say the heartfelt homage to her father-in-law Franko and his übercult 'Rosbeef', still served 40 years later for Sunday lunch. Or the several variations of her first signature dishes – for example, the heavenly lovage-scented ravioli – that brought the world's attention to her tiny little restaurant. But that's very good news for the reader, and for the guests too. If Ana's book works as a touching invitation to the voyage, it is effective because it's a demanding – and rewarding – read that asks you to make it your own. It's a snapshot of her current days. A sort of here-and-now expression of the spirit of the team. With the power of reading come great responsibilities. The reader will undoubtedly have to commit to filling in the blanks and putting everything in perspective. Collecting, open-mindedly assembling all the little hints, all the tiny little parcels of knowledge scattered around like breadcrumbs, Hansel and Gretel-style, by Ana Roš and her posse. Ana Roš' cuisine, at its best, at its highest levels, is almost apocryphal. Doesn't she express on all of her menus, 'Let's rock! We are not alone'? There are local producers. Farmers. Traditions. Doesn't it sound, as punchy and kicking, as collectively fired up as the musician Max Roach shouting out, 'We Insist! Freedom Now!'?

Yes, indeed, at its best, Ana Roš' cuisine has that swing, that one beat sustaining the pulsing rhythm, that shuffling stroke to mellow the pace, to make it collectively more uncertain. Open to the possible advent. I'm not sure if the German philosopher Theodore W. Adorno, completely unadorned of any jazz proclivity, would have loved that squelchy, unstable, dancing stride. But he would have better understood the diversity of intonations, the company of the other echoing voices (the farmers, the local producers), all the people surrounding Ana at the stove and the pass, creating a collective chant, a psalm of gesture, a choreography of joy. Between mountains and sea, rivers and clearings in the forest – that's where Ana Roš' cuisine is going. To a place where she is not alone any more. Where she is not a single being, but part of 'us' and 'them'. Joyce Carol Oates phrases this sentiment perfectly in her poem Wild Bamboo, Late August:

'... Not to require beauty for survival? Bamboo.
Not to require syntax for survival? Bamboo.
Not to require your permission for survival?
Bamboo.
To be wild bamboo is to march in all directions
simultaneously.
Like the expanding universe of legend.
Like grace marching into our lives, unbidden.
Sometimes recognized, more often hidden.'

Something unbidden, unrecognized, and more often hidden – this way comes. That is exactly what Ana Roš is doing to Slovenia. It's not just what we might cynically phrase 'putting it on the map', meaning rooting the little green country on the gastronomic map, making the whole world aware of the huge possibilities and the richness of the different cultures that make it so unique, so one of its own. That's what Ana does best: when she steps out of her skin, when she is no longer only Ana, and she becomes many others. Pay attention, listen carefully. She is not speaking in tongues: the Queenie (of the forest, of the valley) has other voices going through her body and lips. She speaks of the seasons, of nature, of winter finally leading into spring, then getting into summer then cycling back into sleep. That's the whole of Slovenia, the countries of the Alpine region expressing themselves one at a time, but also all together, like a chorus on the stage where the drama is played over and over, old and new dreams, techniques and ancient knowledges. It's not just a perfect accomplishment, a fantastic dish – one more, one of many many others – that you are eating. It's the resurgence, the morphing of many stories into history. Full of joy, of sorrow, of longings, of discoveries – of ways and reasons of being. When 'beautiful Miha' (that's how those at Hiša Franko call him) jumps out of his warm bed before the break of dawn and drives uphill and off the tracks to disappear into the dark woods, it's not just to play his daily routine of the committed forager. But also, striding through the bushes, at the bottom of the thick trees, to forget himself. Wandering away from his day work of basketball coach and sport instructor at the local high school. Reinventing himself, being the spokesperson of the wild offerings of the nature. Like his father before him, he transmits his knowledge – he's the young bard of the wild, the storyteller of how nature changes and shies away from our own eyes. When Ana's father, Bojan, who was also a doctor in his previous life, like Miha's dad, disappears for a couple of days with his long-time friend Božo, hunting up there – where only eagles dare – they nurture their common stories, voicing oral traditions that might soon go missing. 'You can be a mountaineer or a hunter. Or both, but it's a different commitment.

If you are just a mountaineer, you can immerse yourself in contemplation of nature, the different shades of light. If you are a hunter, you can stand still for hours and hours, then trail your prey among rocks for miles. If we are not careful, there will be no passing of ancestral traditions.'

But there is more than enough food for thought even in Ana Roš' tiniest bite. A mouthful, or just a sample, and it's an explosion, an odyssey of flavours. A thunderstorm of intentions. Call it whatever you like. For us, her post-pastoral cuisine has the perfect tense sense of choral narrative, that sharp prose in motion and poetry in action. That trespassing feeling of transcendence that reveals itself, exactly when you least expected it, wrapped in the abrupt clothes of an epiphany. Post-pastoral cuisine draws lines between land and sea, approaches saveurs, foretells flavours, strings together fellows in an up-close dialogue of possibilities. There's the beautiful, ever-changing precarity of late spring in Ana's beautiful tripes cooked in wild game juice with the first summer chanterelles, and all those fried nettles on top of a triple dose of Tolminc cheese, re-fermented in a pit by Valter. There's the slim, fit alertness of the marbled trout, the local treasure from the Soča river, kissed by the gentle touch of reduced whey and poppy seeds along with the earthy acidity of beetroots pickled in tonka vinegar. And even the gentler chant of the forest, the call of the wild – where wild boar roam. A prophetic vision, an anticipation of the cold winter that will be welcomed by the rituals of reassuring food. Check the wild boar cheeks that Ana stews with plums and brown beans – a masterpiece in its own terms that would exorcize, even at the apex of summer time, the rough days that are going to come.

That's pure Ana. Dancing the dance of here and now, along with the faraway. That's the whole of Slovenia, in a way: the past, the present, and the immediate future. Ana is our Slovenian Queenie (and Valter her devoted King). She is a fairy, an angel, a saint and a sinner, an apostle and a witch. She has to endorse all those identities, to be all those characters at once. Add to that the most brilliant cook this part of the world has ever seen. She is, and also represents anything Slovenia might need: an ambassador, a culinary geo-politician. A catalyst of voices of an until now voiceless country. The future is hers, time is definitely on her side. But don't wake up Brigadoon before its time. The fairytale is beyond real, don't sell out the whodunnit. Keep the spell going. And the dream will keep rolling.

Andrea Petrini is a culinary writer and curator,
European Summit creative director
and GELINAZ! road manager.

Recipes

BREAD & MILK

BREAD & MILK p. 15

This dessert is all about bread and milk. Even the apple that appears in the dish has an important role in our breadmaking. Our sourdough is based on fermentation of apple peels. Bread and milk are everyday, while apple stands for joy and emotions.

Serves 12

For the apple cylinders
2 kg   sour red apples
500 ml organic apple juice
150 ml dry white wine
180 g   caster (superfine) sugar
10 g   ground cinnamon
             vegetable oil, for frying

For the apple pâte de fruit
500 g   apple pulp (see above)
180 g   caster (superfine) sugar
70 g   glucose
20 g   pectin + 60 g caster (superfine) sugar
60 ml   lemon juice

For the yeast ice cream
1 l   milk
180 ml cream
80 g   glucose
100 g   caster (superfine) sugar
8 g   super neutrose
100 g   fresh beer yeast
100 ml pale ale

For the smoked milk
400 g   raw mountain milk
30 g   cornflour (cornstarch)
100 g   mascarpone
             salt

For the cumin mousse
350 ml raw milk
2 tbsp cumin seeds
4   egg yolks
100 g   caster (superfine) sugar
2½   soaked gelatine leaves

For the rye bread crumble
300 g   rye bread
1 l   peanut oil
50 g   sugar
30 g   honey
10 g   salt ↗

For the cranberry coulis
200 g   cranberries
50 ml   water
62 g   molasses

To make the apple cylinders, bake the apples with the apple juice, wine, sugar and cinnamon for 7 minutes at 160°C (320°F). Remove from the oven and separate the pulp from the skin and the pits. Do not throw away anything. Blend the pits and the skin, spread over a Silpat and dry at 75°C (165°F) for 45 minutes. Cut the apple leather into 7 x 11 cm (3 x 4½ in) rectangles. Fry them at 160°C (320°F) and when still warm, shape them into perfect cylinders.

Make the pâte de fruit by heating the apple pulp at 35°C (95°F), then add the sugar and glucose. Bring up to 100°C (210°F) and stir in the pectin, well mixed with the 60 g sugar. Keep stirring and bring up to 107°C (224°F), incorporating the lemon juice. Keep stirring for another 5 minutes, then transfer into a plastic box covered with baking paper. Leave to cool overnight.

To make the ice cream, start heating the milk and cream at 35°C (95°F) in a saucepan. Add the glucose and sugar, well mixed with the super neutrose. Bring to a boil while stirring constantly. Cool down the mixture and incorporate the beer yeast and pale ale. Let it ferment for 12 hours at room temperature. Mix again to press out the air. Freeze the mixture in a Pacojet container.

To make the smoked milk, bring it to a boil with the cornflour and blend it with the mascarpone. Season with salt and cold smoke with a smoking gun.

To make the mousse, heat the milk and bring to a boil. Infuse with the cumin and let it sit for 8 hours. Strain and reheat again. Whisk the egg yolks with the sugar and slowly add the milk. Bring the mixture to a bain-marie and slowly bring up to 82°C (180°F). Add the gelatine and cool. Fill the mixture into the canisters.

To make the crumble, cut the bread into small cubes. Fry until golden in the peanut oil, then drain on kitchen paper. Mix with the sugar and caramelize in a non-stick pan. Take another pan, caramelize the honey and stir away from the fire with the bread. Put back on the heat and stir until the bread separates. Season with salt. Cool down and crush.

To make the coulis, cook the three ingredients together until all the liquid evaporates. Blend into a perfect emulsion.

To serve, fill a cylinder with cumin mousse. Place the smoked milk in the centre, put the yeast ice cream over, and place the cylinder, apple pâte de fruit and cranberry.

MILK

CHRISTMAS RED CABBAGE p. 19

Imagine three girls in the car coming back from Vienna, where we cooked an interesting four-hand dinner with Konstanin Filpou. It was mid-December and we were driving through idyllic snowy countryside. I suggested that over the four-hour road trip, we should discuss the upcoming Christmas menu. This dessert has a lot to do with our Austro-Hungarian roots, flavours and traditions.

Serves 6

For the buckwheat sablée
75 g   sugar
150 g   cold butter
150 g   plain (all-purpose) flour
50 g   buckwheat flour
25 g   ground walnuts
1   egg yolk

For the cranberry coulis
100 g   honey
200 g   cranberries
             juice of 1 orange

For the red cabbage chutney
100 g   honey
50 ml   apple vinegar
200 g   red cabbage
150 g   finely diced green apple
50 g   roasted and cut walnuts

For the sabayon
360 ml cream
100 g   honey
120 ml marsala
6   egg yolks
             salt

To serve
             edible gold leaf

To make the sablée, mix the sugar, butter, flours and walnuts. Add the yolk and mix again. Let rest in the refrigerator overnight. Make 8 cm (3 in) discs. Bake at 180°C (350°F) for 8–10 minutes.

For the coulis, boil 200 ml water and the honey, then pour it over the cranberries and let soak for 10 minutes. Add the orange juice. Blend until smooth.

For the chutney, begin by making a light caramel by heating up the honey to 160°C (320°F). Add the cabbage, then the hot vinegar and cook it until soft. Add the apples and walnuts. Allow to cool. ↓

Cook all the sabayon ingredients to 82°C (180°F). Cool it. Charge in the siphon.

To serve, plate the sablée, cover it with cranberry coulis and red cabbage chutney. Finish with the sabayon and some edible gold leaf.

JOŠKO

WILD PLANTS AND JOŠKO SIRK'S VINEGAR p. 34

Spring is one of the most stunning periods to cook. But it is also very challenging because of its bitterness, which I often have trouble facing. I actually hardly drink beer or coffee. The vinegar of Joško Sirk, simply sprayed in front of the diner, gives to the composition a beautiful freshness and a nice contrast.

Serves 15

For the green asparagus and pumpkin oil emulsion
500 g	green asparagus
30 ml	olive oil
60 g	butter
40 g	chopped shallot
20 ml	white wine
150 ml	pumpkin seed oil
	salt

For the pork sausage cream
1 kg	fresh local pork salami (of course I use the one my father and Franko make together)
300 ml	milk
300 ml	cream
150 g	creamy cheese
15 g	chopped black peppercorns
	salt

For the pork crackling
250 g	zaseka (a sort of lard pâté)
60 g	sugar

For the selection of herbs
butcher's broom
wild hops
wild asparagus
wild garlic (ramsons) and buds
plantago
plantago buds
garlic mustard
hermelika
shadow dandelion
dandelion flowers ↗

To serve
rebula vinegar Sirk
in a spray bottle

Cut off the tips of the asparagus and reserve. Chop the rest of the asparagus into small pieces. In a saucepan, add the olive oil and butter, then the chopped shallots. Sauté them until a transparent colour, then add the asparagus stems, deglaze them with white wine and reduce. Place the mix in a bowl and make an inverted bain-marie to keep the colour. In a Thermomix place the asparagus and blend until a purée. Add the pumpkin seed oil to emulsify the mixture. Once creamy, season with salt.

Place the salami, milk, cream and cheese in a Thermomix and blend at 50°C (120°F) for 10 minutes. Season with black peppercorns and salt if necessary. Smoke it 3 times.

Chop the zaseka into small pieces. Place in a pan on medium heat, stirring before it sticks to the pan. Once all the fat of the sausage has come off, reduce to low heat and cook the zaseka until the crackling caramelizes and gets crispy. Strain and reserve the fat to sauté the herbs. Cool the cracklings and mix with the sugar. Cook them together up to 170°C (340°F), stirring all the time. Place on baking paper and let cool. Reserve in a dark, dry place.

To serve, in a hot pan, put 1 tbsp of the pork fat, and once smoky add the blanched asparagus tips, butcher's broom, wild hops and wild asparagus. Sauté them for a few seconds and transfer to paper. Reheat the pan, and add all the wild plants from the above list and sauté them just for 1 second. They need to remain crunchy and green. Season with salt. On a plate, pipe the asparagus purée and the sausage cream. With a small and flat plate in the bottom, press the purée carefully to create the effect. Finish the dish with the sautéed wild plants, 5 pieces of wild plant heads and pork crackling.

BREAD

BREAD p. 41

My sourdough was born four years ago. I fermented apple peels with some flour and spring water. The first bubbles happened pretty late because it was January, and our apartment is never really warm. The first bread was miserable and even today, the bread sometimes gives us unpleasant surprises. It is a living thing – it suffers from rain and sun – and even flowers around Hiša Franko and pollen in the air may change it completely. Breadmaking for me is one of the most fascinating and ↗

challenging moments of the kitchen. And it is also very rewarding.

Makes 8 loaves

1.8 l	water
480 g	sourdough starter
120 g	honey
720 g	roasted khorasan flour
1680 g	strong (bread) flour
120 ml	water
48 g	salt
	oil, for spraying

Eight to 12 hours before making the dough prepare the starter. Mix 240 g of strong bread flour, 240 ml of lukewarm water and 100 g of active sourdough starter. Leave to double in volume and become bubbly, then use to mix the dough. Warm the water to 28°C (82°F). Pour into a mixing bowl, add the starter and mix by hand. Add the honey and whisk again. Weigh the flours and mix. Transfer to a stand mixer with a dough hook and mix for 5 minutes. Add the second amount of water and the salt. Mix for 5 minutes. Take out of the bowl and put in a plastic container sprayed with oil. The dough should be 24–26°C (70–75°F). Next leave the dough for the bulk fermentation. In this period the dough should get stronger, puffed and airy and should also increase in the volume. In the first 2 hours of the bulk fermentation perform a series of stretch and fold (4 times in 30-45 minute intervals). This will help the dough gain strength.

To perform stretch and fold, grab the dough at 1 side, then pull it up and fold over itself. Repeat on 4 sides of the dough. Leave the dough to rise until it increases approximately 80 percent of the initial volume. Divide the loaves into 620 g each for 8 loaves. Preshape, then let rest for 20 minutes. Give them a final shape and place in floured rising baskets. Proof the loaves at the room temperature until the bread approximately doubles in volume and passes the poking test. Make an indent into the dough and observe the reaction - the dough is done proofing when the indent comes to the initial position slowly. If it returns fast, leave the dough to rise longer. Bake for 20 minutes at 230°C (445°F), full steam and fan, and then for 30 minutes at 160°C (320°F) no steam or fan.

NATAŠA DJURIC AND HER SPELT BREAD, CULTURED BUTTER p. 40

Nataša, once again, changed the bread of Hiša Franko, and made it one of the most important dishes of the 22-course tasting ↗

menu. With hindsight, I find the progression of Hiša Franko's bread simply astounding. From Djuro, through Francesca and finally the incredible Nataša Djuric.

Makes 8 loaves

For the dough
846 ml   water
240 g   sourdough starter
480 g   wholegrain spelt flour
711 g   strong bread flour
9 g   malt extract
48 g   molasses sugar
9 g   malt powder
48 ml   water
24 g   salt

For the cultured butter and buttermilk
2 l   heavy cream
70 g   3.5% yogurt

Eight to 12 hours before making the dough prepare the starter. Mix 120 g of strong bread flour, 120 ml of lukewarm water and 50 g of active sourdough starter. Leave to double in volume and become bubbly, then use to mix the dough.

Weigh both flours and the malt and put in a mixer. Weigh the water and dissolve in the molasses at 25–27°C (77–80°F). Add the sourdough starter and dissolve it as well. Add the water, molasses and starter mixture to the flour mixture. Mix the dough for 5 minutes. Add the salt and the second amount of water and mix for another 5 minutes. Transfer the dough to a plastic container and do the first stretch and fold. Let it rest for 30 minutes. Do another fold. Repeat 3 more times. When the bulk fermentation is over and the dough volume increases by approximately 80 percent, transfer the dough to the work surface. Dust lightly with flour and divide into 600 g parts for 4 loaves and 300 g parts for 8 loaves. Pre-shape and let it rest for 20 minutes. Boule it into a final shape and transfer to baskets. Proof the loaves at room temperature until the bread approximately doubles in volume and passes the poking test. Bake for 20 minutes at 230°C (445°F), full steam and fan, and then for 30 minutes at 160°C (320°F) no steam or fan.

Put the cream in a large pot and cook slowly by stirring at 82°C (180°F). Hold the cream at this temperature for 30 minutes. Remove from the heat and let cool at room temperature at 43°C (110°F). Add the yogurt, whisk to combine, strain and put into a plastic container with a lid. Keep it at 41°C (105°F) for 14 hours. Refrigerate until chilled. Whisk until the butter starts coagulating. Strain the buttermilk and press the butter with cold water to squeeze out the remaining buttermilk. Use the buttermilk for other recipes, such as the trout belly.

HOTEL MOO

ČOMPA S SKUTO p. 45

Potatoes feed all Slovenian families, regardless of their social classes. The potato we use in this recipe comes from a little organic farm close to Kobarid. Leo, my Colombian sous chef, calls it Savanera. In Slovenia we rarely name the potatoes. The idea of the dish was to give a platform to this vegetable. With Istrian truffles, early autumn black trumpets, lamb juice and lamb fat, it shows itself to be an incredible partner.

Serves 10

For the potatoes
750 g   hay
1 kg   rock salt
600 g   egg whites

For the smoked chocolate
600 g   dark chocolate 72%
600 g   sugar
40 g   Maldon sea salt flakes

For the fermented cottage cheese
850 ml cream
700 g   fermented cottage cheese
100 g   mascarpone
5 g   salt

For the chamomile powder
20 g   fresh chamomile flowers

For the potato water
10   large potatoes
2 l   water
5 g   chamomile powder (see above)
3 g   salt
        gelespessa (optional)

To serve
10 g   smoked chocolate in the
        bottom of the plate
20 g   fermented cottage cheese
        to pipe on each plate
        chamomile powder to sprinkle on top
        potato water to finish
10   potatoes coated in hay crust

Blend the fresh hay in a blender until it is powder. Mix the powder together with the salt and egg whites, in a metallic bowl and with a whisk. There is no need to foam the egg white. Cover the potatoes with the mixture and bake at 180°C (350°F) for 20–25 minutes. When we ↗

say cover the potatoes with the mixture, we mean to make it like a big egg with a salt crust.

Melt the chocolate over a bain-marie. Wrap the bowl completely in plastic with a spatula inside. Make a small hole on each side and place a smoker nozzle in one. Smoke heavily 3 times, stirring the chocolate to get as much smoky flavour as possible. Melt the sugar and 300 g water together and bring to 116°C (240°F) and let cool to 80°C (175°F). Then place the smoked chocolate in the mixer bowl with the salt and whisk on full, while slowly adding the sugar syrup. Cool down rapidly in a container in the blast chiller, then pulse for 2–5 seconds on maximum speed in a Thermomix. Once blended to resemble soil, place in the blast chiller again and then smoke once more very heavily.

Place the cream and cottage cheese in a Thermomix and blend on speed 4 for 5 minutes at 70°C (160°F), then on maximum speed for another 2 minutes. Add the mascarpone and salt and blend another 30 seconds on speed 5. Strain and cool.

Place the chamomile flowers in a dehydrator at 41°C (105°F) for 2 hours. Remove and blend, using the spice blender, into a fine powder. Pass through a fine sieve and store for serving.

To make the potato water, wash and peel the potatoes. Place the peels in a pot, then chop 3 of the peeled potatoes into dice and place into the pot as well. Cover with 2 l water and let simmer until reduced to 200 ml. Strain the liquid, add the chamomile and salt and let cool to room temperature and infuse. Strain the liquid again and adjust seasoning and consistency, adding a little bit of gelespessa if too liquidy. If you add gelespessa, do this at least 1 hour before serving, as it needs time for the foam to rise to be removed.

CHEESE RIND AND BEEF TONGUE BROTH

p. 60

I always feel like a naughty child when Valter finds out how many cheese rinds are hidden in different corners of the refrigerator – old cheese, young cheese, three-year-old cheese, fermented cheese, pit cheese. If you are not a countryside child, you never understand how much milk you use to make one form of cheese. Welcome to a no-waste recipe.

Serves 6

For the cheese rind and onion broth
2 kg   Tolminc cheese rinds of different
        years
3 l   beef tongue clarified cooking water ↓

2 kg   red onions
100 ml olive oil

For the red onion powder
        cooked red onions (see above)

For the mushroom dumplings
500 g   plain (all-purpose) flour
1 kg   fresh offcuts of the freshest wild
        mushrooms (whatever we would
        normally not use)
50 g   garlic
150 g   shallots
3 g   dried chilli
100 ml olive oil
        salt
20 g   tarragon
20 g   thyme

To serve
12   onion flowers

Vacuum seal the cheese rind with some tongue water and steam it in the oven at 90ºC (195ºF) for 12 hours. Strain the liquid, cool down, remove the fat and reserve the broth, fat and liquid. Halve the onions and roast in the oven with the olive oil at 180ºC (350ºF) for 20 minutes. Bring together the roasted onion and the cheese water and cook sous vide for 12 hours at 75ºC (165ºF). Strain and preserve the onions and the liquid.

Dry the red onions from the previous step at 56ºC (132ºF) for 48 hours. Blitz to a powder in a coffee grinder.

Place the flour in a large bowl, and slowly pour in 265 g water, mixing the flour all the time. Work the dough with your hands for 10 minutes, cover it with a wet towel and let it sit for 3 hours. After 3 hours, dust your hands with flour and work the dough for another 10 minutes. Cover the dough with a wet towel and let sit for 30 minutes. Repeat this process 3 times. Chop the mushroom offcuts and pan fry them with the garlic, shallots and dried chilli in the olive oil. Season with salt and fresh herbs. Do not overcook. Allow to cool, then make the dumplings, taking as a norm the perfect Chinese dumplings.

Steam the dumplings, then roast them in the reserved cheese fat, powder them with the onion powder and pour over the very warm onion and cheese broth. Finish with the onion flowers.

TRIPE THE TRIPE p. 52

I hated tripe as a child. We had it on the school menu every Thursday, and there was no way to avoid that lunch. I can still see the school cooks frowning at every dish that was coming back to the kitchen. Valter once took me to dinner with Fabrizia Leroi, a female chef from the Italian Dolomites. She cooked me tripe that evening, and it ↗

was at the moment, against all odds, that I fell in love with them.

Serves 10

For the tripe
1 kg   mountain beef tripe, blanched
100 g   roasted onions
100 g   carrots
5   bay leaves

For wild jus
20 kg   deer and roebuck bones
2 l   red wine
3 kg   mirepoix
100 g   tomato purée (paste)

For the jamar foam
500 g   pit cheese
500 ml cream
10 g   proespuma (hot)
        salt

For the white asparagus
1 kg   white asparagus
700 g   brown butter
7 g   salt

For the nettles
500 ml sunflower oil
40   big nettle leaves

For the broad beans
1 kg   broad (fava) beans
3 g   bicarbonate of (baking) soda

For the magnolia flowers and stamens
10   magnolia flowers
7 ml   olive oil
3 g   salt
5 ml   vinegar spray

To serve
200 g   chanterelles
30 g   butter
30 g   olive oil

Clean the tripe of all the impurities and fibres. Put the tripe, onions, carrots and bay leaves in a pan, cover with water and bring to the boil. Simmer for 2 hours. Cool them down and cut very finely into long thin slices.

To make the jus, roast the bones in the oven at 230ºC (445ºF) for 30 minutes. Deglaze with red wine. Roast the vegetables and tomato purée in a big pot and combine with the bones with red wine. Reduce. Cover with cold water and 2 kg ice and cook on low heat for 6 hours. Strain and continue cooking for another 2 hours.

To make the jamar foam, cut the cheese into 2 cm (¾ in) chunks. Place in a Thermomix with the cream, proespuma and salt. Blend on speed 3 at 70ºC (160ºF) for 5 minutes, then on maximum for another 4–5 minutes. Check the seasoning and strain into a siphon. ↗

Charge twice and check. Reserve at 55ºC (130ºF) in the sous vide for serving.

Remove the woody end part of the asparagus and peel. Place the asparagus in a vacuum bag with the brown butter and salt and seal in a vacuum bag. Sous vide at 75ºC (165ºF) for 25 minutes and let cool to room temperature. Strain the butter, keeping some for service, and reserve the rest for the next batch of asparagus. Cut the asparagus at a 45-degree angle (7 pieces per portion). Heat the oil to 160ºC (320ºF). Fry the nettle leaves, one by one. Keep in a dark, dry space.

Blanch the beans in salted, boiling water with the bicarb for 10 seconds and cool immediately in an ice bath. De-skin and dry and reserve in the refrigerator until serving.

Pick and wash the flowers if needed, keeping all the small petals and the stamens. To serve, dress the petals with the olive oil, salt and vinegar spray.

To serve, cook the tripe in the wild jus for 20 minutes. Pan fry the chanterelles in butter and olive oil, then add 15 g of water and the broad beans. Heat the siphon canister filled with cheese to 50ºC (120ºF) and place it on the bottom of the dish. Place the asparagus and broad beans in the centre. Cover with the tripe, forming them as spaghetti. Cover with magnolia flowers.

WALNUTS, PORCINI AND COFFEE p. 55

This is Marta's expression of autumn in the Soča Valley. When she applied for a job, I asked her to create a dish that would convince me. Marta is Italian, and I think that the little trick with coffee is so refreshing. It is the way our shepherds drink their coffee in the morning. There are a lot of walnut trees in our valley, and we usually combine them with cheese or use them in desserts. In autumn, you would see white sheets with freshly picked walnuts drying in the sun. They are as valuable gold to us.

Serves 60

For the coffee blend
10 g   Colombian Hiša Franko coffee blend
        Čokl
15 g   toasted, dehydrated, powdered
        walnuts
6 g   dried, powdered porcini

For the cheese and walnut foam
600 ml milk
600 ml cream
200 g   chopped walnuts
305 g   2-year-old cheese
50 g   5-year-old cheese
4   soaked gelatine leaves ↗

For the cheese and walnut shortbread

250 g   unsalted butter
200 g   walnuts
125 g   flour
15 g   sugar
15 g   5-year-old cheese, grated
4 g   salt
1 g   black pepper

For the carrot bites

1 kg   carrots
150 g   butter
15 g   salt
400 ml carrot juice
6   soaked gelatine leaves
300 ml buttermilk

For the carrot glaze

200 ml carrot juice
5 g   black peppercorns
4 g   kappa carrageenan

To serve

20 g   porcini powder

Put all the ingredients and 250 ml water in a cafetiére and bring to a boil until you get the coffee.

Put the milk, cream and walnuts in a sous-vide bag and soak at 52°C (110°F) overnight. Blend in a Thermomix (no temperature) for 4 minutes, and pass through a cheesecloth. Warm the walnut milk to 80°C (175°C) in a Thermomix. Add the 2 different cheeses to the milk, blend on temperature for 5 minutes, add the gelatine and blend again. Put the mix in a siphon with 3 charges.

Cut the butter in pieces and leave it at room temperature to soften. Toast the walnuts and blend them while still hot to make a paste. Add the paste to the butter and emulsify. Roll into a log in clingfilm (plastic wrap) and chill. To make the shortbread, soften 125 g of the chilled butter then add all the remaining ingredients and mix them with a whisk. Mix with your hands, make a ball, wrap in clingfilm (plastic wrap) and leave to rest in the refrigerator for at least 1 hour. With a rolling pin, roll out the dough to 5 mm (¼ in). Cut into 1.5 x 3 cm (½–1¼ in) rectangles and bake at 180°C (350°F) for 8–10 minutes.

Roast the carrots in the butter and 300 ml water until cooked. Blend with the salt and the carrot juice. Bring to 70°C (160°F) while blending and add the soaked gelatine.

Add the buttermilk and correct the salt. The purée needs to be creamy and quite runny. Transfer to moulds and freeze.

To make the glaze, mix all the ingredients together and bring to 82°C (180°F). Put the frozen carrot bites on the toothpick and coat them in the carrot glaze.

To serve, combine the coffee and cheese and walnut foam. Serve the shortbread and carrot lollipops on the side. Powder with porcini powder.

VEAL CONSOMMÉ, CELERIAC AND YOUNG LINDEN LEAVES p. 58

In Slovenia, every Sunday meal starts with soup in the middle of the table. It is usually made out of beef, but the challenge in this dish was to use some parts of mountain veal that did not fit with other recipes. Nevertheless, it was popular.

Serves 16

For the celariac vinegar

30 ml   red wine vinegar
300 ml water
50 g   sugar
20 g   salt

For the veal consommé

15 l   veal stock (made from bones)
10 l   veal demi glace
3 kg   minced (ground) veal
2 kg   mirepoix
600 g   egg whites
500 g   celeriac offcuts
        salt
        kuzu

For the hazelnut cream

20 g   sugar
50 ml   2-year-old red wine vinegar
50 g   celeriac offcuts
150 g   roasted hazelnuts
70 ml   hazelnut oil

For the celeriac rolls

4   celeriac
        hazelnut cream (see above)

For the celeriac and morel candies

50 g   dried and soaked morels
300 g   celeriac peels
200 ml olive oil
50 ml   hazelnut oil
50 ml   celeriac vinegar (see above)
30 g   salt

For the kappa

200 ml celeriac vinegar (see above)
4 g   kappa carrageenan

For the linden leaves and dressing

100 ml lovage oil
50 ml   celeriac vinegar (see above)
20 ml   pear reduction
7 g   salt
50 g   young linden leaves

To serve

1%   kuzu to the quantity of veal consommé
        lovage oil
        pear reduction ↗

To make a celeriac vinegar, heat the red wine vinegar, water, sugar and salt. Add the celeriac and cook for 1 hour. Strain and cool down.

Bring all the consommé ingredients together, roasting the mirepoix in the oven beforehand. The temperature of the oven should be 180°C (350°F). Cook on 80°C (175°F) for a few hours, clarify with the minced meat and egg whites. Thicken with kuzu.

Bring the sugar, vinegar, celeriac offcuts and 50 ml water. Let it infuse for a few hours. Strain and blend with hazelnuts and emulsify with hazelnut oil.

Peel the celeriac and cut it with a Japanese mandoline into equal strips. Spread over the celeriac and roll up. Cut them to single portions.

Confit the morels and peels in olive oil at 80°C (175°F) for 2 hours. Strain the oil and preserve it for the next time. Blend the mushrooms and celeriac peel with the rest of the ingredients. Put into silicone moulds and freeze.

For the kappa, bring the 2 ingredients to 82°C (180°F) and coat in the frozen candies by using a toothpick. The operation needs to be quick, so as not to create a coating that is too thick. Let cool to room temperature, using Styrofoam to hold the stick.

Mix all the ingredients together aside from the linden leaves and dress the linden leaves just before serving.

Add 1% kuzu to the quantity of veal consommé you are using. Bring to a boil and keep simmering for 10 minutes. Roast the celeriac roll on both sides in a non-stick pan. Place the celeriac candy on top and cover with linden leaves. Finish with drops of lovage oil and pear reduction.

I ♥ BEEF TONGUE p. 56

If you ask Svit and Eva Klara about their favourite meat, they would say beef tongue and roebuck. This dish is my contribution to the local farming community. The taste of roasted purslane and borage and the seaside nostalgia of oysters makes this dish one of my favourites, too.

Serves 8

For the red pepper crisps

5 kg   red (bell) peppers
10 g   salt
30 g   brown sugar
30 ml   olive oil
200 ml red pepper juice (from the
        cooked peppers)
3   pepperoncini pieces
50 ml   red wine vinegar
20 g   egg whites
5 g   gelespessa
30 ml   soy sauce ↓

For the red pepper gel

12	gelatine leaves
1 l	red pepper juice (from the cooked peppers above)
7 g	salt
41 ml	red wine vinegar
24 ml	soy sauce
43 ml	fish sauce
10 g	agar agar

For the purslane salad

300 g	wild bunches purslane

For the pickled purslane

150 ml	water
100 ml	apple vinegar
20 g	honey
10 g	salt
1	dried chilli

For the fried borage leaves

16	borage leaves
200 ml	water
10 g	salt
800 ml	peanut oil

For the oyster mayo

446 g	fresh oysters (washed in their own liquid)
30 ml	lemon juice
120 ml	olive oil
200 ml	grapeseed oil
25 ml	soy sauce
5 g	gelespessa

For the tongue brine

120 g	salt
11 g	coriander seeds
18 g	cumin seeds
6	bay leaves
1	head garlic
10 g	peppercorns
15 g	thyme
15 g	rosemary
20 g	star anise
50 g	onion

For the tongue

1	beef tongue
1	clove garlic
1 g	thyme
10	peppercorns
1	bay leaf
1 g	rosemary
1 l	red pepper juice
	cold butter
	salt

To make the pepper crisps, put the peppers on 2 gastronorms (hotel pans) and sprinkle over the salt, sugar and olive oil. Bake them for 20 minutes at 200°C (400°F) and then 40 minutes at 180°C (350°F). Once the peppers are cooked, blend them in a Thermomix and strain through a chinois, reserving all of the juice. Take 200 ml of the strained juice of the peppers and mix in the rest of the ↗

ingredients once cold. Spread the mixture over Silpats and cut out disc shapes (about 2.5 cm/1 in in diameter). Dry at 80°C (175°F) with 5% humidity, and once they are dry, separate the discs. Bake them at 140°C (280°F) for 7 minutes.

Soak the gelatine in water for 5 minutes. Mix the rest of the ingredients together in a saucepan, correct with salt. Bring the mixture to the boil, add the gelatine, boil for 4 minutes and then pour the mixture into flat trays to a thickness of 5 mm (¼ in). Place in the refrigerator and once it is cold and solid, cut into discs (2.5 cm/1 in same size as the chips).

To make the purslane salad, on a barbecue, grill the purslane in a wire mesh basket, making sure the charcoal is red and smoky. Cover the purslane with a bowl and grill the salad, making sure it has a lot of smoky flavour.

To make the pickled purslane, mix all the ingredients in a saucepan and bring to the boil. Let the mixture cool down and add to the purslane salad. Use after 2 days.

To prepare the borage leaves, compress the leaves in a brine twice. Dry the leaves then fry them at 170°C (340°F) until crispy. Season with salt.

To make the oyster mayo, blend the oysters in a Thermomix, add the lemon juice and start to add the olive oil and grapeseed oil, slowly to emulsify the mixture. Once emulsified, season with soy sauce and add the gelespessa.

To make the brine, take 1 l water and pour over the rest of the ingredients, apart from the tongue, in a saucepan. Bring to the boil to release the flavours. Add 5 l water.

Place the tongue in brine for 3 days. Then vacuum seal and cook for 72 hours at 65°C (150°F). Then take out of the bag, keep the liquid and peel the tongue when it is hot. Cut slices of 2.5 cm (1 in) from the tongue, using the red pepper discs as portion guides.

To serve, heat the beef tongue at 70°C (160°F) in a water bath. Reduce the red bell pepper juice down to a syrup consistency, then finish it with 30% cold butter on original consistency. Glaze the beef tongue well with the pepper glaze. Put it on the plate, place the red pepper gel on the plate, topped with the oyster mayo, and cover with a mix of purslane salad seasoned with salt. Finish with fried borage leaves and red pepper crisps.

THE COW IN THE HAY

p. 46

This dish is a homage to a Slovenian tradition of eating beef and potatoes on a daily basis. On Sunday, the beef consommé comes first. Slovenians never get sick of it.

Serves 6 ↗

For the fermented red radishes

25 g	salt
300 g	red radishes
5 g	garlic
10 g	ginger
½	dried habanero chilli without seeds

For the mashed potatoes

300 g	potatoes
50 ml	olive oil
20 g	rosemary
100 g	chopped red onions
30 g	bacon
3	soaked gelatine leaves

For the onion powder

500 g	onions

For the potato chips

500 g	starchy potatoes
10 g	salt
	vegetable oil, for frying

For the grilled leeks

3	leeks
30 ml	olive oil
1 g	salt
1 g	lemon thyme

For the prosciutto mayo

150 g	6-month-old prosciutto skin
2	egg yolks
1 tbsp	fresh lemon juice
150 ml	grapeseed oil
1 tbsp	mustard
8 g	salt

For the pickled mustard seeds

100 g	mustard seeds
200 ml	white vinegar
10 g	salt
10 g	sugar
3 g	lemon thyme
2	bay leaves
2	cloves garlic
1	dried pepperoncino

For the beef cheeks

2 kg	beef cheeks
3	onions
3	carrots
1	celery stick
500 ml	red wine
4	bay leaves
1	bunch thyme
1	sprig fresh rosemary
1	sage branch

For the oxtail croquettes

2 kg	oxtail
3	onions
3	carrots
1	celery stick
500 ml	red wine
4	bay leaves
1	bunch thyme ↗

200 g	leftover green tacos
	vegetable oil, for frying
200 g	flour
4	egg yolks

For the hay glaze

500 g	hay
	remaining stock from beef cheeks (see above)
	remaining stock from oxtail (see above)
	salt

Blend 1 l water with the salt. Put it in a glass jar with the red radishes, garlic, ginger and habanero chilli. Ferment for 3 weeks at room temperature, avoiding higher temperatures. After 3 weeks, place the radishes in the refrigerator to slow down the fermentation.

To make the mash, boil the potatoes and strain, reserving the cooking liquid. Heat the olive oil with the rosemary. Add the chopped onions and bacon, then add the potatoes and keep roasting on medium heat. Blend when still hot with some cooking liquid, then add the gelatine. Fill the siphon.

For the onion powder, bake the onions at 240ºC (465ºF) for 50 minutes, until they are totally black and dry. Then blend them in a spice mixer and strain.

For the potato chips, peel the potatoes and cook in water until totally soft. Strain and blend them in a Thermomix while they are hot, so the starch develops. Season with salt and spread on a Silpat with 200 g in each layer. Dry in the oven overnight at 55ºC (130ºF) with 5% humidity. Once dry, fry in vegetable oil at 220ºC (430ºF). Note: Do not season the chips after frying them, since the mixture already has salt.

Place the leeks in a vacuum bag together with the olive oil, salt and lemon thyme. Cook at 75ºC (165ºF) for 75 minutes. Once cooked, ice shock them. On a super hot grill, place the leeks and burn them until they are totally black. Cut the leeks in slices of 1 cm (½ in).

To make the mayo, cut the skin into small pieces and cook them at very low heat for around 30 minutes, until the skin releases all the fat. It is important to stir very often, so the fat doesn't burn and turn bitter. Strain and cool down. With a hand blender, blend the egg yolks with half the lemon juice. Start to emulsify with the grapeseed oil, adding little by little. Continue with the prosciutto fat the same way, then with the grapeseed oil. Finish and season with the mustard and salt.

To make the pickled mustard seeds, use one saucepan for the mustard seeds and one for the pickling liquid. In the first pot, boil 300 ml water and add the mustard seeds. Cook them for 5 minutes and strain. In the second pan, mix the rest of the ingredients and bring to a boil. Take the pot off the heat and cool down. Strain and add to the mustard seeds. Use after 2 days. ↗

To cook the beef cheeks, roast the cheeks on a flat iron and reserve. In a big pot, brown the onions, carrots and celery stick. Then add the red wine and reduce until there is no more alcohol. Add the beef cheeks previously browned, cover with water, add the aromatic herbs and cook for 4 hours over a medium heat, or until the cheeks are tender. Take out the cheeks out and reserve. Strain the stock and reserve. Portion the meat into 30 g pieces.

To cook the oxtail, brown the oxtail on the flat iron and reserve. In another pan, brown the onions, carrots and celery stick. Then add the red wine and reduce until there is no more alcohol. Add the previously browned meat and aromatic herbs and cover with water. Cook at 140ºC (300ºF) in the oven for 2½ hours, or until the oxtail is tender. Take the oxtail out and reserve, straining and reserving the stock, too. While the oxtail is warm, pull the meat. Season with salt and some of the reserved stock. Mix them well and cool down. Once cold, make croquettes in 25 g portions and freeze them. When ready to serve, fry the tacos until crispy, then blend in the Thermomix to a powder. Use the taco powder, flour and egg yolks to bread the oxtail croquettes.

To make the glaze, wet the hay and heat a large pan until very hot. Add the hay and roast it. Deglaze with the stocks and cook it for 30 minutes. Vacuum seal and cook at 75ºC (165ºF) for 6 hours. Strain. Season with salt.

To serve, place the ring of the leek, already emptied, into the middle of the plate. Fill in with the prosciutto mayo. Put the oxtail croquette on the top. Top it with onion powder. On the other side, place the salad of fermented radish, pickled mustard seeds and cime di rapa. Put on the top a piece of beef cheek, covered with the hay glaze, just quickly heated on the open fire. On the other side, place the cheek with potato foam and chips.

GOAT COTTAGE CHEESE RAVIOLI p. 53

Ah, ravioli. Every time I want to get rid of them, people get upset. Diners seem to be addicted to my pasta. So, who cares about the trends!

Serves 6

For the dough

500 g	semola rimacinata di grano duro
360 g	egg yolks
1	egg
30 ml	olive oil

For the filling

| 500 g | goat cottage cheese |
| 500 ml | cream ↗ |

For the hazelnut and prosciutto broth

1	carrot
1	roasted onion
1	stick celery
350 g	prosciutto
500 ml	hazelnut oil
100 g	brown butter

For the corn

| 300 g | corn |

For the fried polenta

| 100 g | polenta |

For the praline

200 g	peeled hazelnuts
50 ml	hazelnut oil
15 g	salt

For the garnish

| | nasturtium flowers |
| | nasturtium leaves |

Work the dough ingredients together with your hands until the dough is slightly hot. Cover it with clingfilm (plastic wrap) and let it sit in the refrigerator for 1 hour.

Place the filling ingredients in a Thermomix and blend into an emulsion, heating up to 70ºC (160ºF). Cool it down and let it sit in the refrigerator before making the ravioli.

For the broth, cook the vegetables, prosciutto and 2.5 l water in a pressure cooker for 2 hours. Strain. Emulsify with hazelnut oil and brown butter.

Boil the corn for 30 minutes. Drain and roast it in a cast iron pan until golden and smoky. Allow to cool.

Roast the polenta flour in a dry iron pan until brown. Let cool on baking paper.

Roast the hazelnuts in the oven at 175ºC (345ºF) for 10 minutes without adding any fat, just shaking the tray from time to time. Blend with hazelnut oil and salt until smooth.

When you are ready to serve, first cook the ravioli. Pan fry them with hazelnut praline, some cooking water and prosciutto broth. Add the corn. Top with roasted polenta flour. Serve over the prosciutto hazelnut broth.

POLONKA ROCKS – BEER AND CHEESE POPCORN p. 61

Najlepša jutra so zjutraj; the most beautiful mornings are in the morning. So reads a quote from Ivan Volarič-Feo, a local poet to whom Valter dedicated his beer brewing skills. I wonder if Valter ever realized how much I was thinking of him when I created this dessert. Beer, three-year-old cheese ↓

and junk food popcorn – three things you think of when you have a lazy beer in funky and always rock & roll Polonka.

Serves 6

For the walnut crunch
40 g   butter
30 g   glucose
80 g   sugar
100 g   walnuts

For the white choko cream
120 ml milk
240 ml cream
6 g   glucose
3 g   gelatine
175 g   white chocolate

For the beer gel
250 ml FEO beer
2   gelatine leaves

For the cheese ice cream
300 ml milk
50 ml   cream
35 g   sugar
100 g   3-year-old Tolminc cheese
5 g   super neutrose

For the beer chips
160 ml beer
30 g   glucose
4 g   agar agar

For the wild hops
80 g   wild hops

For the cheese popcorn
20 ml   olive oil
40 g   corn grains

First, make the walnut crunch. In a saucepan, melt the butter and add the glucose and sugar. Stir until you get a caramel, then add the walnuts and stir constantly until it crystallizes. Spread out on a Silpat and let it cool down.

In a pan on medium heat, mix the milk, cream and glucose. Add the gelatine and stir to dissolve it. Continue stirring until you reach 85°C (185°F). Take off the heat and add the chocolate, stirring constantly until the chocolate is melted. Let it cool down and then whip in a mixer at high speed.

To make the beer gel, heat the beer until 85°C (185°F), then add the gelatine and stir to dissolve. Heat for 2 more minutes, place in a plastic container and reserve in the refrigerator.

Next, make the cheese ice cream. Place the milk, cream, sugar and cheese in a Thermomix, blending for 6 minutes at 80°C (180°F). Add the super neutrose and blend for 1 more minute. Let the mixture cool down, and place in a Pacojet container. Freeze to be used before serving. ↗

To make the beer chips, place all the ingredients in a mixer and blend for 3 minutes. Place the mixture in a saucepan and bring to a boil. Pour the mixture into a plastic container and let it cool down in the refrigerator for about 1½ hours. Once the gelatine is ready, put it in a Thermomix and blend it until puréed. Spread the mixture on Silpats, with 110 g on each one. Dry overnight at 65°C (150°F).

To prepare the wild hops, chop the stems in small pieces and reserve them in ice water.

To make the cheese popcorn, using a non-stick pan, heat the oil and add the corn grains. Cover the pan and let the popcorn puff. Dress it with caramelized corn and mix with salt. To plate, place the beer gel, then the walnut crunch, followed by white chocolate topped with chopped wild hops. Place the cheese ice cream and beer chips alongside.

CINNAMON AND APPLE ROSETTE, SHEEP CHEESE p. 49

This is a dish we like calling 'pain in the ass' in the kitchen. We took a long time to create a dough that was light, crispy and airy, and to create the right balance between sweetness and cheesiness. This cheese dish meant that Leo had to spend four hours a day frying the rosettes. It was part of a plan for a twelve-course cheese-only menu, but the plan has been abandoned due to so many people needing lactose-free menus.

Serves 8

For the rosette dough
70 g   manioca flour
50 g   tapioca flour
50 g   plain (all-purpose) flour
420 ml water
20 g   sugar, plus extra for sprinkling
14 g   cinnamon

For the sheep cheese emulsion
720 ml cream
180 g   aged Bovec cheese
3   gelatine leaves
105 g   chestnut honey
8 g   salt

For the apple gel
200 ml filtered reduced apple juice
4 g   iota carrageenan

For the compressed apple
6   red sour apples
500 ml water
30 g   citric acid

For the red cabbage chutney powder
50 g   butter ↗

200 g   red cabbage leaves, chopped
150 g   apple brunoise
50 ml   apple vinegar
100 g   honey
50 g   roasted and chopped walnuts

To serve
8   primula flowers
10   primula leaves
12   yarrow leaves

Blend the manioca flour to a fine powder, then mix in the other ingredients with the help of a hand blender. Fry the rosette using the iron mould in the shape of a flower. Fry the rosette at 190°C (375°F), making sure the mould is super hot when you add the dough. Sprinkle over more sugar when still hot and transfer to a dehydrator for 4 hours at 52°C (125°F).

Bring the cream and cheeses to 70°C (160°F) in a Thermomix. Blend for 10 minutes. Add the gelatine, honey and salt. Strain through a cheesecloth and let set at room temperature, covering the top, touching the surface, with baking paper.

To make the apple gel, mix the 2 ingredients together with a hand blender until it reaches a perfect structure of a gel. Vacuum seal many times until all the bubbles are gone. Transfer to a piping (pastry) bag.

Peel the apples. Cut the apples into 4-mm (⅛-in) slices. With a pasta cutter of 2-cm (¾-in) diameter, remove the centre of the apples. Compress the apples in water and citric acid 5 times.

Melt the butter in a pan, then add the cabbage, apple, and vinegar and reduce to a syrup. Then add the honey and cook for 1 hour over a low heat. Add the walnuts and cook for another 20 minutes. Cool down and dehydrate for 4 days at 52°C (125°F) until completely crunchy. Blitz to a powder.

To serve, coat the base of the plate with cheese emulsion. Place the apple, then more cheese, and put on the rosette. Top with the apple gel and finally the red cabbage chutney powder. Finish with the flowers and leaves.

LAND OF LIVING WATERS

TROUT SKIN p. 71

This dish is all about zero waste. We use a lot of trout, and sometimes it's difficult to ↗

think about how much waste we can produce on daily basis; skins, heads, bones, tails and offal are usually the parts that are not used in restaurants. This was created by my Colombian sous chef Leonardo Fonseca Celis, who wanted to recreate chicharrones, but instead of using pork skin, he decided to use trout skin, and replaced lime with bergamot skin purée. In other dishes, we tend to throw away the pickled liquid used for various elements, but Leonardo wanted to find a use for it, bringing up the colour in the dish and adding a unique acidity.

Serves 12

For the habanero salt
20 g   salt
10 g   habanero chilli powder

For the trout skin
8   trout skin
        vegetable oil, for frying
        habanero salt (see above)

For the trout liver purée
100 g   trout livers
        habanero salt (see above)
30 ml   brandy

For the bergamot skin purée
180 g   bergamot skin (without the white part)
30 g   sugar
60 ml   bergamot juice
40 g   butter

To serve
12   nasturtium flowers

To make the salt, blend the ingredients together and reserve to season the skin.

Clean the trout skin and remove the scales, blanch for 3 seconds in boiling water, clean the meat off the skin and dry it at 56ºC (133ºF) for 7 hours. Deep fry it at 220ºC (430ºF) and season with habanero salt.

For the liver purée, sprinkle the livers with habanero salt. In a hot flat pan, sauté the livers to caramelize the surface, deglaze with the brandy and reduce the liquid until the alcohol has disappeared. Blend with a hand blender and season with the habanero salt. Pass through a cheesecloth and reserve in a piping (pastry) bag.

To make the bergamot skin purée, take the bergamot skin and clean all the white parts, making sure you have 180 g of clean skin. Blanch it twice in cold water until boiling, always with new water. Blanch a third time with cold water and cook it for 20 minutes after the water is boiling. Strain and reserve the skin. Blend the skin together with the sugar and bergamot juice. Add the butter gradually, avoiding heating the mixture. Pass through a tamis and reserve. ↗

To plate, make small dots of liver and bergamot purée on the skin and cover them with nasturtium flowers.

MARBLE TROUT ROE, ROSA DI GORIZIA, YEAST p. 70

Marble trout is rare, and impossible to have in the restaurant on a regular basis. Dušan Jesenšek, a former vet and the CEO of the fishing association of Tolmin, saved the trout from extinction. Every year in December and January, a group of men fish out the marble trout from the river and extract eggs from female trout and sperm from male trout. Then it is all about the artificial insemination before the fish are returned to the river at the exact point where they were fished. A part of the fertile trout roe is given to us as the most prestigious caviar. Another delicacy from the Soča Valley is Rosa di Gorizia. The most expensive chicory in the world needs almost a year and a half to grow. And in its last weeks of its life, it is fermented in a dark space under (originally) cow shit. This is why Andrea Petrini calls it 'shitty salad'. The production is limited to the towns of Solkan and Gorizia. My mother's family cultivated it, then sold it at *mercato di Trieste*, making sure the family had enough money for an excellent education for their children.

Serves 16

For the marble trout roe
200 g   marble trout roe
8 g   salt (4%)

For the Rosa di Gorizia
500 ml vegetable stock
100 g   dried black trumpets
50 g   black truffle skin
30 g   dried porcini
3   gelatine leaves
3.5%   salt
8   heads Rosa di Gorizia

For the trout bottarga
2   trout
6%   salt

For the yeast cream
1 l   cream
100 g   roasted beer yeast
12 g   salt
50 ml   hazelnut water

For the pickled cedro lemon
50 g   cedro lemon peel
50 ml   cedro juice ↗

50 ml   water
50 g   sugar

For the trout roe, mix the 2 ingredients together and let the roe sit in the refrigerator.

To make a brine, slowly cook the vegetable stock with all the dried mushrooms and truffle skin at 75ºC (165ºF). Simmer for 6 hours, then add the gelatine and let cool at room temperature. Strain, add 3.5% salt and freeze for 24 hours. Let it strain hanging through a cheesecloth. Compress the Rosa di Gorizia in the liquid and let it set for 2 hours.

Gently remove the trout roe bag and cure it in the salt for 6 hours. Cold smoke it. Transfer to a dry ventilated room and hang until completely dry.

Cook down the cream and yeast until reduced by one third. Emulsify with the salt and hazelnut water. Set in the refrigerator.

Bring the peel to the boil 3 times, changing the water each time. Bring the juice, water and sugar to the boil and let it cool. Infuse the cedro peel and let it set for 1 week. Transfer to a dehydrator at 56ºC (133ºF) for 6 hours.

To serve, assemble all the ingredients at room temperature. Dress the Rosa di Gorizia with cedro, add grated bottarga and serve the trout roe and yeast cream on the side.

TROUT BELLY AND ROSA DI GORIZIA p. 73

In the winter months, the waters in the Soča Valley get ice cold, and this is why the trout get fatter (for the same reasons as human beings, I presume). We had never considered that in the kitchen, then one time, during the staff meal, we grilled trout in a charcoal oven and found out that the trout belly was by far the best part.

Serves 16

For the trout belly
6   trout bellies
300 ml 3.5% brine water
1 kg   ripe pears
2   pieces tonka bean

For the pumpkin oil emulsion
10 g   salt
50 ml   lemon juice
2   egg yolks
150 ml pumpkin seed oil (not cold pressed)
80 ml   rapeseed (canola) oil

For the roasted pumpkin seeds
50 g   pumpkin seeds

For the buttermilk
        buttermilk, leftover from making butter
0.5%   gelespessa ↓

For the compressed Rosa di Gorizia
8 heads Rosa di Gorizia
100 ml clarified pear juice
60 ml pure beetroot (beet) juice

Clean the trout bellies and vacuum seal them in brine water. Juice the pears and cook until reduced by half. Add the tonka bean and continue cooking for another 30 minutes. Cover with clingfilm (plastic wrap) and let sit for 3 hours. Fire the charcoal oven to 300°C (570°F). Remove the tonka bean from the glaze, and also remove the trout belly from the brine water and dry well. Grill the bellies for 30 seconds, making sure that the fat has melted on both sides. The last 10 seconds, glaze them constantly with pear glaze. Put the bellies on paper and give them one last touch of pear glaze.

Blend the salt, lemon and egg yolks together. Slowly emulsify with both oils. Transfer to a squeeze bottle.

Roast the pumpkin seeds in a very hot iron pan until they puff. No oil or any other fat is needed.

Thicken the buttermilk with gelespessa.

Clean the Rosa di Gorizia and remove all the leaves. Compress the leaves with 50 g ice, pear and beetroot juice 3 times. Keep the bag in iced water.

To serve, plate the trout belly with pumpkin emulsion, compressed Rosa di Gorizia and pumpkin seeds. Finish with a 'lagoon' of buttermilk and some drops of pumpkin oil.

LA REGINA p. 74

The trout: although there is a whole chapter about it, making it interesting has been somewhat of a challenge to me. For years, we tried to convince Italians that the river trout was as good as their Mediterranean seafood. And we also needed years to prove to the world that freshwater fish was very high quality. That said, the taste of the trout depends on the quality of the water, the quantity of oxygen in the water and its temperature.

Serves 12

For the whey sauce
3 l whey
1 l cream

For the mint oil
300 g mint leaves
200 g lemon balm leaves
500 ml grapeseed oil

For the poppy seeds
50 g poppy seeds

For the pickled beetroot
300 ml water ↗

200 ml red wine vinegar
20 g salt
50 g sugar
8 tonka beans
300 g red and pink beetroots (beets)

For the trout
2 trout (1 kg each)
olive oil
fleur de sel

To serve
10 galinsoga plants
10 small nasturtium leaves

Mix the whey and cream in a pan and reduce over a medium-low heat, stirring once in a while so the bottom doesn't burn and the mixture doesn't boil. It is important to not boil so the reduction doesn't become a deep brown colour. Keep reducing until the sugars start to caramelize. You will notice it once the reduced whey has a light brown colour, sweet flavour and creamy texture.

Blend all the ingredients for the mint oil in a Thermomix at 70°C (160°F) for 8 minutes. Put the mixture in a metallic bowl and do an inverted bain-marie. Once the mixture is cold, strain it through a cheesecloth.

In a non-stick pan, toast the poppy seeds on medium-low heat and set aside.

Mix all the pickle ingredients, except the beetroot. Bring to a boil, and let the mixture cool down. While the pickle base cools down, slice the beetroot in a mandoline in slices of 0.1 mm. Place the beetroot in a glass jar together with the pickled mixture. Use after 2 days.

Fish the trout 12 hours prior to serving. Portion the trout fillets 120 g each. Place the trout in a tray with olive oil and fleur de sel on the bottom. Cook the trout skin-side up under a salamander for 1 minute. The trout will still be red inside, but cooked on the outside. Remove the skin. To serve, heat the whey, place the trout on it and season it with salt and poppy seeds. Put some drops of mint oil, the beetroots, galinsoga and nasturtium around the fish.

JERUSALEM ARTICHOKE FLOWER p. 69

Not a lot of people know how amazing the flavour of Jerusalem artichoke flowers is. It is one of the tastiest and most beautiful late summer flowers. They grow all along the Nadiža river and are the first sign of autumn. The roots are actually pretty small and very difficult to use.

Serves 6 ↗

For the summer cauliflower cream
500 g cauliflower
300 ml cream
4 g salt
3 g ground pepper

For the summer cauliflower roast
200 g summer cauliflower
30 ml olive oil

For the toasted sunflower seeds
400 g sunflower seeds
50 ml sunflower oil

For the toasted sunflower seeds and cauliflower cream
200 g cauliflower cream (see above)
100 g toasted sunflower seeds (see above)

For the Adriatic sea urchin
12 sea urchins
4.5% brine

To serve
50 Jerusalem artichoke flower leaves
8 ml sunflower oil
3 g salt

First, make the cauliflower cream. Clean the cauliflower and cut it into regular even slices. Cover with the cream and bring to a boil. Simmer for 20 minutes, then blend until smooth. Add the salt and pepper.

To make the cauliflower roast, cut the cauliflower into small pieces. Heat the olive oil and roast the cauliflower until golden. Drain the cauliflower on paper and dry at 65°C (150°F) overnight.

Roast the seeds, then cool them. Set aside half, then blend the rest of the toasted seeds with the oil to make a praline. Blend the cauliflower cream and the remaining toasted sunflower seeds together.

Open the sea urchins and clean out the eggs. Put them in a glass jar, cover with the brine and let them sit for 24 hours in a cold place.

Place the cauliflower cream in the centre of the plate. Top with praline sunflower seeds and roasted cauliflower. Dry the sea urchin and place it in the flower shape. Cover with leaves of Jerusalem artichoke flower.

ARCTIC CHAR p. 76

When my parents-in-law bought Hiša Franko, they used water from a little spring, Ftanca, which passes by the house to feed the fishponds. One fishpond was for the trout, the other one, which was built later on, became home for a family of arctic char. It is a beautiful and very tasty sweet water fish, more common to the alpine lakes than to the rivers. Fallopia japonica, or Asian knotweed, is an invasive plant, and in ↗

Slovenia it is forbidden to grow it. It is a part of the buckwheat family and native to East Asia. It tastes sour and bitter, very similar to the flavour of rhubarb. It is an important antioxidant.

Serves 4

For the knotweed gel

200 g	green apple
200 g	rhubarb
500 g	leaves and stems of young knotweed plants
50 g	sugar
15 g	agar agar
5 g	gelespessa

For the green tea gelatine

200 ml	clarified fish stock
30 g	organic green tea leaves
10 g	agar agar
3	soaked gelatine leaves
5 ml	jasmine green tea

For the buttermilk

300 ml	buttermilk
15 g	gelespessa
3 g	salt

For the puffed buckwheat

10 ml	olive oil
80 g	buckwheat groats

For the arctic char

2	arctic char, approximately 450 g each
50 ml	apple vinegar
200 ml	apple juice
30 ml	honey
20 ml	olive oil

First, prepare the knotweed gel. Push the apple, rhubarb, knotweed (reserving some of the smaller leaves) and sugar through a juicer. Vacuum seal and place the juice in ice water for 2 hours. Blend in the agar agar and gelespessa and bring to a boil. Allow to set for a few hours. Blend and transfer the gel to a piping (pastry) bag.

To make the green tea gelatine, bring the fish stock to the boil and infuse with the green tea. After 10 minutes, strain and cool down. Add the agar agar, bring to the boil, add the gelatine and start cooling it down. When it starts thickening, add the jasmine green tea and let it set. Cut into 1 cm (½ in) cubes.

Reduce the buttermilk by one third and stabilize with gelespessa. Season with salt.

Heat a cast iron pan to maximum heat. Add the olive oil and buckwheat and let it puff by turning the pan around so the buckwheat doesn't burn. Allow to cool and store in a dry place.

Clean the fish and cut fillets to beautiful equal rectangles. Reduce the vinegar, apple juice and honey by half. Add the olive oil, ↗

then brush the fish with the mixture. Cook the fish under a salamander on the highest possible setting, skin-side up, for 45 seconds. Let the skin caramelize completely, but check the cooking of the flesh – it needs to remain pink and juicy. If the fish is not cooked enough after this time, raise the top of the salamander and reduce the heat to minimum.

To serve, pipe the knotweed gel onto the plate and cover with room temperature, slightly foamed buttermilk. Make a salad of green tea and buckwheat, top with the fish and place leaves of knotweed on the side.

BABY TROUT p. 77

This is all about the little – 100 gram – brown trout that live in a small stream in the high mountains. It is a pure and unique fish. The flavour combinations here are extremely light, to let the trout take centre stage.

Serves 4

For the baby trout

2	baby trout, 100 g each
130 g	salt
100 g	white sugar
	zest of 5 tangerines

For the chestnut purée

400 g	peeled chestnuts
1 l	milk
15 g	agar agar
	salt
	white sugar

For the chestnut chips

	cooked chestnuts (see above)
80 g	hot chicken stock
20 g	gelepessa
	peanut or sunflower oil, for frying

For the chestnut powder

	chestnut chips (see above)

For the tangerine segments

20 ml	apple vinegar
25 g	sugar
6 g	salt
50 ml	tangerine juice
8 g	tangerine zest
10 g	mustard seeds
4	tangerines

For the tangerine oil

5	tangerines
200 ml	grapeseed oil

For the salad

	lamb sorrel
	pimpinella leaves
	oxalis ↗

	yarrow
	salt, to taste

To serve

50 g	fresh trout eggs

First, prepare the trout. Clean the fish and make the fillets. Mix the salt and sugar, then add the tangerine zest. Cover the baby trout fillets with the cure and let sit for 25 minutes before rinsing off the mix.

To make the chestnut purée, cook the chestnuts in milk for 1 hour in a saucepan over a low heat. Strain the milk, keeping the chestnuts on the side. Cook 300 g of chestnut milk with 9 g of agar agar for 2 minutes. Cool it down, then blend it until it becomes a smooth purée. Season with salt and sugar.

Blend the reserved chestnuts with the chicken stock, at 70°C (160°F) in a Thermomix and add the gelespessa. Blend until smooth, and if necessary, add more chicken stock. Spread out on a Silpat. Let dry at 72°C (165°F) for 4 hours. Finally, deep fry the chips at 180°C (350°F) until golden and crisp. Use a very precise thermometer. The frying oil should have a high smoke point.

For the chestnut powder, fry some of the chips a bit longer so they become darker, then make a powder out of them.

To prepare the tangerine segments, bring the vinegar, sugar, salt and tangerine juice plus zest to the boil. Cook for 15 minutes. Let cool and strain. Add the mustard seeds. Cut the tangerine into segments, avoiding any seeds and white parts. Marinate them with the tangerine vinaigrette.

To make the tangerine oil, peel off the tangerine zest so it falls right into the oil (also keep all the essential oil of the tangerines). Put the zest and oil into a vacuum bag and keep it for 12 hours in a 70°C (160°F) water bath.

Dress the salad with the tangerine oil and salt.

To serve, put the baby trout fillets on the plate. Then pipe on chestnut purée, combine with tangerine slices and the dressed wild plants and chestnut powder. Finish with chestnut chips.

GARDEN & FOREST WITCHES

CHICKWEED PARADISE p. 81

Chickweed is one of the tastiest and healthiest weeds from our garden and meadows. People from the Soča Valley mostly do not know it, though. It is a great surprise for them how similar it is to the green pea. It grows everywhere, especially in the summer.

Serves 12

For the fermented green strawberries
200 g   green strawberries
300 ml 2.5% brine

For the chickweed salad
500 g   young chickweed plants
3 kg   shell-on green peas
        salt
200 g   cleaned broad (fava) beans
300 g   shelled green almonds
50 g   green strawberries

For the strawberry gel
300 g   ripe strawberries
10 g   agar agar
3   soaked gelatine leaves
300 g   semi-ripe strawberries
15 g   salt
10 g   Madagascar black pepper

To serve
30 g   almond oil
15 g   strawberry seed oil

Clean the strawberries and put them in a glass jar. Pour over the brine and cover with a towel. Let sit for 10 days at 21ºC (70ºF).

Clean the chickweed and remove the green peas from their shells. Blanch the shells, drop into iced water, then pass them through the juicer. Bring this liquid to a boil, adjust the salt, strain, vacuum seal and store in ice water. Boil the green peas for 10 seconds, peel and store in a cold place. Repeat with the broad (fava) beans. Soak 200 g of the green almonds in water and let sit for 24 hours. Blend the soaked green almonds with some of their soaking water and 100 g of broad beans to a perfect purée. Slice the green strawberries.

Juice the ripe strawberries, whisk in the agar agar and bring to a boil. Add the gelatine and blend immediately with the semi-ripe strawberries. Add salt and pepper and place on a Silpat. Let it cool down and form into discs of 2.5 cm (1 in) diameter.

To assemble, heat the green pea shell liquid, adjusting the salt if necessary. Chop the remaining green almonds that have not been soaked. Mix them with green peas and broad beans. Add the diced green strawberries and chickweed and dress with salt and almond oil. Add the fermented green strawberries. ↗

Place the strawberry discs, followed by the green almond purée, on the bottom, then add the salad. The broth should be served at the table. Finish with some drops of strawberry oil.

ABSOLUTE PORCINI p. 102

It looks simple, but it's a very complex dish. The idea was born after my second visit to Niko Romito's Casa Donna. There was a dish that focused on one ingredient only. It was late August, and I got a phone call from Miha, my forager. 'I am in the forest, Ana,' he shouted. 'It is just crazy. Mushrooms! So many of them!' A few hours later he showed up with fifty kilos of them. I was cutting, cleaning and drying them for the entire day, but the day after he came again. We were forced to think quickly, and this beautiful dish is the result of that forest madness.

Serves 8

For the mushroom and porcini glaze
3 kg   onions
1.5 kg parsley root
5 kg   porcini
21 kg   mix of champignons, chanterelles
        and russula, thinly sliced
500 g   salt

For the beetroot purée
1 kg   beetroot (beets)
300 ml mushroom stock
2 g   gelaspessa
30 g   tarragon
        salt

For the smoked egg foam
2   eggs
4   egg yolks
50 ml   soy sauce
40 ml   fish sauce
7   soaked gelatine leaves
600 ml grapeseed oil
        salt

For the mushroom broth
5 kg   rooster mushrooms
500 g   parsley root
1.5 kg onions
30 l   water
15 g   crushed peppercorns
        1.5% salt (for seasoning)
4   bay leaves
5 g   pepper
500 g   dried porcini

For the tarragon oil
200 g   tarragon leaves
300 ml grapeseed oil ↗

To serve
4   beautiful medium porcini mushrooms
        fleur de sel
        trpotec

Roast the onions and parsley root in a big saucepan, until they are very brown. Add the porcini and simmer for about 6 hours. In another pan, place the mix of sliced mushrooms. Add the salt and cook for 20 minutes on very low heat to sweat them. Cover with a lid and simmer for around 6 hours. The mushrooms will release so much water that they will cook in the same liquid. Cook this stock for around 4 hours. Strain both stocks, mix them together and start to reduce slowly to make a glaze. From that amount of mushrooms, you will get around 3.5 l of mushroom glaze.

Wrap the beetroot in aluminium foil and bake at 180ºC (350ºF) for 1 hour. Peel them when they are still hot and then blend them with the rest of the ingredients. Season with salt.

Smoke the eggs and egg yolks in a smoker, at least twice. In a pot, heat 140 ml water, the soy sauce and fish sauce. Add the gelatine. In a Thermomix place the smoked eggs, adding the gelatine mixture. Mix together and slowly add the grapeseed oil to emulsify. Finish with some salt to season it, and reserve in a siphon with 2 chargers.

Roast the roosters in the oven at 230ºC (445ºF) for 20 minutes. In a big saucepan, roast the parsley root and the onions. Add the roosters and cover with the water, then add the spices and simmer for 3 hours. Strain and add the dried porcini to the rooster consommé and simmer for 2 hours over a low heat, without boiling. It is important to not boil it since you don't want to get a bitter flavour, or for it to be a dark and cloudy colour. Strain again and reserve.

Blend the tarragon leaves and grapeseed oil together in a Thermomix at 70ºC (160ºF) for 6 minutes. Then place the mixture in a metallic bowl and cool it down in an ice bath. Then strain it through a cheesecloth. Steam the porcini mushrooms for 2 minutes. Glaze the mushrooms with the mushroom glaze, then roast in a charcoal oven without heating the centre, glazing constantly. Add a pinch of fleur de sel. Serve with egg foam, beetroot purée and leaves of trpotec. Heat the broth and serve it alongside.

SUMMER PUMPKIN AND ELDERBERRIES p. 84

This is one of those happy dishes where the flavours are in perfect harmony; first you taste pumpkin, then elderberries and finally duck. ↗

Serves 8

For the fermented elderberries

2 kg	elderberries
3 l	3% brine
30 g	sugar

For the duck jus

10 kg	duck carcasses
6	onions
6	carrots
3	celery sticks
1 l	red wine
12	bay leaves
3	bunches thyme

For the elderberry jus

70 g	elderberries
350 ml	duck jus (see above)

For the pumpkin

1	whole summer pumpkin
	elderberry jus paste (see above)
300 g	elderberries
60 g	sugar
20 g	salt

For the caramel jus

80 g	sugar
20 ml	water
350 ml	duck jus (see above)

For the foie mousse

350 ml	duck jus (see above)
300 g	foie gras
16 g	salt

For the dry duck breast

100 g	rock salt
100 g	elderberries
30 g	sugar
14 g	coriander seeds
5	skinless duck breasts

For the fermented elderberries, put all the ingredients in a jar. Cover with a clean towel and let it sit for 7 days at at 25°C (77°F).

Roast the duck carcasses at 230°C (445°F) for 20 minutes. In a deep saucepan, roast the vegetables. Add the duck carcass, red wine and herbs. Reduce until there is no more alcohol remaining. Cover with water and simmer for about 8 hours. Strain and start to reduce the stock, until the flavour is more concentrated and the reduction has the texture of a sauce.

For the elderberry jus, bring together the elderberries and duck jus and cook for 2 hours. Strain and keep the paste to cover the pumpkins while baking.

Cut the pumpkins in half and cover with a paste made out of the reserved elderberry jus, elderberries, sugar and salt (simply blend them together). Wrap the pumpkins in aluminium foil and bake at 140°C (285°F) for 25 minutes or until cooked and soft, but not mushy. ↗

Next, make the caramel jus. Mix the sugar and water in a small pan and heat, stirring often, until you get a dark caramel. It is important to not burn it, since you don't want to have a bitter taste in the sauce. Once you have the dark caramel, add the duck jus little by little to not crystallize the caramel. Take off the heat and reserve for the plating.

To make the foie mousse, heat up the duck jus, put in a Thermomix and emulsify with the foie gras on high speed for 5 minutes at 50°C (120°F). Season with salt. Put the mix in silicone bon bon moulds and freeze. Take out of the freezer 10 minutes before using.

Blend all the ingredients for the cure, then rub the duck breasts with the mixture and leave for at least 2 days in the refrigerator without covering. Then dry them at 90°C (195°F) for at least 16 hours.

To serve, put a slice of heated unpeeled pumpkin on the plates. Top with the fermented berries, caramel jus, duck foie and grated dried duck breast.

DANDELION p. 96

Dandelion is one of the humblest plants that grow in the Soča Valley. Slovenians are, in general, crazy about it. In the earliest days of March, we eat it as a salad, and later, when the plant becomes thicker and bitter, we dress it with warm vinegar and pork crackling. This recipe is a simpler version of one of the first dishes I created, strongly influenced by Matej Tomažič. I honestly cannot recall who made it first.

Serves 16

For the dandelion

50 g	buckwheat flour
200 g	plain (all-purpose) flour
50 g	cornflour (cornstarch)
400 ml	mineral water
200 ml	pale ale
8	tender dandelions with roots cut in half
	sunflower oil, for frying
	fleur de sel

For the buckwheat popcorn

20 ml	rapeseed (canola) oil
100 g	buckwheat groats
5 g	salt

For the thick yogurt

200 g	thick yogurt
7 g	salt

To serve

50 g	dandelion honey

To prepare the dandelions, mix all the ingredients, except the dandelion, and let them sit in the refrigerator. Add ice cubes and immerse the dandelion. Rinse well and fry the ↗

dandelions at 180°C (350°F). Let them sit on paper. Season with fleur de sel.

Use a heavy iron pan to toast the buckwheat for 10 minutes. When hot, add the oil and buckwheat. Turn off the heat and stir. When all puffed, transfer to kitchen paper and add the salt.

Mix the yogurt and salt together and hang the yogurt in a cheesecloth in the refrigerator for 24 hours. Strain all the liquid out and keep the solid yogurt in a piping (pastry) bag.

To serve, place the dandelion on the plate, pipe on the yogurt, sprinkle with buckwheat and spread with honey. Invite guests to eat it with their hands.

SMOKED BONE MARROW, SILENE VULGARIS AND GREEN PEAS p. 104

Green pea and silene have very similar flavours – nutty and green. We combine them with strawberries for freshness and smoked bone marrow for its umami-ness. It is to be eaten with your hands, in one bite.

Serves 2

For the green pea meringue

40 g	sugar
150 ml	pea juice
14 g	albumina
0.5 g	xantana
	salt

For the bone marrow spread

1 kg	bone marrow, smoked and brined
in 7% brine	

For the salad

20 g	green peas
15 g	silene
30 g	wild strawberries
15 g	grayling roe (brined)
10 g	chickweed
7 g	white and violet wild violets
10 ml	strawberry seed oil
3 g	salt

Cook the sugar and 100 ml water to a syrup. Cool down. Add the pea juice, albumina, xantana and salt and blend well. Cool for 3 hours. Whisk until soft peaks form. Spread on Silpats 2 cm (¾ in) thick and dehydrate at 50°C (120°F) for 2 hours.

Render the marrow slowly in a pan, constantly stirring until it is a golden colour. Set in the fridge. Return to room temperature and emulsify with the help of a hand blender.

To make the salad, gently bring all the ingredients together. ↓

To serve, break the meringue and spread it over the bone marrow. Place the salad on the top. Serve on the marrow bone.

HOLLY, BLACK SHALLOTS, BLUE CHEESE p. 86

Holly is one of the most intense sprouts in late spring. Its flavours are bitter and balsamic, and they require very careful flavour combinations. The plant is magic, with red, almost Christmas balls. It always reminds us of holidays.

Serves 12

For the blue cheese cream
200 g   sweet Gorgonzola
180 ml   cream

For the black shallots
2 kg   black shallots
         salt

For the clam sauce
1 kg   clams
30 g   garlic
200 ml   white wine
50 g   honey
30 ml   soy sauce
20 g   calamar garum
0.3%   gelespessa

To serve
200 g   holly leaves
12   bigger linden leaves

Blend together the sweet Gorgonzola and cream, bringing to 70°C (160°F). Strain and keep in a squeeze bottle.

Wrap each shallot in aluminium foil and keep at 60°C (140°F) in the oven for 2 months. Peel. Blend with some water and season with salt.

Bring the clams, garlic and white wine to a boil. Cook for 20 minutes. Strain. Return to the pan, add the honey and continue cooking for 20 minutes. Add the soy sauce and garum and thicken with gelespessa.

To serve, blanch the holly for 20 seconds and stop cooking in iced water. Chop. Gently stir in the clam sauce. Open the linden leaves, spread over all the ingredients and close gently to form a wrap.

KALE TACO, WILD PLANTS p. 90 ↗

This is a true taste of wild plants. It could be almost Asian or Mexican, but really, it is so much about the local environment and spring season.

Serves 16

For the green tacos
500 g   plain (all-purpose) flour
250 g   polenta
30 g   plantago powder
50 g   kale powder
10 g   salt
         vegetable oil, for frying

For the egg yolk emulsion
8   egg yolks
8 g   black garlic
2 g   salt

For the salad dressing
100 g   hazelnut miso
120 ml   elderflower syrup
20 ml   hazelnut oil
28 ml   apple cider vinegar

To serve
100 g   crushed roasted hazelnuts
10   varieties of wild herbs and flowers (wild garlic/ramsons sprouts and flowers, garlic mustard, wild watercress, wild hops, acacia flowers, elder flower, potato dandelion, yarrow, dandelion flowers – any herbs that you can find that are soft and full of flavour)

Weigh out all the ingredients, then mix all the dry ingredients in a stand mixer on speed 1, slowly adding 200 ml water little by little. Mix for a maximum of 1 minute – the dough shouldn't become elastic. When it starts to form a ball, transfer to a lightly floured work surface and gently fold into a smooth even ball. Wrap in clingfilm (plastic wrap) and keep in the refrigerator. Leave for at least 12 hours. To make the tacos, roll the dough really thinly, around 1 mm, and cut with a mould. Fry at 170°C (340°F), then fold into shape before it cools. Keep in the dehydrator until needed.

For the emulsion, put the egg yolks in a vacuum bag, add the black garlic and seal. Cook in a sous-vide or steam oven at 63.5°C (146°F) for 2 hours. While still hot, transfer to a blending cup and blend with a hand blender until smooth. Season with salt and place in a piping (pastry) bag. Cool rapidly.

For the dressing, mix everything together in a Thermomix at speed 7 for 5 minutes. Strain and keep in the refrigerator.

Dress the herbs and flowers with the salad dressing and crushed hazelnuts. Place the emulsion of egg yolk in the bottom of the taco and place the salad on top.

CORNFIELD IN THE MOUNTAIN p. 94

Young corn is available maybe only two weeks in the busiest month for the restaurant, when we all deal more with tourists and guests than what is going on in our natural surroundings. But when we work so closely with nature, we have to act and react fast. This dish has been dreamed and realized by my Colombian chef, Leonardo. I rarely give place to other chefs in my team for the creative process.

Serves 4

For the achiote salt
100 g   salt
10 g   achiote

For the corn
8   young corn cobs in husk
50 g   brown butter
6 g   achiote salt (see above)

For the Tolminc cheese foam
300 ml milk
300 ml cream
550 g   3-month-old Tolminc cheese
4   soaked gelatine leaves
6 g   salt

For the corn curd
10   big mature corn cobs

For the husk powder
300 g   corn husks
10 g   salt

Mix the 2 ingredients and blend them in a spice blender to a powder. Vacuum seal the corn in their husks and cook them in the oven at 95°C (200°F) for 90 minutes. Remove them from the bag and grill them over charcoal for 8 minutes, until almost burnt on the outside. Note: it is important that the charcoal is only embers, so you can get a cleaner charcoal flavour in the corn. Open the husk, brush the corn with brown butter and season with achiote salt once grilled and ready to serve.

Heat the milk and cream together in the Thermomix to 60°C (140°F). Add the cheese and blend until smooth, maintaining the temperature. Add the gelatine and salt. Fill the siphon and charge 2 chargers.

Pass all the corn through a juicer. Cook all the juice down until reduced by one-third. Keep in the refrigerator.

Roast the husks in the oven at 230°C (445°F) for 30 minutes. Cool down to room temperature, then blend in the spice blender to a powder. Mix with the salt and reserve.

To serve, plate each very hot corn in the husk, inviting people to eat it with their hands. ↗

Serve the Tolminc foam on the side along with the corn curd and husk powder.

MEADOWSWEET IS A QUEEN OF SUMMER FIELDS p. 93

Two weeks after the original cucumber dish was on the menu, we ran out of fermented green strawberries. I tried to replace them with pickled carrots and fermented goose-berries, but it somehow did not work out. I was away at an event when my sous chef Leonardo called to tell me he was put-ting the cucumber dish off the menu. 'There is no more balance, Chef.' The fields were full of meadowsweet in that period – so we came up with this. Meadowsweet is an intense flower – you may easily hate it. But with cucumber, watermelon and tomato it is simply striking.

Serves 8

For the meadowsweet oil
500 g meadowsweet
600 ml rapeseed (canola) oil

For the watermelon
200 ml watermelon, seeds removed
20 g sugar
20 g salt

For the tomatoes
300 g date tomatoes
12 g salt
35 g sugar
200 ml meadowsweet oil (see above)

For the cucumbers
200 g hard garden cucumbers
20 ml tomato cooking liquid (see above)
10 ml olive oil
2 g salt

For the roasted tomato and watermelon emulsion
400 g yellow ripe date tomatoes
300 g ripe watermelon
10 g salt
20 g sugar
50 ml olive oil

For the chocolate sauce
200 g dark chocolate 72%
50 ml olive oil
10 g salt
18 ml umeboshi liquid

To serve
  fleur de sel
  green and black basil leaves
  drops of meadowsweet oil (see above) ↗

Blend the meadowsweet with oil in a Thermo-mix, heating up to 70ºC (160ºF) for 10 minutes. Strain well over iced water. Chill in the refriger-ator until ready to serve.

Cut the watermelon into perfect rectan-gles approximately 5 cm (2 in) long, 2 cm (¾ in) wide and 3 cm (1¼ in) thick. Sprinkle them with sugar and salt and compress 3 times. Close in a vacuum bag, compressing all the air outside, and store in an ice bath for a few hours.

Place the date tomatoes on baking paper and sprinkle with salt and sugar. Cover with the meadowsweet oil. Bake at 140ºC (285ºF) for 1 hour 40 minutes. Let them cool down at room temperature and peel them gently when cold. Dry the peels at 60ºC (140ºF) in a dehy-drator. Store the peeled tomatoes in the refrig-erator. Store any residual cooking liquids there as well.

Slice the cucumbers with a mandoline as thinly as possible. Dress with a bit of tomato cooking liquid, tomatoes, meadowsweet oil, olive oil and salt.

To make the emulsion, put all the ingredi-ents together on a tray covered with baking paper. Bake at 200ºC (400ºF) for 25 minutes, then reduce the temperature to 135ºC (275ºF) for 40 minutes. Blend in a Thermomix on the highest speed.

Melt the chocolate, emulsify with olive oil, add the salt and close with umeboshi liquid. Let it set at room temperature.

To serve, place the watermelon on a dish, cover with slices of date tomatoes, peeled tomatoes and cucumber. Add the tempered chocolate sauce and the tomato and water-melon emulsion. Finish with some fleur de sel, green and black basil leaves and drops of meadowsweet oil.

WALNUT, 21 DAY-AGED KEFIR, POLLEN AND HONEY p. 83

This dish has been with us for more than a year. I created it for a four-hand dinner, and it is very natural in both its visual appeal and flavour.

Serves 10

For the kefir
1 l farmer's raw milk
200 g kefir mushrooms

For the walnut cake
135 g sugar
15 g plain (all-purpose) flour
160 g walnuts
160 g egg whites

For the honey ice cream
6 egg yolks ↗

180 g forest honey
100 g organic bee pollen
600 ml milk
300 ml cream

For the chamomile syrup
300 ml water
300 g sugar
120 g fresh chamomile flowers

For the pears
  thinly sliced pears

To garnish
  fresh chamomile leaves and flowers

Bring the milk to the boil and let it cool down. Pour it into a glass jar, add the kefir-mushrooms, cover with a cloth and leave it to ferment at room temperature (around 22ºC/72ºF) for 21 days. The result is very cheesy.

Strain through a plastic chinois and store the kefir in a glass jar in the refrigerator. Wash the soaked mushrooms with unchlorinated water and restart a new kefir. The kefir has a very nice, jellyfied structure.

Put 105 g of sugar with the flour and wal-nuts in a blender, pulsing until you obtain a granulated texture. Set aside.

Whip the egg whites with 30 g of sugar until stiff peaks appear. Fold the flour mixture into the egg whites in 2 parts. Pour over a paper lined tray and bake at 180ºC (350ºF) for 17–20 minutes.

Whisk the egg yolks with the honey and the bee pollen for 5 minutes (the pollen doesn't dissolve, don't worry!). Heat the milk and cream to 35ºC (95ºF). Temper into the egg yolk mixture bit by bit, then transfer to a bain-marie and bring up to 82ºC (180ºF). Pour into a bowl over an ice bath to immediately cool. Put into your ice cream maker and churn.

Bring the water and sugar to the boil, or until all the sugar is dissolved. Add the cham-omile, cover with clingfilm (plastic wrap) and leave it to infuse for 2 days at room tempera-ture. Strain and divide the liquid in half – half will be used for the gel, and half for marinating the pears compressed in camomile syrup.

To serve, Pacojet the ice cream, place the kefir in the centre and place the sponge cake on the side. Set the chamomile jelly and finish with the ice cream, pears taken out of the syrup and placed next to the ice cream and fresh chamomile leaves and flowers.

SWEETCORN GARDEN

p. 103

This is all about the sourness of the kombu-cha, the umami-ness of buckwheat and the sweetness of the corn. ↓

Serves 4

For the sweetcorn
3   corn cobs

For the puffed buckwheat
15 ml   sunflower oil
60 g   buckwheat groats

For the corn husk and puffed buckwheat meringue
2   egg whites
125 g   sugar
125 g   icing (confectioners') sugar
60 g   puffed buckwheat (see above)
1 tbsp   corn husk powder (see above)

For the corncob kombucha
15 g   black tea
3   roasted corn cobs (see above)
125 g   sugar
100 ml   old kombucha

For the corn mousse
250 g   fresh corn kernels (see above)
15 g   sugar
1 g   salt
250 ml   cream
70 g   mascarpone

To serve
liquid nitrogen

The corn husks are burnt for the meringue, the kernels are for the mousse, and the cobs for the kombucha.

Remove the husks of the corn and place on a flat tray. Bake at 240°C (465°F) until totally black. Blend in a spice blender and reserve for the meringue. Cut off the kernels and reserve them for the mousse. Place the corn cobs in a flat tray and bake them at 220°C (430°F). Reserve for the kombucha.

Heat the oil in a lyonnaise (iron) pan to 220°C (430°F). Add the buckwheat and cover with a lid until it puffs. Reserve.

Place the egg whites in a bowl over a bain-marie with the sugar. Start to whisk until it reaches 50°C (120°F), and make sure there are no grains of sugar. Place the mixture in a stand mixer on full speed. Start to add the icing sugar slowly and whisk until medium point – not yet too firm. Add the corn husk powder and with a silicone spatula, make sure you incorporate the powder properly. Lastly, add the puffed buckwheat and mix gently to incorporate all ingredients together. Then take 1 flat tray and 2 Silpats. Place 1 Silpat on the flat tray and spread on 120 g of the meringue, then put the other Silpat on top of the meringue, making sure it has the same thickness. Bake the meringue for 25 minutes at 160°C (320°F) with a medium fan. It is important to not put the fan on full, to avoid the meringue losing its the shape. Once baked, place in the dehydrator at 52°C (125°F) until you need to use it. ↗

Infuse 1.5 l water with the black tea and the roasted corn cobs for 1 hour at 80°C (175°F). Strain and cool down, then add the sugar and old kombucha plus the scoby – a symbiotic mixed culture of yeast and bacteria used in the production of kombucha. Let sit at room temperature for at least 5 days. Once the kombucha has a good flavour, keep in the refrigerator.

Combine the corn kernels, sugar, salt and three-quarters of the cream and bring just to the boil. Simmer over moderate heat, stirring the corn until tender, around 5 minutes. Transfer to a blender and purée until smooth. Strain the purée through a fine sieve, pressing on the solids. Let cool completely, then whisk in the mascarpone. In a bowl, beat the remaining one-quarter of the cream until stiff. Fold into the corn mixture until no streaks remain.

To serve, freeze the kombucha with liquid nitrogen and place it in the bottom of the bowl. Cover with corn mousse and serve with the meringue.

RHUBARB AND ELDERFLOWER p. 98

I know it is kitsch. But sometimes kitsch is nice. Rhubarb is one of the few plants that survive our hard winters. And elderflower... Slovenians are mad about them. We do litres of elderflower syrup to mix with water and drink throughout the year.

Serves 4

For the rhubarb
200 g   cleaned rhubarb
100 ml   elderflower syrup
3   gelatine leaves

For the elder 'marshmallow'
100 ml   elderflower syrup
juice of 1 lime
10 g   gelatine

For the rhubarb-strawberry sorbet
400 ml   rhubarb juice
75 g   sugar
200 g   strawberries
25 ml   liquid glucose
100 g   stabilizer

For the lime curd
275 g   sugar
5   eggs
5   limes, juice and zest
2   soaked gelatine leaves
375 g   softened butter

For the dehydrated strawberries
200 g   strawberries
100 ml   elderflower syrup ↗

To serve
8   stems and leaves of knotweed

Cook the rhubarb in the syrup at 60°C (140°F) for 15–20 minutes, or until soft.

Add the soaked gelatine and cool. Mix in a stand mixer.

To make the 'marshmallow', assemble the elderflower syrup and lime juice and bring to a boil. Add the previously soaked gelatine. Cool and start mixing in a stand mixer. Mix for 30 minutes keeping the mixing bowl in ice. When the mixture is almost firm, take it out and place in the silicone mould. Freeze. Once frozen, cut into 3½-cm (1⅜-in) cubes.

To make the sorbet, take the rhubarb juice, add the sugar, strawberries and stabilizer and start cooking. At 40°C (105°F), add the liquid glucose and bring to a boil. Cool it down and blend in the remaining ingredients.

To make the curd, cook the sugar, eggs and lime juice/zest in a bain-marie until thick. Add the gelatine and strain. Add the butter little by little. Cool it. Blend and fill in a piping (pastry) bag.

Cut the strawberries in quarters and compress them in syrup 4-5 times. Dry in a dehydrator until they are dry outside and still moist in the middle.

Compose all the ingredients together and finish with fresh knotweed stems and leaves.

THE PEACH AND THE WOODRUFF p. 89

I have discovered woodruff recently. Unlike Scandinavian countries, we have plenty of it, yet we do not have the tradition of using it. But there is plenty of woodruff, especially in the dense forest above the Soča river. That forest is on my running trail, and in the hot summer evenings there is an intense aroma of bitter almonds in the air. And we have a lot of peaches. It is one of the most precious fruits of the western part of Slovenia. Barley may not be originally from here, but it is the base for a lot of traditional recipes. I have a bit of a love-hate relationship with it, but in this version of raw ice cream, I find it incredibly interesting.

Serves 8

For the woodruff syrup
1 kg   sugar
100   pieces sweet woodruff

For the sweet woodruff gel
250 ml   sweet woodruff syrup (see above)
4 g   agar agar

For the peach gelatine
2   gelatine leaves
250 g   peach purée ↗

For the saffron whey
600 ml whey
100 ml cream
2 g   saffron

For the milk crumble
100 g   brown butter
100 g   sugar
100 ml milk powder

For the barley ice cream
100 g   pearl barley
600 ml milk
100 ml cream
60 g   sugar
10 g   ice cream stabilizer

For the peaches in sweet woodruff syrup
200 g   peaches (cut in thin slices)
200 ml woodruff syrup (see above)

Cook the sugar with 1 l water, then allow to cool. Add the sweet woodruff. Let it sit for 3 days. Strain.
    Cook the syrup with the agar agar, allow to cool then blend.
    Soak the gelatine leaves in cold water, melt them, and add it to the purée.
    Reduce the whey and cream to 350 ml, then add the saffron. Let it sit, then blend and strain.
    To make the milk crumble, mix the brown butter with the sugar and milk powder. Bake it in an oven at 200ºC (400ºF) until caramelized.
    Roast the pearl barley for 30 minutes at 190ºC (375ºF). Soak the barley with the milk and cream and let it sit overnight. Strain it, add the sugar and stabilizer and bring to a boil. Freeze the mix in a Pacojet container.
    Add the peaches to the syrup and compress it in a vacuum machine 3–4 times. Keep in an ice bath until serving.
    To serve, place gel with piping bags, then place the gelatines on the plate. Cover with saffron whey. Serve with crumble, ice cream and slices of peach. Finish with leaves of fresh woodruff.

BEESWAX, PEACHES AND ELDERFLOWER

p. 101

We source beeswax and some honeys from Marija. She lives less than 2 kilometres (¾ mile) from Hiša Franko and has an incredible knowledge about the material. She has been nominated a Slovenian of the year for her work with bees. This dish has been created for a four-hand dinner in Quintonil in Mexico City with my amazing friends Alejandra and Jorge.

Serves 16 ↗

For the beeswax infusion
350 g   melted beeswax
300 ml cream
       salt

For the beeswax crème anglais
60 g   egg yolks
45 g   sugar
250 g   beeswax infusion (see above)
       salt

For the peach salad
3 kg   sweet, hard peaches
500 kg sugar
3   vanilla pods
70 ml elderflower vinegar

For the peach and elderflower gel
1.2 l   peach juice
1 l   peach syrup
1 l   elderflower syrup
25 g   agar agar
10 g   gelespessa

For the peach kernel ice cream
2 l   milk
2 l   cream
750 g peach kernels
20 g   salt
5   egg yolks
75 g   sugar
30 g   cornflower (cornstarch)
300 ml milk
300 ml cold peach kernel infusion

To serve
       elderflowers

Mix the beeswax infusion ingredients and infuse them on a bain-marie for 3 hours. Cool the infusion at room temperature for 24 hours. After 1 day, strain through the cheesecloth.
    Proceed with crème anglaise. Beat the yolks and sugar on the bain-marie until it reaches 70ºC (158ºF), whipping the egg yolks with sugar. Add the warm infusion of beeswax and bring to 83ºC (181ºF) while mixing all the time on a bain-marie. Add the soaked gelatine leaves. Cool it down, while covered.
    Peel the peaches and cut into 5 mm (¼ in) squares. Keep the offcuts. Bring the sugar and 800 ml water to a boil. Add the vanilla pods, peach offcuts and vinegar. Let it infuse for 24 hours. Strain. Vacuum seal the peaches with the liquid and preserve in iced water.
    To make the peach and elderflower gel, put all the ingredients in a pan, bring to the boil and allow to set. When cold, blend, pass through a tamis 3 times and place in a piping (pastry) bag.
    Let the milk, cream, peach kernels and salt infuse for 24 hours. Blend and strain through a cheesecloth. Mix all the ingredients and freeze in Pacojet containers.
    To serve, place the peaches and gel on the plates, add the ice cream and pour the beeswax English cream over the top. Finish with fresh elderflowers.

(RE)EVOLUTION OF KOBARIŠKI ŠTRUKLJI p. 99

Kobariški štruklji is the most traditional dish from our area of Slovenia. It has been here for generations. The recipe has never been written down, and every house makes it in a bit of a different way. Štruklji have very thick and sticky pastry and are traditionally filled with walnuts, raisins and cinnamon. I wanted to create a linear evolution, especially regarding the dough. The pork crème brûlée is a surprising end to the meal. With horseradish and oxalis, it makes for an amazing combination.

Serves 16

For the plum jam
25 g   sugar
500 g dried plums
300 ml red wine
5 g   salt

For the smoked pork crème brûlée
3 kg   smoked ham
3 l   cream
160 g egg yolks
40 g   sugar
5 g   salt
       plum jam (see above)

For the filling
50 g   sugar
150 g ground walnut
300 ml cream
180 g semi-dried apples (see below)
220 g sauteed parsnips (see below)
160 g caramelized pork cracklings
       (see below)
160 g walnut crumble (see below)

For the semi-dried apples
1 kg   ripe red apples

For the sauteed parsnip dices
1 kg   parsnips
250 g butter

For the caramelized pork cracklings
200 g zaseka (pork fat)

For the walnut crumble
120 g sugar
45 g   glucose
60 g   butter
150 g ground walnuts

For the štruklji dough
270 g plain (all-purpose) flour
150 g starch
200 ml cold water ↓

For the apple cocktail

10 l	fresh apple juice
3	cinnamon sticks
3	pieces star anise
150 ml	single malt whisky
	smoked ice cubes

To serve

100 g	pork fat
	demerara sugar
	fresh horseradish
	wood sorrel

Caramelize the sugar, add the plums, deglaze with red wine and add the salt. Simmer for 30–40 minutes. Cool down and cut the plums into dice – it should look like a coarse-textured paste.

Chop the ham into small pieces. Bring to a boil with the cream, simmer for 30 minutes, and cool down at room temperature. Strain. Heat 600 g of the pork infusion to 70°C (160°C). Whisk the yolks with the sugar until they are dissolved. Add a spoon of the plum jam to the crème brûlée jars. Slowly pour the pork infusion into the egg mixture to temper it, then add salt and strain. Bake in an oven on convection at 100% humidity and 80°C (170°F) for 45 minutes. Cool down in an ice bath.

Place the dry ingredients into a mixer with the hook attachment and slowly add the water. Mix for 4 minutes on medium speed to develop the gluten. Cover the dough with clingfilm (plastic wrap) and let it rest for 30 minutes. Work the dough in the pasta machine starting at 10 mm (⅛ in) and going down to 2 mm (1/16 in). Once you reach the 2 mm (1/16 in) thickness with the dough, use a cutter of 5 cm (2 in) diameter to get the size and shape needed to form the štruklji.

Place the the filling portions (previously made) in the center of the 5 cm (2 in) diameter dough you previously cut. Wet the rim of the wrapper with water, enough to moisten. With the wrapper in your palm press the filling into it with your index finger. Use your palm to begin closing the wrapper around the filling. Where the wrapper begins to meet, crimp the top of the semi-circle, and continue crimping from the top towards the edges. Once sealed, place the dumpling on a surface with the crimp facing up, and use your pinky to make an indent on top of the dumpling.

To make the semi-dried apples, cut the apples in half and take out the seeds. Place the apples in the dehydrator at 65°C (149°F) and dry them for 12 hours. Take the apples out of the dehydrator and cut them into dices of 1 x 1 cm (⅓ x ⅓ in), then reserve.

Peel the parnips and cut into dices of 1 x 1 cm (⅓ x ⅓ in). Place the butter in a sauce pan on medium-high heat. Once the butter is melted, slowly add the parsnips and stir constantly, so the butter doesn't burn. Strain and reserve.

To make the cracklings, place the zaseka in a sauce pan and cook at medium heat ↗

for around 10 minutes. All the fat should be melted and it will form cracklings, crispy fat that becomes solid. Stir often and cook for 10 more minutes to avoid the fat burning and getting bitter. Strain and reserve.

To make the walnut crumble, melt the sugar, glucose and butte. Then add the ground walnuts, rolling the mixture between 2 baking papers. Bake at 200°C (392 °F) for 10 minutes.

To make the filling, mix the semi-dried apples, sauteed parsnips, caramelized pork cracklings and walnut crumble. To finish the filling, in a saucepan, melt 50 g of the sugar and 150 g of ground walnuts on medium heat. Once the sugar and walnuts are combined, add 300 ml of the cream and add the filling. Cook for 5 minutes until the mixture is fully combined. Allow to cool and set the mixture. Portion the mixture into pieces of 10 g each and reserve.

Reduce the apple juice to 3 l with the spices. Allow to cool. To make the cocktail, combine 500 ml of the reduced apple juice and the whisky. Finish with a smoked ice cube.

Steam the štruklji and dress them with pork fat. Serve together with the apple cocktail and use demerara brown sugar to caramelize the top of the brûlée. Grate fresh horseradish on top and finish with wood sorrel.

MY DAD IS A HUNTER

WILD BOAR, PLUMS AND BROWN BEANS FROM LIVEK p. 123

This is about brown beans and plums. They grow in the same period of time, late August. When you see high wooden sticks in the middle of nowhere in the Slovenian countryside, it's the brown beans. This dish has an admittedly unusual and strong flavour combination. Brown beans need a strong-tasting and fat meat, and the wild boar cheek turned out to be the ideal partner.

Serves 12

For the fresh brown bean purée

80 g	shallots
100 ml	olive oil, plus extra for frying ↗

500 g	brown beans
30 g	thyme
30 g	marjoram
30 ml	red wine vinegar
30 ml	soy sauce

For the smoked plum purée

500 g	plums, stones (pits) removed
40 g	butter
10 g	salt
80 g	sugar

For the pickled plums

400 ml	red wine vinegar
20 g	salt
15 g	sugar
10 g	thyme
2	bay leaves
2 g	chilli

For the bean salad

500 g	brown beans
	vegetable oil, for frying

For the wild boar cheeks

625 g	plums
250 ml	sake
1 kg	wild boar cheeks

For the pork glaze

20 kg	pork bones
2 l	red wine
5 kg	mirepoix
300 g	tomato purée (paste)
200 g	thyme
150 g	marjoram

To serve

	fresh hibiscus flowers
	dried green juniper
	green juniper oil

Sauté the shallots in a little olive oil and cook until translucent. Soak the beans overnight and cook in 300 ml of the same water with some salt, until soft. Blend in a Thermomix at 70°C with the herbs. Finish with the vinegar and soy sauce. Emulsify with the 100 ml olive oil.

To make the plum purée, halve the plums, put them in a gastronorm (hotel pan) together with the butter and bake at 180°C (350°F) for 25 minutes. Strain the remaining liquid and blend the pulp in a Thermomix at 60°C for 5 minutes at high speed. Add the salt and sugar to the purée to season it. Smoke twice and reserve.

To make the pickled plums, bring 600 ml water to the boil with the vinegar, salt and sugar. Add the thyme, bay leaves and chilli and let cool. Vacuum seal the plums in the liquid and repeat the same procedure 3 times. Place the vacuum bag in iced water. Let it sit for 6 hours, keeping the water always icy. Cut beautiful thin slices of plums.

To make the salad, soak the beans in 1 l water overnight, then clean them out of the ↗

skins. Fry the skin at 150ºC (310ºF) until crunchy. Cut the beans in thin slices (like almonds), reserving half of the beans raw and toasting the other half in a pan until they are brown in colour and crunchy in texture.

To make the wild boar cheeks, rinse the plums a few times in warm water. Put in a container with the sake for 24 hours in the refrigerator. Remove the stones (pits) and blend for 2 minutes in a Thermomix on cold till smooth. (Add approximately 150 g of soaking liquid.) Rub the cheeks with the plum mix and cook at 72ºC (162ºF) for 32 hours.

Roast the bones in the oven at 230ºC (445ºF) for 30 minutes. Deglaze with red wine. Roast the mirepoix vegetables and tomato purée (paste) in a huge pan. Deglaze with bones and red wine, then reduce. Cover with ice and water, then add the herbs. Cook for 6 hours on a very low heat. Strain and cool down. Remove the fat and cook for another 2 hours.

To serve, place the smoked plum purée at room temperature, combined with the slightly heated bean purée, pickled plums and gently glazed cheeks. Top with the brown bean salad and hibiscus flowers. Season with green juniper and green juniper oil.

ROEBUCK ON THE SURF OF KOLOVRAT p. 119

I am in love with the flavour of roebuck. My children think it is the best meat in the world, and there is never enough for them. I like the idea of spicing it up with the taste of the sea. Our forests and meadows face the gulf of Trieste, and therefore the grass that the roebuck eats has more mineral and intense flavour.

Serves 8

For the roebuck
800 g   roebuck loin
2 kg   cow's kidney fat

For the parsnip chips
2 kg   parsnips
450 ml cream
        vegetable oil, for frying

For the wild mushroom brunoise
150 g   porcini mushrooms
50 g   chanterelles
50 g   black trumpets

For the pickled spruce sprouts
200 g   spruce sprouts
50 g   sugar
10 g   salt
50 ml apple vinegar ↗

50 ml   lemon juice
30 g   lemon zest

For the spruce powder
200 g   mature spruce needles

For the spruce oil
600 ml grapeseed oil
400 g   spruce branches and needles

For the mushroom stock
5 kg   champignons
5 kg   mature big porcini and porcini stems, preserved from other dishes
3 kg   chanterelles
200 ml olive oil
20 l   chicken stock
500 g   dried black trumpets and porcini mushrooms
200 g   cold butter

For the smoked anchovy butter
300 g   salted anchovies in oil
250 g   anchovies
50 ml   anchovy oil
50 ml   oyster water

To serve
50 ml   olive oil
20 g   butter
        fleur de sel
        colatura di alici
        spruce oil
        parsnip chips
        spruce powder

Clean the roebuck and cover it with melted kidney fat. Hang it in a dry age refrigerator for 1 month.

Peel the parsnips, reserving the peel, and cook them on a low heat in 300 ml cream. When the cream is almost caramelized, add the remaining cream and cook until soft. Blend well. Cook the parsnip peel for 20 minutes, then dry in a dehydrator at 80ºC (175ºF) until completely dry. Then fry them at 230ºC (445ºF) for a few seconds, or until they puff.

Clean the mushrooms and cut them into brunoise.

Boil the sprouts for 1 minute. Bring the sugar, salt, vinegar, lemon juice and 50 ml water to the boil and cool down. Add the lemon zest and spruce, and close in glass jars.

Dry the spruce needles at 56ºC (132ºF) until completely dry. Blend to a powder. Keep in a dry place.

To make the spruce oil, put the oil and spruce in a Thermomix. Blend at 70ºC (160ºF) for 20 minutes. Strain into a bowl over iced water.

Cut all the fresh mushrooms and roast gently in the olive oil. Deglaze with the warm chicken stock and cook down for 4 hours. Add the dried mushrooms and continue cooking for another 3 hours, or until dark and pretty thick. Strain and emulsify with butter.

Blend all the anchovy butter ingredients together at 60ºC (140ºF) until smooth. ↗

Cold smoke it 3 times. To serve, heat an iron pan until very hot, add a drop of olive oil and roast the roebuck loin for 1½ minutes on every side. Add the melted anchovy butter and let the meat sit for 3 minutes, then cut. It must be still red, almost raw inside. Pan fry the mushroom brunoise for a few seconds in an equal mix of heated butter and olive oil. Season with salt. Heat all the other ingredients and plate. Finish with some drops of colatura di alici, spruce oil, parsnip chips and spruce powder.

DEER HEART p. 117

This dish was created as a collaborative dish with Leonardo Pereira. I really like those intense moments when two completely different philosophies melt into one single dish. The idea was to play around the last winter chicory in the garden, bitter as hell and really challenging. After that super funny eight-hand dinner, the deer heart dish was adapted for the regular menu.

Serves 4

For the deer heart
100 g   deer heart

For the juniper salt
20 g   salt
10   juniper berries

For the autumn chicory salad
1   head bitter chicory

For the hazelnut
40 g   hazelnuts

For the rowan berries
50 g   frozen rowan berries
30 g   sugar

For the yeast oil
100 g   fresh beer yeast
100 ml grapeseed oil
5 g   salt

For the buckwheat tacos
25 g   butter
50 g   plain (all-purpose) flour
50 g   buckwheat flour
1   pinch salt

For the smoked egg mayo
3   eggs
15 ml   soy sauce
15 ml   water
2   leaves gelatine
100 ml grapeseed oil

Devein the meat and take away the silver skin. Blast freeze the heart to -5ºC (23ºF) and cut to perfect 2 mm (generous ¹⁄₁₆ cubes). ↓

In a coffee grinder, blend the salt with the juniper berries. Pass through a sieve.

Clean the chicory and slice it very finely.

Toast the hazelnuts at 180°C (350°F) for 8 minutes. Remove the skins and roughly chop.

Rowan berries must be frozen to get rid of toxins. Heat 30 ml water and add the sugar, stirring until dissolved. Add the berries and simmer for 10 minutes. Cool down.

Break apart the fresh yeast on a baking tray lined with baking paper. Roast in the oven at 150°C (300°F) for 20 minutes, then allow to cool.

Blend the yeast with the grapeseed oil and the salt. Slowly add 1 tbsp warm water. Blend at 70°C (160°F) for 20 minutes. Do not strain.

Temper the butter. Sift the 2 flours and add a pinch of salt. Use your hands to mix the butter and flour mixture; it should reach a wet, sand-like consistency. Little by little, add cold water while working the dough. Use just enough water to bind the dough, and fold by hand for 8–10 minutes. Cover in clingfilm (plastic wrap) and let rest in the fridge for 1 hour. Afterwards, using a pasta roller, roll the dough thin and use cutters to punch out large circles. In a dry hot pan, toast the dough on either side until crispy.

Cook the eggs in the shell in a water bath at 65°C (150°F) for 20 minutes. Afterwards, peel the eggs into a bowl and cold smoke very heavily, at least 3 times. Blend the eggs with the warm soy sauce and water (in which you previously dissolved the bloomed gelatine), then emulsify with the grapeseed oil. Fill the siphon with 2 chargers.

To serve, put the deer heart in a bowl and season with the juniper salt. In another bowl, put the chicory, chopped hazelnuts and rowan berries and dress with the yeast oil. Assemble the deer heart tartare and salad on top of your toasted buckwheat taco.

DEER BLACK PUDDING WITH CHESTNUTS AND TANGERINES p. 115

My father shot a beautiful huge deer. We decided to buy it through the local hunting association (these are the rules – the hunter can never sell you the animal directly). The only parts that belong to the hunter are the offal.

Serves 20

For the black pudding

100 g	deer lungs
300 g	deer heart
300 g	deer liver
150 g	deer kidneys
5 g	peppercorns
2 g	red cardamom ↗

5 g	allspice
1	star anise
3 g	fennel seeds
2 g	Sichuan peppercorns
300 ml	deer blood
150 g	dark chocolate 72%
30 ml	whisky
1 kg	cooked, peeled and chopped chestnuts
68 g	wild duck fat, melted
	zest of 3 tangerines
	zest of 1 lemon
300 g	cleaned pork intestines (for sausage casings)

For the tangerine sauce

1 kg	tangerines
75 g	sugar
20 g	pinus mugo needles
80 g	butter

For the chestnut chips

300 g	peeled chestnuts
100 ml	black truffle jus
1.5 l	water
15 g	sugar
12 g	salt

To serve

30 g	grayling roe
50 g	brined raw chestnuts
20 ml	pinus mugo oil
2 g	pinus mugo salt

Boil the lungs, then chop them. Dice to small cubes all the other innards, cleaned carefully. Grind the spices to a powder and cook with the blood, chocolate and whisky at 62°C (144°F) for 1 hour. Emulsify. Add all the chestnuts and cool. Add the melted wild duck fat then season with salt if necessary. Add the zest and put the filling in the pork intestines. Cook for 7 minutes. Cool. Roast in a very hot pan until caramelized, then slice.

Peel the tangerines and bring the peels to the boil 3 times. Juice the tangerines, and add to the sugar and peel and cook for 20 minutes. Add the pinus mugo needles and infuse for 2 hours. Reheat again. Blend, then strain. Add the butter, emulsify and let it sit.

To make the chestnut chips, cook all the ingredients together slowly for 2 hours. Blend, then spread over a Silpat and dry for 1½ hours at 70°C (160°F). Fry until crisp.

To serve, place the black pudding on the corner of the dish. Top it with the grayling roe, brined raw chestnuts and chestnut chips. Serve the tangerine sauce on the side. Finish with drops of pinus mugo oil and salt.

WILD BOAR, BLACK PUDDING AND QUINCE p. 118 ↗

This is inspired by the famous blood pudding so common in all the countryside across Europe. Here, we've tried to recreate the nostalgia of the past.

Serves 8

For the braised wild boar

2 kg	wild boar
3	onions
3	carrots
2	celery sticks
500 ml	red wine
2	bay leaves
1	bunch thyme

For the blood sausage and sourdough

300 g	onions
1 kg	wild boar meat (see above)
120 g	dried plums
180 ml	pig's blood
10 g	agar agar
	salt
1 pinch	juniper powder
	frozen sourdough bread

For the blood sauce

1	onion
100 g	dried plums
60 g	butter
500 ml	wild boar stock
150 ml	pig's blood
10 g	star anise
5	cloves
15	peppercorns
10 g	cardamom pods

For the wine brûlée

350 ml	merlot wine
100 ml	orange juice
100 g	sugar
10 g	agar agar
	peel of ½ orange

For the pickled apple and quince

2	firm apples
2	firm quinces
500 ml	lemon juice
500 g	sugar
100 ml	apple vinegar
2	strips lemon zest

For the quince purée

4	big quinces
200 g	sugar

To braise the wild boar, use 2 big separate pots. Brown the wild boar in the flat iron and reserve. In the large rondeau on the griddle, brown the onions, carrots and celery sticks. Add the red wine and aromatics and reduce until there is no more alcohol. Add the previously browned boar and cover with water. Cook for 4 hours on medium heat, or until the boar is tender. Take the meat out and reserve. Strain the stock and reserve. Pull off the wild boar meat after cooking and reserve. ↗

To make the blood sausage, first finely chop the onions. In a big pan, caramelize the onions until they are soft and translucent. Add the meat and cook for 20 minutes on a medium-low heat. Add the dried plums, chopped into small pieces, and the blood. Cook for around 2 hours on low heat. Take 200 g of the cooking liquid and blend together with the agar agar in cold water. Add water to the pan and cook for 20 more minutes. Season with salt if necessary and finish with juniper powder.

Once cooked, place all the meat in a gastronorm (hotel pan) and place in the blast chiller for 15 minutes, until cooled down. Portion the meat in 115 g sizes. Place the mix in clingfilm (plastic wrap) and make rolls that are tight and firm, then freeze them. In a meat slicer, cut the frozen sourdough bread into 2.5 mm (scant ⅛ in) pieces. Cut the blood sausage into 6 cm (2½ in) long pieces. Put them inside the sourdough bread slices and wrap to make a tight roll. Reserve and keep in the refrigerator.

To make the blood sauce, in a saucepan, brown the onion and dried plums, together with butter. Add the stock and cook for 20 minutes. Add the blood and the spices and cook for 30 minutes on low heat. Strain, then blend the sauce and reserve it.

To make the wine brûlée, mix the merlot, orange juice, sugar and agar agar. Blend together when cold, then place in a pot and bring up to 90°C (195°F) to activate the agar agar. Add the orange peel and cook for 10 minutes over a low heat, stirring often. Strain and place the mixture in a gastronorm (hotel pan). Freeze, then cut the gel into 5 mm (¼ in) cubes.

To pickle the apple and quince, make small balls (with a melon baller) with the apple and quince and reserve separately. In a saucepan, mix the lemon juice, sugar, vinegar, 1 l water and the lemon zest. Bring to the boil and then let cool. Strain and add to the Parisienne of quince and apple, keeping the fruit separate still. Use after 2 days.

To make the purée, chop the quinces into small pieces and place them in a saucepan. Add the sugar and cook over a low heat for 2 hours, stirring very often, as it's important not to burn the bottom of the pan. Once the fruit is completely cooked and sweeter, blend in a blender and reserve in piping bags.

To plate, put the bread and wild boar roll in the centre, then add the apple and quince balls and serve with the blood sauce.

BEAR p. 114

Oh yes, we do eat bear. Bear meat is a part of Slovenian traditional cuisine. But Slovenian hunting is very regulated – we are not monsters, shooting bears at will, and I believe that is why we are one of the few European countries still left with a large bear population. Bear meat must be cooked ↗

through; it is very red and strongly flavoured. This recipe is the result of a conversation between myself, Leonardo and Andrea. I asked them to close their eyes and imagine the bear.

Serves 10

For the bear
4 kg	bear shoulder
6	onions
6	carrots
2	celery sticks
2	bay leaves
500 ml	red wine
1	bunch thyme

For the bear sauce
20 kg	bear bones
	bear stock (see above)
2 l	red wine

For the berry salad
30 g	redcurrants
30 g	blackcurrants
30 g	gooseberries
20 g	trout roe
5 g	green juniper powder (from dehydrated green juniper berries)
20 g	honey
3 g	salt

For the green juniper oil
200 g	green juniper leaves
300 ml	grapeseed oil

For the crystallized berry leaves
100 g	raspberry and blackcurrant leaves
1 l	peanut oil

For the smoked trout sauce
1	carrot
1	onion
1	celery stick
500 ml	white wine
4 kg	smoked trout bones and heads
2 l	water
2 l	cream

For the trout skin chicharrón
500 g	trout skins
	vegetable oil, for frying
	salt

To cook the bear, I use 1 big pot and 1 big flat iron for this. Brown the bear meat in the flat iron and reserve. In the large rondeau, brown the onions, carrots and celery. Add the red wine and reduce until all alcohol evaporates. Add the previously browned bear meat and cover with 5 l water. Cook for 4 hours on medium heat, or until the bear is tender. Take the bear out and reserve. Strain the stock and keep to one side.

To make the bear sauce, brown the bear bones in a roasting tin in the oven at 230°C ↗

(445°F) for 20 minutes. Deglaze with red wine and cook down. Add some ice cubes and cover with 3 l stock. Simmer for 5 hours over a low heat. Strain and reduce the stock to one-quarter.

To make the berry salad, gently mix all the ingredients together.

For the green juniper oil, blend the ingredients all together in the Thermomix at 70°C (160°F) for 6 minutes. Then place the mixture in a metallic bowl and cool it down in an ice bath. Once cold, strain through a cheesecloth.

To make the crystallized berry leaves, clean the leaves by submerging them in ice water, then dry them. Heat the oil to 160°C (320°F) and fry the leaves without changing their colour.

To make the smoked trout sauce, brown the vegetables in a saucepan over a medium heat, then add the white wine and reduce until there is no more alcohol. Add 2 kg of the smoked trout bones and cover with the water. Simmer for 3 hours on low heat. Strain and reduce half the remaining stock. Add the cream and the remaining 2 kg of smoked trout bones. Simmer for another 1½ hours on low heat, strain and reserve.

To make the chicharrón, blanch the skins in boiling water for 1½ minutes. Then remove the excess of meat and fat on the skin. Dry for 10 hours at 52°C (125°F). Then fry in vegetable oil at 220°C (430°F). Season with salt and reserve in a dry place.

To serve, heat the meat in the bear sauce, covering it all the time with the sauce. Put in the berry salad, crystallized berry leaves and crispy trout skin. Foam the sauce and set on the side. Then add a few drops of green juniper oil.

THE WILD DUCK COLOURFUL WORLD

p. 122

Imagine the late summer heat. Imagine the freshness of mountain green juniper. Imagine the flavour of roses and beetroot. Imagine the green notes of unripe chestnuts and black walnuts. Do you know how many walnut and chestnut trees are around us? This is the wild duck salad.

Serves 8

For the wild duck
30 g	salt
25 g	crushed green juniper
100 g	wild duck breast

For the beetroot salad
80 g	red beetroot (beets)
70 g	pink beetroot (beets)
70 g	yellow beetroot (beets) ↓

120 g brown butter
80 g green kohlrabi
70 g yellow kohlrabi
50 g black radishes
200 ml 2-year-old apple vinegar
100 ml apple juice (from fresh apples)
50 g honey

For the walnuts
50 g black walnuts
50 g green chestnuts
50 g English walnuts
25 g sugar

For the salad leaves
garden chicory
nasturtium
tarragon
lovage
sorrel
calendula
beetroot leaves
chicory flowers
garden violets
rose petals
2.5% brine

For the rose and beetroot coulis
200 g small beetroot (beets)
100 ml rose water
100 ml fresh beetroot juice
60 g sugar
80 ml light apple vinegar
salt
3 g gelespessa

For the dressing
100 ml rose water and beetroot pickling liquid
(see above)
50 ml olive oil
salt

To serve
40 g duck fat mayo
15 g crushed green juniper

Mix the salt and juniper, and cover the cleaned wild duck breast. Leave for 1 day at 12°C (54°F). Remove the salt and store the duck breast in a cold place.

Wrap all the beetroot with some brown butter in aluminium foil and bake at 180°C (350°F) for 30 minutes. Peel when still hot and let it sit at room temperature. Cut to perfect 5 mm cubes. Peel the rest of the vegetables. Bring the green kohlrabi peels with vinegar, apple juice and sugar to the boil and cook for 10 minutes. Strain and add the last two vegetables, sliced to 1 mm thickness, to the hot liquid. Compress a few times.

Slice the black walnuts. Peel the green chestnuts and slice them. Toast the English walnuts at 175°C (345°F) for 12 minutes. Cool down. Mix with sugar and caramelize until golden. Remove from the heat, stir again and put over the heat, stirring until the walnuts separate. Cool down on baking paper. ↗

Compress the leaves in 2.5% brine with ice. Dry on kitchen paper.

Cook the peeled beetroots for the coulis in salted water. The water should be just enough to cover. When cooked, drain and reserve 100 g of the cooking liquid. Slice the beetroot. Bring the rose water with the beetroot juice, sugar, vinegar and cooking liquid to the boil. Season with salt and compress the sliced beetroots. Let it sit for 24 hours. Strain the liquid, and keep it for the next step. Blend the beetroots with some of the liquid heating up to 70°C (160°F) until smooth. Stabilize with gelespessa.

To make the dressing, mix all the ingredients apart from the brine together and whisk.

To serve, cut the duck into thin slices. Pipe the duck fat mayo and the beetroot coulis on the plate. Combine the salads and nuts. Then dress with the rose vinaigrette and crushed green juniper.

DREŽNICA

LAMB TARTARE p. 140

When I first visited Istanbul, a friend of mine, a famous Turkish chef, Maksut Askar, brought me to a few secret markets. I fell in love with those squares full of lamb butchers; I found out how little I knew about the meat I loved the most. In a corner, I noticed a huge amount of white fat. I wanted to understand what it was and what it was for. This is how I discovered the interior lamb fat, the one that is found around the lamb kidneys. It is the tastiest part of the animal. When we started thinking about creating a good lamb tartare, we faced the problem of the flavour. The taste of raw lamb meat isn't strong enough – this is how we found out that if we dress the raw lamb meat with cooked interior lamb fat, we get the perfect result: raw meat that tastes like perfectly roasted lamb.

Serves 12

For the hydro honey
45 g hydro-fermented honey
250 g linden honey

For the tartare
1.2 kg lamb kidney fat
1 lamb shoulder
15 g salt

For the roasted onions
2 yellow onions
8 g salt ↗

For the tomato-thyme jelly
300 ml Tomato Water (page 251)
200 g thyme
3 soaked gelatine leaves
10 g salt

For the smoked lamb zabaione
2 eggs
300 g interior lamb fat, cooked for 3 hours
80 ml chicken stock
3 soaked gelatine leaves
15 g salt
5 g black peppercorns

For the Jerusalem artichoke salad and chips
200 g Jerusalem artichokes
vegetable oil, for frying
50 ml olive oil
salt

To serve
60 g chickweed
60 g arctic char roe

To make the honey, mix the 2 ingredients together and let them ferment for 1 month at room temperature.

Melt 1 kg of the kidney fat and coat the lamb shoulder with it. Dry age the lamb shoulder for 10 days. Remove the veins from the meat and use a fork to scratch it clean. Cook the rest of the lamb kidney fat for 2 hours on very low heat until the colour is similar to that of brown butter. Dress the lamb tartare (which is cut with a very sharp knife into small cubes) with salt and warm lamb fat 20 minutes before serving. Leave at room temperature.

Wrap the onions in aluminium foil and roast them at 180°C (350°F) until they reach 92°C (195°F) in the centre. Cut them and keep the outer layer. Torch them, then marinate with the hydro honey 1 hour before serving and add the salt.

Heat the tomato water, add the thyme and let it infuse for 6 hours. Strain, heat again and add the gelatine and salt. Allow to cool.

To make the smoked lamb zabaione, cook the eggs at 62°C (144°F) for 1 hour. Peel and smoke them 3 times. Warm the lamb fat and slowly add it to the eggs, keeping it warm set over a bain-marie. Whisk intensely. Warm the chicken stock, add the gelatine and add it to the egg mixture. Add the salt and pepper.

Cut 100 g of the artichokes into thin slices. Fry them at 160°C (320°F) and put them in the dehydrator. Cut the remaining artichokes brunoise-style and pan fry them for 1 minute in olive oil over a very high heat. Season with salt.

To serve, put the onions on the plate and combine all the ingredients. Finish with chickweed and char roe. The portions should be bite-size. Eat with your hands.

LAMB AND CRAB p. 131

This is a 2019 sister dish of the 'kid goat and crayfish' dish from spring 2018. The meadows of Drežnica are a lot closer to the sea than most people might imagine. The sea breeze changes the minerality of the soil, and therefore the flavour of plants and animals. Lamb and crab meat have very similar flavour notes. Jerusalem artichokes (sunchokes) from the valleys work as a connection point between the two.

Serves 10

For the crab
3	crabs (500 g each)

For the lamb
200 g	salt
2	whole lamb legs
20 g	black peppercorns
2	medium onions
30 g	thyme
30 g	rosemary

For the roasted Jerusalem artichoke reduction
10 kg	Jerusalem artichokes

For the dressing
300 g	roasted Jerusalem artichoke reduction (see above)
100 g	extra virgin olive oil
	salt

For the lamb roll
60%	of the lamb meat (see above)
40%	of the crab meat (see above)
10	chard leaves

For the egg yolk and Jerusalem artichoke juice
10	whole eggs
100 g	roasted Jerusalem artichoke reduction (see above)

For the lamb consommé
25 kg	lamb bones
1.2 kg	carrots
1.2 kg	celery
1.2 kg	leeks
1.2 kg	onions
200 ml	vegetable oil
20	egg whites
3 kg	minced (ground) lamb
300 g	carrots, diced
300 g	celery, diced
300 g	leeks, diced
300 g	onions, diced

Bring water to a boil and cook the crabs for 10 minutes. Stop the cooking in ice water. Clean the meat.

Mix 5 l water and salt with a hand blender and make sure all the salt is dissolved. ↗

Place the legs in and brine them for 12 hours. Take the legs out of the brine. In a very hot flat cast iron pan, brown the legs on all sides. Then place them in a gastronorm (hotel pan). Add the rest of the ingredients and cover the legs with water – three-quarters should be covered. Cover the pan with a lid and cook at 120°C (250°F) for 8 hours.

Pull the meat off the bone and chop it into small pieces. Reserve.

Place the Jerusalem artichokes in flat trays and roast them in the oven at 200°C (400°F) for 10 minutes. Pass them through a juicer and strain the juice, then once again and start to reduce it in a pan down to one quarter. Dehydrate the artichoke dust and fry at 160°C (320°F), then reserve for serving.

To make the dressing, mix all 3 ingredients.

Mix 60% of the lamb meat and 40% of the crab meat. Season it with the dressing. Blanch the chard leaves in hot water with salt for 3 seconds and right afterwards put in a cold bath. Take out the leaves and pat dry. Place the leaves on a chopping (cutting) board and place the meat on it. Carefully start to roll the leaves, making sure they're tight.

Cook the whole eggs at 62°C (144°F) for 30 minutes. Place in an ice bath. Crack the eggs and keep only the egg yolks. With the help of a syringe, take 10 g of the egg yolk out of each egg yolk, and at the same point, with another syringe, insert 10 g of the reduction.

To make the consommé, roast the bones in an oven at 220°C (430°F) for 20 minutes. Chop all the vegetables and roast them in a pot together with the oil, making sure the vegetables are brown and not burnt. Add the lamb bones and cover with water. Simmer for 12 hours. Strain, cool down the stock and reserve.

In a big bowl, break the egg whites with a whisk. Then add the remaining ingredients. In a big pan, place the just-made lamb stock and the previously made mixture. Cook on medium-low heat and avoid a boil. Stir for the first 20 minutes until you see the egg white start to float to the top with the rest of the ingredients. Then stop stirring, but keep on low heat for 30 minutes, or until the consommé is completely clarified. Strain and reserve.

To serve, put the egg yolk in a small bowl and cover with lamb consommé. Heat the lamb-crab rolls under the salamander and put 120 g of fried artichoke dust on top. Invite people to drink the broth without mixing the egg yolk, and to eat the rolls with their hands.

LAMB BRAIN AND PRESERVED BLACKCURRANT BEIGNET p. 130 ↗

This dish was inspired by the famous caviar and sour cream fried bread of Disfrutar. Experiments were long and painful. There were days our hands were all burnt and there were days the dough simply did not work.

Serves 12

For the lamb brain
300 g	lamb brain
80 g	butter
15 g	salt
25 ml	port wine
80 ml	lamb jus

For the beignet dough
1	egg
3 g	salt
9 g	sugar
130 g	plain (all-purpose) flour
15 g	cornflour (cornstarch)

For the preserved blackcurrant
1 kg	cleaned blackcurrants
50 g	salt
5	star anise
2	cinnamon sticks
10	crushed green cardamoms

For the blackcurrant glaze
200 g	preserved blackcurrant (see above)
3%	agar agar

To serve
	vegetable oil, for frying

Clean the lamb brain and cook it in butter, deglaze with port wine and blend with warm lamb jus until a perfect emulsion. Fill into small round spheres 1.5 cm in diameter.

Place the egg and 115 ml water together and blend well. Add all the dry ingredients and blend again with a hand blender. Do not blend too much, as you do not want to develop gluten. Place in a siphon and charge. The recipe is enough for a small siphon, which you should charge 4 times, or if using a large siphon, charge 5–6 times. Keep in the refrigerator at least 1 hour before serving.

Bring all the preserved blackcurrant ingredients together, mix well and leave for 3 weeks in a glass jar, covered with a clean towel. Remove the spices and strain through a cheesecloth.

For the glaze, blend the preserved blackcurrent and 400 ml water together and strain through a chinois. Weigh and add the agar agar. Bring to 80°C (175°F) while whisking constantly. Glaze the frozen 'brain' balls in the mixture at 80°C (175°F) and refreeze rapidly.

Preheat the oil to 190°C (375°F). Heat a 5 cm (2 in) diameter ladle in the oil until super hot. Make the first layer of the dough with a canister. Place the frozen 'brain' in the centre and cover with more dough. Fry. Drain it on kitchen paper.

CHICORY AND PLUMS p. 126

Sometimes the simple things are the things that amaze me. I am crazy about the salads. I could eat greens every day, especially in the summertime. Late summer chicories are one of those special garden stories; bitter and hard but very tasty and healthy.

Serves 8

For the chicory

70 g	brown butter
4	heads summer chicory
50 ml	red wine
13 g	salt

For the plum purée

500 g	plums (yellow and sour)
30 g	butter
5 g	salt

For the horseradish-flavoured buttermilk

1 l	buttermilk
30 g	sugar
50 g	chestnut honey
100 g	fresh horseradish
15 g	salt
3 g	gelespessa

For the sunflower seeds

30 g	sunflower seeds

For the chicory root jus

3 kg	chicory roots
50 g	flower honey

For the chicory root chips

500 g	chicory roots
200 ml	apple syrup
15 g	fleur de sel

To serve

30 ml	aged apple vinegar
15 g	honey
8	wild chicory flowers

Heat the butter and roast the whole chicory in it. Deglaze with red wine and cook until soft. Season with salt. Let it sit on paper for 10 minutes. Before serving, roast it under the salamander, until the chicory is hot and soft inside and crunchy on the outside.

Cover the plums with aluminium foil with a bit of butter. Bake at 200°C (400°F) for 30 minutes. Let them hang in a cheesecloth for 1 hour. Reduce the liquid by half. Add the salt. Discard the plum stones (pits) and blend the flesh with skin and liquid until creamy.

Cook the buttermilk for 3 hours. Strain and reserve both liquid and solid. Melt the sugar with the honey until a dark caramel and deglaze with the hot buttermilk liquid. Cook for another 30 minutes. ↗

Grate in the horseradish and let it infuse until cold. Strain and stabilize with gelespessa.

Roast the sunflower seeds and cool them down.

Juice the chicory roots. Combine the liquid with 100 ml water and the honey and reduce until almost syrupy.

Cut the chicory roots with a mandoline into very thin slices. Blanch and stop cooking in ice water. Dry well. Soak in the apple syrup. Dehydrate at 50°C (122°F) for 48 hours. Finish with fleur de sel.

To serve, bring the vinegar, honey and 15 ml water to the boil and cook for 15 minutes. Cool down and dress the flowers with some drops of the liquid. When plating, the only hot ingredient is the chicory. Put the plum purée to one side, and cover with sunflower seeds, chips and flowers. Put the chicory in the centre and pour the horseradish buttermilk on the side. Finish with drops of super bitter chicory root jus.

MOUNTAIN RABBIT ON HOLIDAYS IN MEXICO 2.0 p. 127

I had never been in Mexico at the time that I created this dish. It is based on dreams and on the idea that rabbit can be more than just a healthy but boring piece of meat.

Serves 12

For the black garlic

1 kg	local organic garlic

For the rabbit

20	whole rabbits

For the rabbit jus

20 kg	rabbit bones
6	onions
6	carrots
3	celery sticks
1 l	red wine
10 g	black peppercorns
12	bay leaves
3	bunches thyme
15 g	long pepper
10 g	cloves
10 g	star anise
10 g	cinnamon sticks
15 g	green cardamoms
7 g	dried pepperoncini
120 g	dark chocolate 72%

For the pickled peppers

250 ml	white wine vinegar
80 g	honey
20 g	cinnamon powder
20 g	chilli ↗

70 ml	water
500 g	red (bell) peppers

For the roasted carrots, parsley root and parsnips

200 g	carrots
200 g	parsnips
110 g	parsley root
200 ml	olive oil
	salt

For the bean salad

200 g	local brown beans, ideally from Idrsko
200 g	curry leaves
200 g	lovage
50 g	salted peanuts
1 kg	black garlic (see above)

For the fried kale

1 l	peanut oil
100 g	fresh curly kale
	salt

To serve

380 g	rabbit saddle and legs (no bones)
50 g	butter
30 ml	olive oil
	salt

To make the black garlic, wrap every single garlic bulb in aluminium foil and place them in the dehydrator at 52°C (125°F) for 4 weeks. It is important to use a higher temperature since you want to ferment the garlic and not dry it. After 3–5 weeks, you will see that the garlic is black and soft, then you will know it is ready. Take the garlic out of the dehydrator and squish to take the garlic cloves out. Reserve half of them in the refrigerator and the other half in a dehydrator to grate it on the dish.

Break down the rabbits and debone the legs, but reserve the bones and rest of the rabbit for the jus. The leg meat will form a main component of the dish.

Roast the rabbit bones in the oven at 230°C (445°F) for 20 minutes. In a deep saucepan, roast the vegetables. Add the rabbit bones, red wine, peppercorns and herbs, reducing until there is no more alcohol remaining. Cover with water and simmer for about 8 hours. Strain and start to reduce the stock ntil the flavour and texture are more concentrated and the reduction has the texture of a sauce. You will get around 5 l of jus. Add the long pepper, cloves, star anise, cinnamon, cardamom, pepperoncini and chocolate. Let infuse for 2 hours, then strain and reserve.

Place all the ingredients in a saucepan, aside from the red peppers, and bring to a boil. Let it cool down, then strain and reserve. Take the peppers and place directly on the fire, until they are completely black, burned and cooked. Then put them in a gastronorm (hotel pan) and cover with clingfilm (plastic wrap). Leave for 15 minutes, then peel. Quickly rinse them afterwards with cold water. Cut julienne of 4 cm (1½ in) long. Place the peppers in the ↗

pickling liquid and use them after 2 days.

Place the carrots, parsnips and parsleyroot in a tray. Add the olive oil all around and season with some salt. Bake at 180°C (350°F) for 20 minutes. Cool at room temperature and slice.

To make the bean salad, cook the brown beans in cold water until it boils, then cook for 15 more minutes. Strain them and let them cool down without using any cold water, since you don't want the skin to fall off. Once cold, slice them in thin slices like almond flakes. Dry the curry leaves in a dehydrator for 12 hours at 62°C (144°F) and blend them in a spice mixer. Pass the powder through a tamis. Dry the lovage for 12 hours at 62°C (144°F) and blend them in a spice mixer. Pass the powder through a tamis. To assemble the salad, take the sliced beans and peanuts and season with black garlic, lovage powder and curry leaf powder.

To fry the kale, heat the oil to 190°C (375°F). Clean the kale leaves and remove the stems. Fry the leaves and season with salt.

To serve, warm the butter and oil and cook the rabbit meat from all sides to let it get pink inside. Season with salt. Let it sit for 2 minutes. Cut, then place the rabbit jus on the dish. Follow with red peppers, bean salad and roasted roots. Add the meat and cover with fried kale leaves.

KID GOAT AND CRAYFISH p. 133

This was my favourite dish of 2018. The delicate balance of two meats, one coming from the meadows under the Krn mountain, and the other from the nearby rivers, is simply incredible.

Serves 8

For the kid goat and crayfish bites

100 g	salt
	olive oil
1	kid goat leg (Drežnica kid goat, 7 kg animal total weight max)
1	kid goat shoulder (Drežnica kid goat, 7 kg animal total weight max)
1.5 kg	crayfish
	pepper
8	large endive (chicory) leaves, steamed

For the kid goat consommé

3	kid goat heads, tongue and brain removed
4	kid goat ribs with meat and skin on it
4	kid goat tails
200 g	roasted onions
200 g	carrots
200 g	leeks
250 g	celeriac ↗

2 kg	minced (ground) kid goat meat (from the legs and shoulders)
50 g	carrots, brunoise
50 g	onions, brunoise
50 g	celery, brunoise
300 g	egg whites

For the fried young potato

200 g	young potatoes
7 g	salt
	rapeseed (canola) oil

For the lamb mayo

60 g	egg yolk
30 ml	lemon juice
200 g	roasted lamb fat
15 g	salt
2 g	ground black pepper

For the dumpling dough

500 g	plain (all-purpose) flour
250 ml	boiling water
20 g	salt
50 ml	olive oil

For the dumpling filling

100 g	kid goat sweetbreads
100 g	kid goat brain
200 g	cooked kid goat tongue
100 g	kid goat liver
50 g	kid goat heart
100 g	shallots
50 ml	olive oil
20 g	salt
10 g	black peppercorns, chopped

For the mint oil

200 g	mint
50 g	verbena
50 g	lemon balm
300 ml	leccino olive oil
50 g	lemon zest

For the mint

30 g	fresh mint leaves

Heat the charcoal oven to 140°C (285°F).

Sprinkle the salt and a bit of oil over the meat. Roast the leg and the shoulder of goat kid in a roasting tin. Wrap in aluminium foil and continue cooking in the charcoal oven for 2½ hours. Open the aluminium foil and proceed cooking for 1 more hour.

Boil the live crayfish for 2 minutes, then remove the heads and clean the meat. Slice it. Blend the heads and pass through a chinois, pressing hard to extract the liquids. Dress the tails with it.

Pull the meat from the goat kid bones and when still hot, mix it with the crayfish meat. Season with salt and pepper. Cut the endive (chicory) leaves into 15 cm (6 in) squares. Make wraps with the endive and cut down the portions to a roll of 8 cm (3 in).

Roast all the meat with bones in the oven at 180°C (350°F) for 15 minutes. The fat will caramelize a bit. Add the roasted onions, ↗

carrots, leeks and celariac and cover with cold water. Cook for 12 hours. Let it cool down at room temperature. Strain the stock. Remove the fat and reserve half the fat. Mix together half of the fat, the minced meat, brunoise vegetables and egg whites. Add the mix to the cold stock and simmer for another 3 hours. Cool down and strain.

Cut the potatoes very thinly and keep in ice water. Dry and fry at 160°C (320°F) until crisp in oil.

Make a mayonnaise out of the egg and lamb fat: whisk the egg yolks with lemon, start dripping in lamb fat at 40°C (105°F). Season with pepper and salt.

Work the dough ingredients for 10 minutes on a minimum speed. Let the dough rest for 20 minutes.

Bring the sweetbreads to a boil and clean them of all fibres. Blanch the brain and clean it of all fibres. Chop all the meat, then add the finely chopped shallot, olive oil, salt and pepper. Cool down well. Roll the dough as thin as possible, place the filling in the middle and close in a form of štruklji (similar to Chinese dumplings).

Blanch the herbs for a few seconds and stop cooking in ice water. Dry the herbs and blend them slowly with the olive oil in a Thermomix, reaching 70°C (160°F). Then at maximum speed, blend for 10 minutes. Add the lemon zest and strain over ice.

Chop the mint.

To serve, heat the wraps in a steam oven, cover with clingfilm (plastic wrap), making sure they do not lose shape. Place a wrap on a plate, top with the mayonnaise and cover with fried potato. Steam the dumplings for 10 minutes in a Chinese steam pot, and cover with chopped mint and mint oil. Pour over the boiling consommé.

SQUID AND LAMB SWEETBREAD p. 134

This is a favourite dish of many guests. The original dish was created a few years ago, and what is presented here is its natural evolution. Jadranski kalamar squid from the Adriatic is one of the tastiest squid in the world, with a very firm texture and intense flavour.

Serves 12

For the squid

1 kg	Adriatic squid, approximately 8 cm (3 in) each
	salt
30 ml	olive oil

For the lamb sweetbread stuffed squid

400 g	lamb sweetbreads
70 g	butter ↓

50 ml   port wine
1 l   pomegranate juice
100 ml very reduced lamb jus
50 g   egg whites
15 g   salt
9 g   ground pepper
        salted squid (see method)

For the cheese
200 ml double cream
2   soaked gelatine leaves
200 g   Valter's pit cheese (jamar)

For the wild watercress salad
400 ml pomegranate juice
70 ml   wine vinegar
30 g   sugar
15 ml   olive oil
7 g   salt
300 g   wild watercress

For the black ink sauce
30 g   butter
50 ml   olive oil
200 g   chopped red onions
200 g   chopped carrots
2 kg   squid entrails and ink (see first step)
150 ml white wine
        salt

For the calamar garum
        calamar garum

This step needs to be planned a month in advance: clean the squid and reserve all the entrails and ink. Cover with 20% of the salt and let sit at 20°C (68°F) for 28 days. Strain and reserve the fermented liquid. Quickly roast the cleaned squid and let them rest in their own juices, with the reserved fermented liquid, for 3 days.

To prepare the sweetbreads, blanch them in salted water and clean well. Roast the sweetbreads in 20 g butter on a very high heat and deglaze with the port wine and pomegranate. Stop cooking after the sweetbreads have absorbed all the liquid. Add half the lamb jus and cook for 10 minutes. Cool down and mix in the egg white, salt and pepper. Reduce the remaining lamb jus and butter until glazed.

Remove the squid from the liquid, dry them and fill with sweetbreads. Brush the squid with the rest of the lamb jus and roast under the salamander by brushing it continuously. Prepare the rest of the elements of the dish before the final cooking of the squid.

To prepare the cheese, heat the cream to 60°C (140°F), add the gelatine and blend with the pit cheese. Season with salt if necessary and let it set until gelified.

To make the salad, reduce the pomegranate, vinegar and sugar by two-thirds. Combine the olive oil and salt. Use to dress the watercress salad.

Melt the butter and olive oil, then slowly cook the onions and carrots until soft. Add the squid entrails, roast on all sides and deglaze ↗

with white wine. Cook for 20 minutes, add 3 l iced water and cook slowly for 4 hours. Strain into a bowl set over ice and add salt to taste.

To serve, once the squid is cooked, make sure it has rested on a chopping (cutting) board for at least 3 minutes. Glaze it with calamar garum and cut in half with a very sharp knife. Serve with a spoon of the pit cheese and the watercress with pomegranate dressing. Warm the ink sauce and serve.

SWEET PORCINI MUSHROOM p. 138

You cannot ask nature to give a few kilos of mushrooms every day of the same size, same flavour, same type. You cannot ask for the best plums in the world. When there are too many plums and too many mushrooms, a dessert happens. This dessert is a complete balance of umami-ness, sweetness and sourness. This dessert is not sweet at all; it could easily be one of the starters.

Serves 6

For the plum chutney
2   red onions
200 g   sugar
300 ml plum vinegar
2 kg   fresh plums
60 g   chopped plum stones (pits)

For the porcini crumble
100 g   sugar
13 ml   white vinegar
2 g   salt
1.1 g   bicarbonate of (baking) soda
200 g   butter
30 g   dried porcini
100 g   powdered milk
35 g   maltodextrin

For the sour milk ice cream
875 ml sour milk
25 g   glucose
375 ml cream
5 g   super neutrose
200 g   sugar
420 g   egg yolks

For the parsley granita
85 g   sugar
15 g   glucose
2   soaked gelatine leaves
30 g   parsley leaves
30 ml   lime juice
10 ml   lemon juice

To serve
20   pieces crystallized parsley ↗

Chop the onions in julienne. Cook them with the sugar and plum vinegar until reduced, then add the plums and cook for around 40 minutes on a low heat, stirring often to not burn it. Mix in the plum stones (pits). Cook for 20 more minutes, cool down and reserve.

To make the porcini crumble, put the sugar, 30 g water, vinegar and salt in a saucepan and make a caramel. When it reaches 150°C (300°F) add the bicarbonate of (baking) soda and mix – be careful in this step, since the bicarbonate of soda is going to make the caramel grow out of the pot. Spread it in a Silpat and freeze it. Once completely cold, chop it in small pieces and reserve. Vacuum the butter and porcini and infuse for 1 hour at 80°C (175°F). Strain and reserve the butter and the porcini. Place the butter in a pan and add the powdered milk. On low heat, stir very frequently for about 10 minutes. The mixture is going to become more liquid, so you don't need to add more butter to the mixture. Once the powdered milk gets a brown colour, take it off the heat and strain it through a cheesecloth. Chop the porcini and add the strained powdered milk solids. Place it in a bowl, add the maltodextrin and mix with a whisk. Finely chop the caramel and add to the powdered milk solids. Mix once again and reserve. Keep it frozen.

Mix the sour milk, glucose and cream and bring to a boil. Add the super neutrose and sugar and make sure everything is dissolved. Add the mixture to the egg yolks, little by little, then cook all together at 82°C (180°C). Strain and reserve in a Pacojet container.

Blend together 450 ml water, the sugar, glucose and gelatine. Place it a gastronorm (hotel pan) and freeze it. Once frozen, break it and place in a blender. Add the parsley leaves and blend until smooth and green. Season with the lime juice and lemon juice. Place it in a gastronorm and put it in the blast chiller, scratching with a fork every 5 minutes until you have an airy granita.

To serve, Pacojet the ice cream. Cool the plates. Plate the chutney and cover with crumble. Serve the ice cream and granita. Top with crystallized parsley.

MOUNTAIN RASPBERRY AND GOAT CHEESE p. 135

Summer is a fantastic time for little wild raspberries. They're almost impossible to eat because they have so many seeds in them. Valter's uncle Marko, a very special man, forages them for us. They mostly grow in Kovrat, and tend to ferment very quickly. Wild raspberries are very sour and match well with the strong-tasting goat's cheese from Drežnica. ↗

Serves 6

For the beurre noisette crackers
2   eggs
80 g   sugar
200 g   plain (all-purpose) flour
120 g   very dark brown butter
           salt

For the raspberry ice cream
200 ml sugar syrup
70 g   glucose
500 g   wild mountain raspberries

For the raspberry jelly
500 g   wild mountain raspberries
150 g   sugar
4   soaked gelatine leaves

For the raspberry tuiles
           raspberry pulp and seeds (see above)
100 ml sugar syrup
30 g   glucose

For the lemon curd
2   organic lemons, juiced and zested
2½   eggs
135 g   sugar
1   soaked gelatine leaf
185 g   butter

For the goat cheese ganache
300 g   very fermented soft goat cheese
250 ml cream

For the lemon meringue
90 ml   organic lemon juice
60 g   sugar
2   soaked gelatine leaves
250 g   egg whites

To serve
120 g   fresh raspberries
150 ml beurre noisette

Whisk the eggs and sugar, then incorporate the flour gradually. Add the tempered brown butter and a pinch of salt at the end. Wrap in clingfilm (plastic wrap) and leave to rest for 2 hours in the refrigerator. Roll out the dough using a pasta machine with the help of a little bit of flour – it should be 3 mm (⅛-in) thick. Cut into 5 cm (2 in) circles and bake on baking paper in a ventilated oven at 170°C (340°F) for 10 minutes.

Warm up the syrup, add the glucose at 35°C (95°F) and bring to the boil. Cool down the syrup and mix it with the raspberries until smooth. Fill the Pacojet container.

Freeze the raspberries, place them in a chinois and squeeze them until all the juice is separated from the pulp and seeds. Keep the pulp and seeds for the raspberry tuiles. Bring the liquid and sugar to the boil, add the gelatine and leave to set in the refrigerator for a few hours. ↗

Mix all the tuile ingredients together in a Thermomix at 100°C (210°F) for 10 minutes (because the wild raspberries have a lot of seeds). Spread over a Silpat and dehydrate in a food dehydrator at 70°C (160°F) for 48 hours.

Mix together the lemon juice, lemon zest, eggs and sugar. Bring to 82°C (180°F) in a bain-marie while whisking continuously. Off the heat, fold in the gelatine and slowly add the butter, cut into small pieces. Store in the refrigerator.

Blend the ganache ingredients together in a Thermomix at 70°C (160°F) until the emulsion is smooth.

Heat the lemon juice with the sugar and 20 ml water and reduce. Add the gelatine and cool down to 30°C (86°F). Slowly fold in the egg whites. Fill the siphon with 2 chargers.

To serve, Pacojet the ice cream, place a cracker on the dish, then pipe the lemon curd and the goat's cheese ganache. Place the raspberry ice cream and rasperry jelly on top, foam the lemon meringue, torch it and finish with fresh raspberries and a raspberry tuile. Heat the beurre noisette to 45°C (115°F), foam with a hand blender and pour alongside. Add 1 teaspoon of raspberry jelly on the opposite side.

PETRINI LOVE(AGE) p. 141

One of the main reasons why Andrea Petrini fell in love with the restaurant was lovage ravioli. There were days I had a feeling he would rather eat them at the table or steal them from the pan than talk to me. Lovage ravioli was off the menu for a few years; now they are back, mostly because of this book. I generally do not like signature dishes. But the thin pasta that explodes under your tongue in the perfect lovage-potato umami-ness is always so challenging.

Serves 8

For the pasta dough
500 g   plain (all-purpose) flour
400 g   egg yolks
50 ml   olive oil

For the lovage filling
500 g   white potatoes (not too starchy)
200 g   freshly picked lovage
10   soaked gelatine leaves
100 g   butter
12 g   salt

For the potato glass
200 g   potatoes
           vegetable oil, for frying ↗

For the rabbit jus and rabbit fat
100 ml olive oil
300 g   shallots ↗

500 g   carrots
1 kg   interior fat of rabbits
           (around the kidney)
4   rabbit carcasses
700 ml dry white wine
50 g   rosemary
200 g   garlic

For the black olive powder
200 g   taggiasca olives in olive oil

To garnish
15 g   rosemary

Slowly work all the pasta dough ingredients together, and let sit in a vacuum bag in the refrigerator for a few hours.

Peel the potatoes and cut them into thin slices. Cook them covered with salted water, then remove from the heat. Blanch the lovage, refresh in iced water, then chop it. Blend the potatoes with the cooking water and the lovage. Continue mixing for 10 minutes. Add the gelatine and butter. Adjust the butter if necessary. Add the salt.

Roll the pasta dough on size 1. Place the jellified filling in the middle. Close well, because the filling will turn liquid with cooking.

Overcook the potatoes in 800 ml water. Blend into a transparent mix. Dry at room temperature for 2 days. Fry at 160°C (320°F) until crispy.

In a large frying pan, heat the olive oil and fry the chopped shallots and carrots. Add the rabbit fat and rabbit carcasses and roast well. Deglaze with the white wine, reduce and add 10 l of cold water. Cook for 5 hours and cool down. Store in the refrigerator overnight. Remove all the fat. Reduce the fat with rosemary until brown – the colour should look similar to brown butter. Add the garlic to the rabbit jus and cook down for another 2 hours. Cool and strain.

Bake the black olives at 180°C (350°F) for 12 minutes. Dry them at 70°C (160°F) for 24 hours. Blitz to a powder.

Cook the ravioli, pan fry them in the rabbit fat with rosemary, deglaze with rabbit jus and powder with black olives. Cover with a layer of potato glass.

MEDITER–RANEAN TERRACE

BEEF TONGUE UMAMI p. 167

This dish was born in a taxi somewhere between London, Manchester and Moscow. I was getting ready for my exciting four-hand dinner in Moscow. I always challenged myself for events like this to create something new and open a new horizon. I believe in adrenaline! It had been a year with so many flights and a lot of dishes created while driving, in an airport, or on a train. This was first supposed to be a lamb, but when I cooked the lamb it did not have the flavour I was searching for, but there were only a few hours left before the dinner. Do you have any other meat I could use, guys? Surf and turf cow. Just imagine cattle on pastures overlooking the sea.

Serves 10

For the pickled celeriac
400 ml apple vinegar
400 g sugar
1 kg celeriac

For the Mediterranean dashi
300 g sardines
300 g mackerel heads and bones
salt
500 g dried local seaweed
300 g scallop membranes
200 g dried forest mushrooms
80 ml soy sauce
500 ml fish sauce

For the smoked celeriac purée
1 kg celeriac
1 l cream
salt
hay, for smoking

For the sliced beef tongue
2 kg beef tongue
2 kg rock salt
2 carrots
2 onions
1 celery stick

For the seaweed and sea fennel salad
50 g sea fennel
30 g seaweed
20 g sugar
30 ml fish sauce
15 ml wine vinegar
50 ml beef tongue stock (see above)
15 ml olive oil

For the scallops
3 kg scallops

For the coral mayo
50 g coral from scallops (see above)
15 ml fresh lime juice ↗

salt
250 ml grapeseed oil

To make the pickled celeriac, mix 600 ml water with the vinegar and sugar in a saucepan, bring to the boil and stir until the sugar has dissolved. Peel, halve and cut the celeriac into 1-mm (⅓-in) slices. Add to the pickling liquid and use after 2 days.

Debone the sardines and the mackerel. Salt them with 20% of their weight for 5 days. Rinse them in cold water, smoke them and dry them at 65°C (150°F) for 16 hours. Bring 15 l water and the seaweed to a boil in a saucepan and simmer for 2 hours. Add the smoked and dried fish and simmer for another 3 hours. Strain, add the mushrooms and let cool. It is very important to not boil the dashi, because you need to make a tea infusion and not a stock or soup. Once the flavour is concentrated enough, take it off the heat and strain. Season with the soy sauce and fish sauce.

Peel the celeriac and chop into small pieces. Cook with the cream over a low heat until soft. It is important to not boil the cream, to avoid a yellow colour in the purée. Strain and blend only the celeriac in a Thermomix for 6 minutes at 70°C (160°F). Season with salt. Place the purée in a gastronorm (hotel pan) and smoke it with hay with the help of a small smoker. Cover with clingfilm (plastic wrap) while smoking and do this process twice.

Cover the tongue with rock salt and quick cure it overnight. Rinse with cold water before putting in a saucepan with the rest of the ingredients, then cover with water. Do not brown the vegetables since we want a clear flavour in the tongue. Cook for around 2–3 hours, depending on the size of the tongue – it needs to be soft enough to put a knife through it. Take the tongue out of the stock and peel while hot. Strain the stock and reserve. Once the tongue is peeled and cold, slice it in slices of 1.5 mm (1/16 in).

To make the salad, blanch the fennel and seaweed then refresh in iced water. Simmer the sugar, fish sauce, vinegar and beef tongue stock and reduce by one-third. Whisk in the olive oil, then use this to dress the blanched greens.

Open the scallops and separate them into 3 parts – the coral for the mayonnaise, membrane for the Mediterranean dashi, and scallops for the dish.

To make the mayo, blend the coral from the scallops and add the lime juice and around 3–4 g of salt. Add the grapeseed oil slowly and emulsify. Add more lime juice if necessary.

Heat the beef tongue in some reserved stock.

To serve, plate the celeriac purée, the beef tongue, the greens and the scallops over the pickled celeriac. Serve the dashi at the table.

LA LAGUNA p. 162

When you land in the airport of Trieste or Venice, you fly over the lagoon. From the air it is incredibly beautiful to observe the intense contrasts and colours of the lagoon plants. In this dish, I tried to recreate La Laguna.

Serves 10

For the dirty cuttlefish
2 kg dirty cuttlefish
500 g 3% brine
200 ml olive oil, plus extra for the pan
50 g rosemary
300 g shallots
200 g carrots
60 g cleaned garlic
400 ml white wine
3 bay leaves

For the spring onions
400 g spring onions (scallions)
60 ml olive oil
10 g salt

For the potato foam
300 g potatoes
3 soaked gelatine leaves
100 g butter

For the tomato sauce
250 g date tomatoes
60 ml olive oil
15 g salt
30 g sugar
5 g sun-dried oregano
250 ml reduced strong red mullet stock

To serve
50 g salicornia
30 g purslane

Clean the cuttlefish and reserve all the interiors and heads. Compress the cuttlefish meat in brine 3 times and strain. Vacuum seal with olive oil and rosemary and cook in a water bath at 52°C (125°F) for 25 minutes. Remove the meat and cut the surface with very sharp knife. Chop the shallots and carrots, then soften them in a big flat pan in olive oil with garlic. Add the cuttlefish offal and its black ink, deglaze with white wine, reduce, then cover with ice, 5 l water and the bay leaves. Simmer slowly for 2 hours. Strain and reduce by half.

Roast the spring onions (scallions) in a charcoal oven until very soft, then salt them. Strain all the liquids through a cheesecloth and work hard on it. Let the onions hang during the night in the refrigerator. The next day, blend them into a perfect purée (use some drops of liquid in case it is too dry).

To make the potato foam, peel the potatoes, reserving the skins. Cook the potatoes in very salty water and strain, keeping the ↗

water and potatoes. Roast the peels, vacuum seal them with the potato cooking water and cook them in a water bath at 75ºC (165ºF) for 4 hours. Strain, then blend in a Thermomix 600 g of the liquid and 300 g of cooked potato. Bring to 70ºC (160ºF), then add the gelatine and butter. Fill a siphon with this mixture and charge with 2 chargers.

To make the tomato sauce, confit the tomatoes with the olive oil, salt, sugar and oregano for 20 minutes at 200ºC (400ºF), then 45 minutes at 135ºC (280ºF). Blend them when still warm, without removing the skins, with the warm red mullet stock.

To serve, blanch the salicornia for a few seconds in salted water and stop the cooking in ice water. Roast the cuttlefish in a hot iron pan, pressing it with another pan. Heat all the sauces and splatter them on the plate as though they were colours.

APRICOTISSIMO p. 146

Kobarid is a border region to Goriška Brda, one of Slovenia's most important fruit-growing areas. It is a kingdom of peaches, wine, apricots, persimmons, figs, cherries and sour cherries. My grandmother had a huge old apricot tree in her garden that overlooked the sea. That tree produced the most incredible fruit – sweet, sour and crunchy. In this dish, I treat the apricot as a vegetable.

Serves 10

For the cooked apricots and strained apricot juice
2 kg   apricots, stones (pits) reserved
300 g   sugar
400 ml water
8 g   salt

For the apricot cones
630 g cooked apricots (see above)
0.3%   gelespessa

For the apricot bloody Mary
2 l   strained apricot juice (see above)
200 ml vodka
½   dried habanero chilli without seeds
5   tonka beans

For the apricot stones
20   apricot stones (pits), with their
      kernels (see above)

For the dried apricots
20   apricots

For the apricot vinaigrette
250 g apricots
30 g   honey
40 ml apricot vinegar
30 g   Dijon mustard ↗

For the smoked apricots
20   apricots

For the fermented apricots
20   apricots
      4% brine

For the rosemary oil
300 ml grapeseed oil
200 g rosemary

For the fermented cottage cheese mousse
300 g fermented cottage cheese, aged for
      6 months
300 ml fresh double cream

For the crystallized red onions
300 g red onions
100 ml apricot vinaigrette (see above)

For the wild lily flowers
10   wild orange lily flowers

For the apricot juice, put all the ingredients together in a saucepan and bring to the boil. Simmer for 20 minutes. Separate the fruit and the liquid part by straining the apricots well. The fruit part is used for the rolls, the liquid for the bloody Mary.

For the apricot cones, blend all the ingredients together together in a Thermomix. Spread them out on a Silpat, then dry in a dehydrator set at 80ºC (175ºF) for 1 hour. Cut them into perfect 5 cm (2 in) squares. Roll them around into a cone and bake at 160ºC (320ºF) for 8 minutes. Store in a dry place.

To make the apricot bloody Mary, blend all the ingredients together for 5 minutes in a blender. Strain. Correct the salt. Chill down to –1ºC (25ºF).

Since we are serving the dish on the apricot stones (pits), we need to actually work them. To prepare the apricot stones, dry them for a half day in the sun. Break the stones and leave them in the sun until completely pale and clean. Dry the kernels in the top of the oven for 1 day. Chop the kernels very finely. For 1 cone, you will need 10 g of chopped kernels.

To make the dried apricots, cut them in half and dry them for 15 hours at 55ºC (130ºF).

For the apricot vinaigrette, place everything in a saucepan and cook over a low heat until reduced by one-third. Strain. Vacuum seal the apricots and then repeat this process three times.

For the smoked apricots, halve and roast them on a charcoal grill. When still soft but well grilled on the outside, smoke them with applewood twice. Keep them in a cold place.

To ferment the apricots, halve them and spoon into glass jars and leave in the brine for 5 days at 25ºC (75ºF), covered with a kitchen towel. Remove them from the brine and pat dry. Cut into very thin slices. For 1 cone, you will need ¼ fermented apricot. ↗

To make the rosemary oil, blend the ingredients together for 6 minutes at 70ºC (160ºF) in a Thermomix. Refresh in iced water and strain through a cheesecloth.

To make the fermented cottage cheese mousse, put the two ingredients together in a Thermomix, heated to 70ºC (160ºF). Place in a piping (pastry) bag.

Slice the onions in beautifully thin slices. Soak them in the cold apricot vinaigrette. Dry them at 65ºC (150ºF) until completely crunchy. Store in a dry place.

Finally, ask your forager to pick you the freshest wild orange lily flowers. Cut them half and use both pieces for the dish.

To serve, use the chopped and toasted apricot pieces as the base for the dish. Fill the apricot kernels with fermented cottage cheese, apricot kernels, smoked apricot, dried and resoaked apricot and the fermented one. Alternate all the ingredients twice, using very small quantities each time, and making sure your guests can have all the flavours in one bite. Place the red onion and lily flowers on the top of the cone. Serve it with chilled apricot bloody Mary with some drops of rosemary oil on the top.

FERMENTED BEAN AND KALE ROLL p. 160

Brown beans are the beans of the valley. Our protein bank, they are so often added to bitter chicory or dandelion salad. With kale, they match into a perfectly balanced bite.

Makes 80

For the fermented beans
1.5 kg beans (from Livek/Idrsko)
2 l   whey
200 g salt
160 g inoculated koji barley
10 g   fennel seeds

For the roasted kale
2 kg   cleaned kale
50 g   chestnut honey
60 ml charcoal oil
15 g   salt

For the smoked eel
3 kg   lagoon eel
      7% brine
300 g mirepoix
150 ml white wine
20 g   anchovy garum
1   piece kombu
50 ml cream
40 g   butter

To serve
8   rice flour steamed paper ↓

Put all the ingredients for the fermented beans into a sterilized glass jar and cover with a cloth. Let them start fermenting and keep for 4 weeks minimum, depending on the room temperature.

Wash the kale and blanch it for a few seconds in boiling water. Roast it over a yakitori grill until it's golden with a nice smoky flavour. When still hot, dress it with honey and charcoal oil. Season with salt.

Clean the eel and brine it entirely for 30 minutes. Warm smoke it. Remove the skin and the head and keep the meat separately. Roast the mirepoix, deglaze with the white wine and add the eel heads and skin. Cover with 300 ml water and simmer for 5 hours. Strain, add the kombu and leave simmering at 80°C (175°F) for 1 more hour. Add the cream, bring to a boil and emulsify in the butter. Carefully clean the eel meat, removing all the bones. Add it to the kale and fermented beans. Dress with the smoked eel sauce.

To serve, place the papers on a worktop, wet them with the eel sauce and add the fermented bean-eel-kale filling. Roll tight and let them set. Cut to perfect rolls. Serve cold.

MOUNTAIN VEAL AND SOLE p. 161

This is my version of vitello tonnato. Well, we got the whole baby veal. It was also high season for lagoon sole. Have you ever tried a really good vitello tonnato? You should.

Serves 12

For the sole
3 kg sole (around 250 g each)
0.3% xantana
1.3 l very light virgin olive oil

For the vitello
1.5 kg veal leg
10 kg kidney fat

For the pil pil sauce
2 kg fish heads and gelatinous parts and bones all cracked
2 l olive oil

For the oyster mayo
70 g oysters
1 egg yolk
40 ml lemon juice
300 ml grapeseed oil
200 ml olive oil
salt
oyster water

For the rice foam
100 g risotto rice (good quality)
3 l tomato water
250 g unpeeled almonds ↗

salt
habanero powder
2 % proespuma (hot)

For the compressed tomatoes
1 kg green tomatoes
200 g yellow date tomatoes
8 basil leaves

For the tomato liquid
2 kg red date tomatoes
30 g salt
60 g sugar
150 ml olive oil
20 g oregano

For the tomato glaze
1.2 l Tomato Water (page 251)
100 ml apple vinegar
200 ml vodka
1.7% kappa carrageenan
10 ml Worcestershire sauce
salt
2 g peppercorns

To serve
300 g butter
chive flowers

Clean the fillets from the bones, reserving the bones for pil pil sauce. Out of 1 fillet you should get around 3 portions. Put the offcuts and the meat, bones and wings in a pan with the parts with more collagen with the olive oil. Cook at 80°C (175°F) for 12 hours. Then let it rest for another 12 hours in the refrigerator, bringing back to 80°C (175°F). Strain though a chinois, making sure you get all the juice out of the fish by pushing hard. Emulsify with a hand blender, add the xantana and correct with the salt and pepper. For serving, it is important to keep the sauce in a bain-marie, but not boiling, otherwise it will split.

Dry age the veal for 6 days at 1.5°C (35°F) and 82% humidity. Cover with kidney fat for 5 weeks at 1.5°C (35°F) and 82% humidity. Debone and clean. Wrap into rolls, then cook at 65°C (150°F) for 1 hour in a thermal water circulator.

To make the pil pil sauce, simmer the ingredients for 12 hours, let it set at 10°C (50°F) for 12 hours. Bring back to 80°C (176°F) and strain by pushing all through a metal strainer, trying to extract the fish liquids and emulsify.

In a Thermomix, blend the oysters, egg yolk and lemon juice, then add the grapeseed oil very slowly while whisking – first making sure you get an emulsion, then add the olive oil doing the same. Correct the seasoning with salt and oyster water.

Cook the rice with the tomato water until the rice is on cooking point. Place in a Thermomix 1 kg of the cooked rice, then blend it with extra tomato water and almonds until smooth. Pass through a chinois, place the mixture again in the Thermomix and season with the salt and habanero powder. ↗

Add the proespum and blend at 70°C (160°F) for 5 minutes on full speed. Charge the siphons with the foam and 2–3 chargers (for serving keep the siphon in a bath at 58°C (136°F). The foam should have a high note of spiciness.

For the compressed tomatoes, make a brine with 1 l water and 25 g salt, place the tomatoes and basil leaves in a vacuum bag, add the brine and vacuum seal. Use after 2 days. For serving, cut the whole tomatoes in quarters. It is important to cut a la minute, to keep the shape and the seeds.

To make the tomato liquid, put the whole tomatoes in a gastronorm (hotel pan) and mix them with the salt, sugar, olive oil and oregano. Cook at 200°C (400°F) for 20 minutes, then at 140°C (285°F) for 30 minutes. Blend the tomatoes in a Thermomix, adding more salt if necessary, then strain through a chinois. Place the mixture in a spherical silicone mould and freeze in the blast chiller.

Bring the tomato water and vinegar to a boil, then add the vodka. Add the kappa, blend with a hand blender and bring to a quick boil, keeping the mixture in a bain-marie while glazing the frozen spheres.

Melt the butter at 80°C (175°F). Confit the sole in it for 3 minutes, then place it on kitchen paper. Put the sole on the bottom of the plate and the oyster mayo on the sole. Cover with pil pil and place the veal slices on the top. Serve with tomato salad and finish with rice foam on the side.

ONE BITE OF KALAMARI NA ŽARU, SMOKED PIT CHEESE

p. 155

When I was a child, *kalamari na žaru* was the dish to order whether you were on the seaside or in the mountains. It was about a cheap version of calamari covered with garlic and parsley oil, and probably this was the flavour that people really loved.

Serves 16

For the calamari sheet
1 kg calamari
10 g salt

For the parsley and garlic oil
500 g parsley leaves
350 ml grapeseed oil
15 g garlic

For the parsley oil aioli
2 egg yolks
10 ml lemon juice
150 ml parsley garlic oil (see above) ↗

```
        lukewarm water
5 g     garlic
```

For the parsley root purée
```
375 g   parsley root
65 ml   olive oil
        salt
```

For the parsley crispies
```
        small parsley leaves
        rapeseed (canola) oil
        salt
```

For the smoked pit cheese
```
500 g   pit cheese
12 g    gelatine leaves
500 ml  cream
1 g     agar agar
5 g     salt
```

Remove the head, guts, fins and skin of the calamari and clean well. Open up the tubes and scrape away any slime or moisture, then dry each one very well. Once dry, chop with a knife until almost minced (work fast). Place the minced calamari in a Thermomix and blend on maximum for no more than 50 seconds at a time (the calamari cannot become too hot). Once it has blended enough to resemble a smooth white paste, pass it through a tamis into a bowl set over an ice bath. Divide the mixture into 400 g portions and season each with 5 g salt. Mix very well. Place each batch in a separate medium-sized vacuum bag and seal, trying to remove as much air as possible. Flatten the mixture in the bag to about 5 mm (¼ in) thick, then place on a tray with another tray on top and a weight to keep it flat. Steam on 100% steam at 90°C (195°F) for 10 minutes and cool rapidly in an ice bath. Once cool, remove from the bag and dry well with paper towels, then portion, into 2-cm (¾-in) squares. Keep in the refrigerator until serving.

Blanch the parsley leaves for 5 seconds, then place in an ice bath. Strain and pat dry. Place 300 g of the blanched parsley in a Pacojet container together with the oil, then freeze in the blast chiller. It's very important that the mixture is completely frozen. Spin 3 times in the Pacojet container and freeze. Repeat this process 3 times – that means you need to spin the mixture 9 times and freeze it 3 times. Cut the garlic in half and remove the centre. Brunoise the garlic and add it to the oil as well. Let it infuse for 24 hours, then strain. Keep some in the refrigerator in a squeeze bottle, and the rest can be used for the aioli.

Place the egg yolks and lemon juice in a blending cup and blend with a hand blender. Slowly add in the parsley garlic oil while blending to get a green mayo. Use some lukewarm water if too thick. Once the mayonnaise consistency is achieved, finely chop the garlic and mix it into the mayonnaise. Let it rest for at least 20–30 minutes, then pass through a tamis or sieve, place in a piping (pastry) bag and reserve in the refrigerator. ↗

Wash and peel the parsley root, and soak on steam 100% at 100°C (210°F) until soft (about 10–15 minutes). Blend in a Thermomix on maximum speed at 70°C (160°F). Slowly add the olive oil, adjusting the consistency with up to 25 ml water and season with salt. Strain through a chinois and reserve in a piping (pastry) bag for service.

Pick small parsley leaves, enough for 1 g per portion. Wrap a plate in clingfilm (plastic wrap) and brush it with a bit of rapeseed oil. Dip your fingers in oil and coat each and every leaf as you lay them flat on the plate. Sprinkle with a little bit of salt and wrap the plate again as tight as possible to keep the leaves flat. Microwave on full power for 35 seconds. Take it out for 10 seconds and return to the microwave for another 35 seconds. Repeat twice. Remove the layer of plastic covering the parsley and return to the microwave for 20 seconds. Repeat until crispy.

Place the pit cheese in foil with an opening and place in a large pan. In the meantime, hydrate the gelatine leaves in ice water for 10–25 minutes. Light the charcoal oven and when it has died down to 200°C (400°F), place the cheese inside and spray the coal with oil. Do this 4–5 times in 5-minute intervals. The cheese needs to be melted and smoky. Remove the cheese from the oven and let cool to about 70°C (160°F). Weigh and add the same amount in cream – 500 g cheese to 500 ml cream. Place in a Thermomix and bring to 80°C (175°F) on speed 8. Add the agar agar, salt and gelatine and let blend 1 more minute. Strain onto a tray using 700 g per normal size gastronorm (hotel pan). Let set in the refrigerator and when set, cut into portions using the smallest ring cutter.

To serve, seal the calamari in a very hot pan with 1 drop of oil, and quickly plate the remaining elements.

PITURALKA p. 150

Pituralka is a forgotten pear that grows in a very restricted area of western Slovenia. The pear is almost inedible as a classical fruit; the flavour is tannic, almost like a turnip. We did several experiments and found out that a slow cooking process underlines its best characteristics.

Serves 8

For pituralka
```
500 g   butter
150 ml  white wine
8       pituralka pears
```

For the pear filling
```
200 g   cena meat of Croatian langoustines
200 g   wild hazelnut mix
        salt ↗
```

```
2       lemon zest
25 ml   hazelnut oil
```

For the pear broth
```
3 kg    William pears
        chestnut honey
```

For the lovage oil
```
150 g   lovage leaves
100 ml  grapeseed oil
```

For the pickled pear salad
```
300 ml  apple vinegar
20 g    lovage leaves
200 g   abate pears
200 g   Treviso chicory leaves
50 ml   lovage oil (see above)
30 ml   hazelnut oil
10 g    salt
```

Place the butter, wine and pituralka pears in a saucepan. Cook them for 3 hours, avoiding burning the butter, but to brown it and add more richness to the pear. Once cooked all the way through, open a small hole in the bottom and take out some of the pulp, making sure you also remove the seeds.

Chop the peeled langoustine meat and the wild hazelnut mix. Season with salt, lemon zest and hazelnut oil. Fill the pear with this mixture and close with the cut button. Heat under the salamander and finish, very gently, with the blowtorch.

Juice the pears and place in a flat gastronorm (hotel pan). Cut into squares of 5 cm (2 in) and place them in a cheesecloth above a perforated, deep gastronorm. Let it sit 36 hours to clarify the juice. Once the juice is clear, place it in a pot and add a 3.5% ratio of chestnut honey. Let simmer for 5 minutes. Cool down and reserve the juice.

To make the lovage oil, blend the ingredients together in a Thermomix at 70°C (160°F) and strain into a bowl over ice.

To make the salad, blend the vinegar, 200 ml water and lovage. Cut the pears into thin slices and add the chicory leaves. Dress with both oils and salt.

To serve, heat the pear until it's 60°C (140°F) in the centre. Caramelize it with a blowtorch. Place it in a bowl and combine with the salad. Pour the broth and sprinkle with the oils.

PICKERELS p. 151

This dish was created after my first visit to Marano Lagunare at the moment the agoon started the famous *fermo pesca* – stop fishing. It is the politics of the northern Adriatic to allow the sea to recover from overfishing. I was allowed to take part in the 2 p.m. auction and the fish selection was so unexpected. There were bags of sweet clams, razor clams and pickerels. ↓

This dish is composed of two dishes; you are first invited to enjoy the seaweed salad, and subsequently to eat the pickerels with your hands.

Serves 4

200 g	capers in salt
1	egg
1	egg yolk
200 ml	light olive oil
15 g	mustard
20 ml	lemon juice
200 g	pickerels
300 g	cornflour (cornstarch)
5 l	peanut oil
100 g	mixed seaweed

Wash the capers under cold water. Put 100 g of capers and the seaweed at 65°C (150°F) in a dehydrator for 16 hours. Leave the other 100 g of capers on the side. Make a basic mayonnaise with the egg, egg yolk, olive oil, mustard and lemon. Blend with the remaining capers. Coat the pickerels in cornflour and fry them for a few seconds at 190°C (375°F). Powder the dehydrated capers and seaweed.

To serve, place the fried pickerels on the side of the dish, looking as though they were swimming in the same direction. Finish with caper mayo and sprinkle with some dried capers and seaweed.

CUTTLEFISH LARD p. 165

Cuttlefish from the lagoon is very sweet, close to lard in flavour. With this dish, we wanted to create a lard consistency, and make our guests feel they were eating something comforting, like toasted bread with garlic and lard. This was also one of the most popular dishes of spring 2019.

Serves 8

For the cuttlefish lard
6 kg	cuttlefish
	2.5% brine
30 ml	olive oil
20 g	pink peppercorns
	salt

For the white asparagus milk
600 ml	milk
30 g	salt
300 g	white asparagus peels and offcuts

For the pine nut milk
300 ml	water
300 g	pine nuts
5 g	salt ↗

For the bread
300 g	old bread
500 g	brown butter
	salt

For the wild garlic oil
150 g	wild garlic (ramsons) leaves
100 ml	rapeseed (canola) oil

For the black sauce
220 g	peeled shallots
250 g	carrots
200 ml	olive oil
1	clove garlic
700 ml	white wine
3 kg	cuttlefish trimmings
200 ml	carrot juice
1 g	bay leaves
21 g	brown sugar
350 ml	cuttlefish ink
50 g	salt

For the aioli
2	egg yolks
30 ml	lemon juice
750 ml	grapeseed oil
175 g	black sauce (see above)

To serve
8	wild garlic (ramsons) leaves
8	wild garlic (ramsons) flowers

Clean the cuttlefish, preserving all the innards. Place the cuttlefish in iced water until it's completely white. Brine the cuttlefish for 1 hour in the brine. Rinse under cold water and dry. Vacuum seal and cook at 51°C (124°F) for 1 hour. Cool in an ice bath. Roast over hot charcoal while spraying with olive oil.

Press the cuttlefish together tightly and wrap in clingfilm (plastic wrap). Press between 2 gastronorms (hotel pans) and freeze. Remove the plastic and slice on a meat slicer into thin slices. Sprinkle with pink peppercorns and salt.

Vacuum the milk, salt and asparagus offcuts. Keep this in the refrigerator for 3 days.

Infuse the water, pine nuts and salt for 24 hours. Blend for 7 minutes and strain. Reserve and keep in the refrigerator.

Cut the bread into 1.5 cm (¾ in) cubes and fry in the brown butter. Drain on paper, then salt.

Blend the oil and wild garlic leaves for 3 minutes at 70°C (160°F) on medium speed. Blend for 2 more minutes on maximum speed. Strain in an ice bath.

Fry the shallots and carrots in a little olive oil until transparent. Add the garlic and 600 ml of wine and reduce until it tastes sweet. Reserve the vegetables in another pot. Add the rest of the olive oil and the cuttlefish trimmings. Caramelize them, deglaze with a little white wine and the carrot juice, add the bay leaves and return the vegetables to the pan. Reduce/simmer for 1 hour, then add the rest of the wine with the sugar. Cover with 750 g ice and water, then add the ink and reduce by ↗

half. Add salt to season (not all the salt at once, taste first).

In the blender, whizz the egg yolks and lemon juice. Add the grapeseed oil slowly and start to emulsify. Then add the finished sauce and correct the salt if necessary.

Refry the bread again at 200°C (400°F) for 30 seconds, then take out and dry on kitchen paper. Coat with the cuttlefish, and put a dot of the aioli on the centre of the plate. Cover with the pine nut milk, add 4 drops of wild garlic oil and garnish with the wild garlic leaves and flowers.

PORCINI, BERRIES AND CRISPY CHICKEN SKIN

p.156

Summer porcini are less tasty than autumn ones, and they grow for just a week or two in summer. They usually appear after the first August rain.

Serves 6

For the porcini
500 g	small summer porcini

For the mushroom broth
200 g	onions
200 g	carrots
150 g	celery
30 g	garlic
80 g	fennel bulb
1	piece kombu
200 g	mix of dried morels, black trumpets and porcini mushrooms
3 l	water

For the forest mushroom curd
100 ml	mushroom broth (see above)
4 g	shallot
6 g	dried forest mushrooms
2	eggs
18 ml	cream
25 g	clarified butter
0.4 g	salt
2 ml	apple vinegar

For the forest oil
200 g	forest oxalis
100 g	spruce needles
300 ml	grapeseed oil

For the berry salad
30 g	blueberries
20 g	elderberries
20 g	cranberries
	forest oil (see above)

For the chicken skin
200 g	chicken skin
300 ml	peanut oil ↗

To serve

          small summer porcini (see above)
20   oxalis leaves

Cut 400 g of porcini and dry them in a dehydrator at 52°C (125°F) for 24 hours. Reserve the remaining porcini for the salad.

Slice all the vegetables on a mandoline except the mushrooms. Place on a tray together with the kombu and roast them at 130°C (266°F) for 20 minutes. Place all the ingredients in a deep pan. Bring to a boil and simmer for 2 hours. Let it cool down and strain through a cheesecloth.

Place the mushroom broth in a saucepan with the shallot and forest mushrooms. Bring to the boil and simmer for 30 minutes. Strain and blend together with the eggs. While blending, add the cream first and start to emulsify, and then add the melted clarified butter. To finish, add the salt and vinegar. Place the mixture in a bowl and cover with clingfilm (plastic wrap).

To make the forest oil, blend the 3 ingredients together in a Thermomix, heating to 70°C (160°F). Strain over iced water.

To make the salad, gently mix the 3 berries together and season with forest oil.

Clean the chicken skin well with a knife, making sure you remove all the fat on the bottom. Cook the skins for 10 minutes in salted water. Strain and dry well. Place on baking paper and open all the skins carefully. Dry at 80°C (175°F) with full ventilation for 6 hours. When completely dry, heat the oil to 230°C (445°F) and puff the skins.

To serve, cut the remaining 100 g of mushrooms into thin slices. Heat the mushroom broth. Plate the berry salad, porcini and oxalis. Pour over the broth and dress with forest oil.

ROSE HIP AND GREEN JUNIPER p. 152

This is a symbiosis of two wild plants growing together on Kolovrat mountain and very difficult to collect. Green juniper is really just normal juniper, but in its unripe version it has a lot of beautiful natural acidity. Rose hip is very common in Slovenia, especially in its dry version of a warm infusion in long cold winters. It is a pain in the ass to pick and process it.

Serves 20

For the rose hip purée
1.5 kg   rose hips
3 l   apple juice

For the rose hip glaze
50 g   rose hip purée (see above)
400 ml apple juice
60 g   sugar ↗

50 g   glucose
5 g   salt

For the rose hip tea gel
1 l   water
200 g   dried rose hips
5   cinnamon sticks
4   star anise
100 g   sugar
12   soaked gelatine leaves

For the green juniper powder
20 g   green juniper berries
1 l   liquid nitrogen

For the green juniper ice cream
60 g   powdered milk
20 g   maltodextrin
270 g   sugar
3 g   super neutrose
20 g   eggs
          pinch of salt
50 g   green juniper powder
1 l   milk
300 ml cream

For the chocolate bubbles
350 g   cocoa butter
650 g   dark chocolate 70%
20 g   lecithin

For the green juniper salt
100 g   green juniper powder
200 g   salt

For the red cabbage chips
          red cabbage leaves
          simple syrup

Cook freshly picked rose hips in apple juice for 2½ hours and then blend in a blender and strain. Keep the strained purée in the refrigerator.

To make the glaze, combine all the ingredients and cook until the glaze is reduced. Keep the glaze in the refrigerator.

To make the gel, cook the first 5 ingredients at 80°C (175°C) until reduced. Then add the gelatine leaves and cool.

Dry green juniper berries in liquid nitrogen, so the berries keep their green colour. Blend to a powder, then freeze.

Mix the powdered milk, maltodextrin, sugar, super neutrose, eggs, salt and green juniper powder, and slowly add milk to ensure there are no lumps. Cook the mixture to 60–70°C (140–160°C). Reduce the temperature to 55°C (130°F) and quickly add the cream. Strain, cool and freeze.

Melt the cocoa butter to 65°C (150°F) and the chocolate to 45°C (115°F). Combine the melted ingredients with lecithin in a bain-marie and use a bubble maker machine (one that would deliver oxygen to fish in an aquarium) for 20 minutes. Freeze the bubble mixture. ↗

To make the green juniper salt, mix the ingredients, then freeze. Keep the salt in the freezer.

Roll out fresh red cabbage leaves. Blanch the rolled leaves in simple syrup. Dry the blanched leaves in the dehydrator overnight until they become crispy.

To serve, on a previously frozen plate, put a big dot of the rose hip glaze. Put a dot of rose hip purée on top of the rose hip glaze. Add a small amount of rose hip tea gel on the rose hip purée. Next, add a tiny quenelle of green juniper ice cream (in the middle of the rose hip purée or next to the rose hip glaze). On top of the ice cream, add a piece of bubble chocolate. Garnish with red cabbage chips and sprinkle a pinch of green juniper salt over the top.

ROSE HIP PRALINE p. 157

This sweet bite is a continuation of the rose hip dessert that I have presented before. I loved that flavour combination so much that I wanted to leave it on the menu for longer.

Serves 120

For the juniper salt
100 g   juniper powder
50 g   salt

For the rose hip purée
1.5 kg   rose hips
3 l   apple juice

For the coating
300 g   dark chocolate 72%
300 g   cocoa butter

To make the salt, blend the ingredients together and freeze.

To make the purée, cook the rose hips and apple juice on a low heat for 3 hours, then blend and strain. Fill up the silicone moulds and freeze.

To make the coating, melt both ingredients separately, keeping them on a bain-marie. Coat the frozen rose hip first in cocoa butter, then in chocolate. Let it cook and finish with juniper salt.

WILD ROWAN BERRY DESSERT AND BONE MARROW p. 149

I have often tasted rowan berries in Austria and Germany and I found them pleasant and very easy to work it. This is why I thought every rowan berry would be easy to work with. I was very wrong. The wild ↓

rowan berries from our mountains are smaller and extremely bitter. And extremely difficult to harvest because of the time competition with birds. Birds love them and when the rowan berry gets the right colour it is too late for us. Due to their tannins and strong bitterness, rowan berries need to be frozen before use.

Serves 12

For the sorbet

3.4 kg	frozen rowan berries
1 kg	glucose
520 g	sugar
9 l	apple juice

For the apple foam

2.35 l	apple juice
2	pieces cinnamon
23	soaked gelatine leaves
25 g	albumina
3 g	salt

For the bergamot cream

180 g	bergamot peel
180 g	sugar
75 ml	water
210 ml	bergamot juice
45 g	butter

For the bone marrow caramel

100 g	sugar
115 g	glucose
200 ml	cream
6 g	salt
45 g	butter
65 g	smoked bone marrow
7 ml	apple vinegar

For the meringue

100 g	egg whites
100 g	sugar
100 g	icing (confectioners') sugar
8 g	cream of tartar
15 g	spice mix powder (clove, star anise and cinnamon)
15 g	dried and powdered rowan berries

To serve

100 g	red sour apple brunoise
200 ml	ice water
30 ml	lemon juice
60 g	fried and diced pancetta
50 g	thin slices of smoked and salted bone marrow
	rowan berry clusters, to decorate

Boil all the sorbet ingredients with 6 l apple juice for 2 hours. Blend and pass through a tamis. Cool down and mix in the remaining quantity of apple juice. Pour into Pacojet containers and freeze for at least 24 hours.

To make the foam, boil 2 l apple juice with the cinnamon until it has reduced to 800 g. Add the gelatine leaves, albumina and salt. Blend well and transfer to a siphon. ↗

Blend the peel 3 times. Add all the other ingredients, except the butter, and cook slowly for 1 hour. Blend with the butter and preserve.

Bring the sugar, glucose, cream and salt to 108°C (226°F). Add the butter, bone marrow and vinegar. Whisk well, emulsify and set aside.

Warm the egg whites with the sugar to 50°C (120°F) and start whisking, slowly adding the icing sugar and cream of tartar. Add the spice powder and powdered rowan berries. Spread over a Silpat and bake for 16 minutes at 170°C (340°F).

Cut the red sour apples to brunoise and compress them in the ice water and lemon juice.

To serve, put all the ingredients on plates, finishing with the ice cream, and present with a big cluster of ripe rowan berries.

SUMMER PEAR p. 166

When I was a kid I was addicted to the summer pears in my grandmother's garden overlooking the seaside. These are green, sweet and delicate.

Serves 4

For the nasturtium granita

80 g	sugar
15 g	glucose
2	soaked gelatine leaves
100 g	nasturtium leaves
10 g	oxalis

For the poached pears

200 g	summer pears
100 g	butter
35 g	honey
10 g	salt

For the blackcurrant coulis

700 ml	blackcurrant juice
70 g	sugar
8 g	agar agar

For the whey coulis

100 ml	whey
20 g	honey
5 g	gelespessa

For the whey ice cream

875 ml	whey
25 g	glucose
375 ml	cream
200 g	sugar
5 g	super neutrose
420 g	egg yolks

For the caramelized white chocolate

100 g	white chocolate

Boil 450 g water, the sugar and glucose. Add the gelatine and cool it down. ↗

Blend the nasturtium, oxalis and cold base. Freeze it and stir every 5–10 minutes.

Clean and halve the pears. Melt the butter and add the honey. Vacuum bag the pear with butter. Cook at 62° C (144°F) for 15–20 minutes.

To make the blackcurrant coulis, combine all the ingredients and boil. Cool it down, then blend.

To make the whey coulis, blend all the ingredients together.

Boil the whey, glucose and cream. Mix the sugar and super neutrose. Add the sugar to the cream and whey. Pour everything over the yolks and cook all together to 82°C (180°F). Strain.

Bake the chocolate in an oven at 160°C (320°F) for 6–8 minutes.

To serve, cool the plates to -5°C (23°F). Pacojet the ice cream. Take a frozen plate and plate the 2 coulis and the caramelized white chocolate. Centralize the ice cream, cover with granita, compose the pears and finish with 2 spoons of granita.

ISTRIA
ISTRIAN GOAT WHEY, HAZELNUTS AND CARDAMOM, SALTED BUTTER AND WALNUTS p. 179

An amazing sweet, local bite that was made for the menu that did not have a real dessert.

Serves 100

For the cardamom reduction

2 l	milk
1 l	whey
2 l	cream
660 g	FEO IPA beer
1 g	Thai chili
1 g	saffron
1 piece	star anise
20 g	cardamom, green
5 g	salt
3 g	pink pepper
20 g	salt
100 g	sugar

For the hazelnut caramels

450 g	cardamon reduction
450 g	sugar
100 g	butter
150 g	hazelnuts ↗

For the whey reduction
10 l whey
5 l cream

For the walnut caramels
400 g whey reduction
12 g maldon salt
550 g sugar
100 ml glucose syrup
300 g butter
100 g walnuts

To make the cardamom and hazelnut caramels: combine the cardamom reduction ingredients in a deep pot on medium heat. Bring to a simmer and stir every 5 minutes to avoid the burning of the bottom of the pot. Reduce to one-quarter or until you reach a texture similar to a syrup. Strain and reserve.

To make the hazelnut caramels, bring the cardamom reduction to 90°C (194°F) in a pot and keep at this temperature. In another pot, melt the sugar and bring to 125°C (257°F). Once you reach this temperature add the cardamom reduction. Make sure your mixture reaches 115°C (239°F). Cook at this temperature for 8 minutes. Allow the caramel mixture to cool to 70°C (158°F), add the butter little by little and add the hazelnuts. Pour the caramel mixture in the tray with fat spray in the bottom and allow to cool. Portion in parts of 5 g each.

To make the butter and walnut caramels: in a large saucepan, mix the whey and the cream and bring them to a boil over high heat and reduce to 1.5 l of its original volume, approximately 5 hours. Allow to cool and reserve.

Bring the whey reduction together with the salt to 90°C (194°F) in a pot and keep at this temperature. In another pot, melt the sugar and glucose syrup and bring to 125°C (257°F). Once you reach this temperature, add the whey reduction. Make sure your mixture reaches 115°C (239°F) and cook at this temperature for 8 minutes. Allow the caramel mixture to cool to 70°C (158°F), add the butter little by little, then add the walnuts. Pour the caramel mixture in the tray with fat spray in the bottom and allow to cool. Portion in parts of 5 g each.

EVOLUTION OF SARDA IN ŠAVOR p. 175

Sardele v šavorju (sarda in šavor) is one of the most amazing dishes of the northern Adriatic area and there are many different versions found along the Croatian, Slovenian and Italian coasts. The sweet-sour combination of flavours has a lot to do with our Austro-Hungarian history.

Serves 6 ↗

For the pickling liquid
500 ml red wine vinegar
40 g colatura di alici
30 g salt
50 g sugar
100 ml water

For the sardines
200 g sardines, heads and bones removed
        pickling liquid (see above)
70 ml leccino olive oil
40 g chopped garlic

For the tomato bottoms
2 kg ripe pelati tomatoes
30 g salt
30 g sugar
70 g fresh basil leaves
250 g green celery
60 g chopped garlic
50 g chopped onion
12 g agar agar

For the red onion pickle
300 ml red wine vinegar
100 ml water
42 g sugar
3 bay leaves
3 cinnamon sticks
5 star anise
30 g black peppercorns
4 red onions

For the colourful carrots
100 g yellow carrots
100 g orange carrots
100 g purple carrots
        pickling liquid (see above)
1 l apple cider
500 g sugar
5 cinnamon sticks
4 star anise
20 cloves
15 g dry ginger

For the red onion jam
80 g red wine
60 ml wine vinegar
50 g raisins
100 g brown sugar
6 chopped red onions

For the mustard mayo
2 egg yolks
150 ml leccino olive oil
30 g mustard seeds
30 g finely chopped shallot
10 ml lemon juice
10 g salt
7 g ground pepper

For the walnut crumble
100 g walnuts
100 g fried and dried brown bread
180 g brown sugar
18 g salt ↗

120 g butter
120 g glucose

First, make the pickling liquid. Cook all the ingredients for 30 minutes, then allow to cool.

Clean the sardines well, then pat dry. Cover with pickling liquid, olive oil and garlic. Place in the refrigerator for 12 hours.

Bring all the ingredients aside from the agar agar together with 200 g water and cook for 25 minutes. Strain the water through a cheesecloth. Keep the water, adjust with salt and sugar (it needs to be a very intense tomato flavour). Cool down. Then take 200 g tomato water, stir in agar agar and bring to a boil. Pour the liquid on a 30 x 30 cm (12 x 12 in) tray. The layer should be around 3 mm. When cold, cut out the perfect bottoms of 1 cm (½ in).

To make the red onion pickle, cook all the ingredients except the red onions together for 30 minutes. Let it cool, then strain. Reserve some of the pickling liquid to pickle the carrots. Cook the unpeeled onions in a water bath for 30 minutes at 85°C (185°F). Peel the onions and cut them in regular slices. Compress them 3 times in the pickling liquid and store in the liquid overnight.

Peel the carrots, then slice them and vacuum seal with the pickling liquid. Simmer the rest of the ingredients for 20 minutes. Compress when still hot with carrots.

For the jam, reduce the wine, vinegar and raisins by half. Add the sugar and onions and cook slowly for 45 minutes. Cool down.

To make the mayo, emulsify the egg yolks with the olive oil, then whisk in the other ingredients.

To make the walnut crumble, grind the walnuts and bread with the sugar and salt. Whip the butter, then add the glucose and the dried elements. Cool down for 2 hours in the refrigerator. Crumble it with your fingers and bake at 175°C (345°F) for 20 minutes with a fan.

To serve, lightly torch the skin of the sardines. Place the red onion jam and mayonnaise. Cover the sardines with tomato jelly and carrots.

THE FIG p. 186

When we started discussions about this dish, Emily, my sous chef at the time, reminded me I was becoming very repetitive in my thinking. 'Forget fig-meadow-sweet-buckwheat.' Fig is one of the fruits of my childhood. In my Istrian summers we almost never cooked breakfast – we just ate from the fig trees, as they were so rich and abundant.

Serves 8

For the fermented figs
120 g salt ↓

240 g fresh beer yeast
1 kg ripe but hard figs

For the fermented fig water
300 ml fermented fig liquid (see above)
1½ figs
20 g fresh beer yeast
2 tsp nutritional yeast

For the yeast chips
100 g fresh beer yeast
80 g cornflour (cornstarch)
200 ml water
  vegetable oil, for frying

For the fig chips
300 g ripe figs
100 ml sugar
100 ml water
15 g agar agar
20 ml liquid glucose

To serve
12 clove flowers

To make the fermented figs, dissolve the salt and yeast in 3 l water. Put the mixture in glass jars and add the figs. Cover with a napkin and let it sit for 48 hours at 25°C (77°F). Take out 600 g of figs and let them rest for another 48 hours.

To make the fig water, blend the remaining 400 g figs with the fermented fig liquid and the other ingredients and strain.

To make the yeast chips, bring the ingredients to a boil and blend. Spread over a Silpat and dry at 65°C (150°F) for 4 hours. Fry at 160°C (320°F) until they puff.

To make the fig chips, wrap the figs in aluminium foil and bake at 180°C (350°F) for 20 minutes. Bring the sugar, water, agar agar, and figs with their liquid and glucose to boil. Blend quickly and spread over a Silpat. Dry at 70°C (160°F) until crispy.

To plate, cut a beautiful slice of fig, put sauce on the plate, then combine with a fig and the two chips. Finish with clove flowers.

GOLDEN MACKEREL

p. 180

This dish is inspired by savor, a typical sweet and sour combination of the Northern Mediterranean, especially in our Adriatic region. Vinegar, Istrian tomato water and cinnamon bring all the flavours from the Mediterranean to our valley. Spices are traditionally used in the western part of Slovenia, since we are a part of the old spice trade road between Venice and Vienna.

Serves 8 ↗

For the mackerel
4 mackerel, 100 g each
1 l Tomato Water (page 251)
25 ml soy sauce
100 ml apple vinegar
30 g caster (superfine) sugar
1 tsp ground cinnamon

For the candied tomatoes
500 g datterini tomatoes
2 pinches salt
3 pinches caster (superfine) sugar
20 ml olive oil
1 pinch dried oregano

For the candied shallots
12 shallots
30 ml olive oil
  salt

For the rice clouds
100 g sticky rice
  peanut oil, for frying

For the caramelized white radish
200 g caster (superfine) sugar
100 ml white wine vinegar
500 g white radish

To serve
  edible gold leaf

Clean the mackerel. If there are some eggs, reserve them. Bring to a boil the tomato water, soy sauce, vinegar, sugar and cinnamon. Cool down and vacuum seal the mackerel fillets. Keep in the refrigerator for 2 hours. Remove the fish from the liquid and put them on a rack.

Put the tomatoes on a tray lined with baking paper and spread over all the ingredients. Bake them first at 200°C (400°F) for 20 minutes, then continue baking at 140°C (285°F) for 30 minutes. When cold, peel them and store in a cold place.

Wrap each shallot, sprinkled with olive oil, in aluminium foil and bake at 160°C (320°F) for 40 minutes. Blend in a Thermomix and adjust the salt. Store in a cold place.

To make the clouds, overcook the rice, blend it into a perfect paste, spread it over a Silpat and dehydrate at 60°C (140°F) until dry. Break the dried rice into pieces and fry at 240°C (465°F) just for a few seconds. Remove from the oil and put them on absorbing paper.

To make the radishes, caramelize the sugar, deglaze with 100 ml hot water and the vinegar and reduce. Cool down. Cut the white radish with a Japanese mandoline and put it into the cool liquid, compress and store in the refrigerator for 6 hours.

To serve, torch the mackerels and cook them under the salamander for 15 seconds at the highest temperature. Put them on an absorbing paper and then place at the centre of a very warm dish. Set on the top 3 pieces of candied tomatoes, followed by a bouquet of caramelized white radish. On the side ↗

of the dish, place the candied shallots. Finish with a rice cloud and a sheet of edible gold leaf. In case of no salamander, toast the mackerels in a non-stick frying pan, skin down, until the temperature goes through, but paying attention that the fish does not completely coagulate.

GREEN KOHLRABI, SAUSAGE AND RICCIOLA p. 188

Istria of course has some amazing fish. In Novigrad, at sunset, the fishermen's boats return to port loaded with wild oysters, scallops and wild fish. But in Istria, people make sausages too. In Istria they ferment. When we think Mediterranean, we wrongly think only about plates full of seafood. In Srbani, fish was almost never on the menu.

Serves 60

For the pickled green kohlrabi
8 green kohlrabi
500 g zeljnica
15 g salt
50 ml olive oil

For the ricciola tartare
400 g cleaned ricciola fillet
200 g sugar
20 g bay leaf powder
500 g salt
200 g fresh sausage
  olive oil
  salt

For the brodetto sauce
300 g shallots
20 g fresh rosemary
20 g thyme
3 g pepperoncini
200 g carrots
5 kg fresh crab heads
3 kg langoustine heads
3 kg scorpion fish heads
150 ml whisky
200 ml dry white wine
2 kg ripe tomatoes, halved
200 ml olive oil
70 ml cream
15 g butter
  salt

To serve
20 g kohlrabi pickling liquid
4 g agar agar (on the quantity of pickling liquid)
0.3% xantana (on the total amount)
  pork mayonnaise (see above) ↗

Peel the kolhrabi. Preserve the peels. Cut the kohlrabi to paper thin slices and compress it with icy zeljnica, salt and olive oil. Leave it in an ice bath for 12 hours.

Clean the ricciola of all fibres. Cure the ricciola with the sugar, bay leaf powder and salt for 1 hour at 15°C (60°F). Wipe away the curing mix. Wrap the fillet and cool it to -5°C (23°F). Cut into a fine tartare with a very sharp knife. Cook the sausage. Open it, clean out the meat and slowly pan fry with olive oil on medium heat. Strain and reserve the fat and the sausage meat. Make a mayonnaise out of the sausage fat and dry the meat on paper. Dress the tartare with sausage and correct with salt.

Cook the shallots, herbs, pepperoncini and carrots in a big pan. Add all the seafood heads (cut, but with all brains and liquids). Use a big wooden spoon to smash them. Deglaze with whisky and white wine. Reduce. Cover with water and ice and add the tomatoes. Cook slowly for 4 hours. Remove the herbs. Blend, then strain through a cheesecloth into an ice bath. Bring to 70°C (160°F) and incorporate the cream and butter, then emulsify. Correct with salt.

Make a gel out of the pickling liquid with a classic recipe using agar agar and xantana. Remove the kohlrabi from the pickling liquid. Put the pork mayonnaise on the bottom of the kohlrabi. Top with the ricciola and sausage mixture. Close the wrap. Warm the sauce at 60°C (140°F) then serve with the wrap.

GREEN BEAN SCOGLIERA p. 189

La scogliera – my favourite pasta. When I am down, stressed or depressed and I need some comfort food and company, I head to Hotel Hvala in Kobarid for my spaghetti scogliera. This is my interpretation of that dish.

Serves 10

For the toasted pumpkin seeds
100 g   pumpkin seeds

For the yellow and green beans
60 g   salt
200 g   mixed beans

For the mussel stock
650 g   onions
1 l   white wine
3 kg   blue mussels
3 kg   clams
3 kg   razor clams
3 kg   sea snails
2   garlic bulbs

For the mussel sauce
300 ml mussel stock (see above) ↗

100 g   penne pasta
80 g   butter

For the black garlic emulsion
100 g   mussel sauce (see above)
30 g   black garlic paste
30 ml   fish sauce

For the chicken skin
100 g   chicken skin

For the apple glaze
500 ml apple juice
14 g   crushed ginger
3 g   garlic
1 g   pepperoncini

To serve
10   steamed and cleaned mussels
10   steamed and cleaned razor clams
10   steamed and cleaned sweet clams
10   steamed and cleaned clams
     fresh green coriander seeds
20   borage flowers

Toast the pumpkin seeds in a pan on m,edium heat, you will see the seeds are ready when they puff. Be careful to not toast them on high heat, otherwise they burn easily.

Bring 2 l water to a boil and cook the beans for 3½ minutes, then refresh them in iced water. Once the beans are cold, take out the seeds and cut the beans as thin as possible, around the thickness of spaghetti.

In a saucepan, brown the onions very gently and without burning since you don't want a dark colour in the sauce. Once the onions are cooked, add the white wine and reduce until the alcohol is gone. Add the seafood and garlic and cover them with water. Bring to a boil for 5 minutes, then put on medium heat and simmer for 5 hours. Strain and reduce the juice by around two thirds, or until even less, depending on the level of salt when you taste it.

Bring the stock to the boil and overcook the pasta in it. Let it sit until cold and then strain. Since the pasta has released all the starch into the stock, you can throw it away. Bring the stock to a boil and gradually add the butter and start to emulsify. Note: the sauce may need more butter depending how salty the stock is. It is important to know that the sauce is a little thicker than usual, but not syrup-like.

Bring the mussel sauce to a boil and add the black garlic paste, gradually emulsifying. Once emulsified, season with the fish sauce.

Clean the fat off the chicken skins, and place them fat-side down and between two Silpats. Place the Silpat in a flat tray and put one more tray on top of the Silpat. Put a rook or heavy weight on top of the tray and bake at 180°C (350°F) for 30 minutes.

To make the glaze, reduce the apple juice by half, then add the crushed ginger, garlic and pepperoncini. Reduce until syrupy. Glaze the chicken skin and put under the salamander. ↗

To serve, heat the beans in the mussel stock. At the bottom of the bowl, spoon in a little of the black garlic emulsion, adding some mussel stock, steamed mussels, razor clams, sweet clams and clams. Cover with beans as if they were spaghetti and place the chicken skin on top. Top with green coriander seeds and borage flowers.

DUCK LIVER, BERGAMOT AND RIESLING p. 185

It was December, there were shadows, and it was cold. Franco, our vegetable man, brought a few kilos of fresh bergamot; Laški riesling is from the wine cellar Dukal from the Slovenian Štajersdka region, with intense notes of petroleum; duck foie gras from the eastern part of Slovenia, a beautiful region of Prekmurje, which is only a couple of hours by car from the Soča Valley, but the food culture and the products drastically change, and the oysters here are Istrian wild Kamenice. Truly, this dish is a roller coaster ride around Slovenia.

Serves 15

For the duck livers
1.2 kg   fresh duck foie gras
100 g   rough salt
20 g   ground pepper
18 g   bergamot zest
400 ml duck jus

For the bergamot dressing
150 ml   riesling
60 g   sugar
150 ml   bergamot juice
2 g   bergamot zest
13 g   salt
50 ml   olive oil

For the riesling gel
300 ml   dry riesling
15 g   bergamot zest
120 ml   water
50 g   sugar
5   soaked gelatine leaves

For the oyster and Brussels sprout salad
8   oysters
200 g   green and purple Brussels sprouts

For the Brussels sprout and oyster emulsion
500 g   purple Brussels sprouts
10   oysters
     salt and pepper

Clean the livers and cover with salt, pepper and zest. Let sit in the refrigerator for 3 hours. ↓

Wipe away the salt. Wrap the livers in clingfilm (plastic wrap) and aluminium foil and poach them in the jus at 75°C (165°F) for 6 minutes. Cool in iced water.

To make the dressing, bring the riesling, sugar and bergamot juice to a boil and cook for 20 minutes. Cool down, grate in the bergamot zest, add the salt and olive oil.

Bring all the ingredients for the gel, except the gelatine, to a boil, cook for 20 minutes, strain and stir in the gelatine. Let sit for 24 hours in the refrigerator.

Open the oysters and poach them quickly in their own liquid. Gently open the sprouts in leaves and blanch them in boiling water.

Cook the sprouts for 15 minutes. Cut them into slices and squeeze out all the water. Help yourself with a cheesecloth. Blend them and add the oysters and oyster water. Season with salt and pepper.

To serve, cut the foie gras. Start putting down the Brussels sprout and oyster emulsion. Dress the Brussels sprout and oyster salad with bergamot dressing. Place the riesling gel.

SEA SALAD p. 184

The Northern Adriatic is a shallow sea, and its seafood has intense flavours. Here, we spice up the best it has to offer with some green tomatoes.

Serves 8

For the scallop and sweet clam salad
8	scallops
18	sweet clams

For the fish sauce
2 kg	clams
2 kg	sweet clams
2 kg	mussels
500 ml	white wine
200 ml	water
200 g	garlic
50 ml	fish sauce
100 ml	vinegar
50 g	dried local seaweed
50 g	dried scallop offal (see above)
50 g	sugar
50 g	green basil
100 ml	olive oil

For the brined green tomatoes
1 kg	hard green tomatoes
1 l	5% brine
200 g	tomato leaves

For the seaweed salad
20 g	salted sea lettuce
20 g	sea asparagus
20 g	haricots de mer
20 g	salted wakame
50 g	yellow tomatoes ↗

To serve
30 ml	olive oil

Soak the sweet clams in cold water and steam for 5 minutes. Open them gently and reserve the meat. Open the scallops and put the offal in the dehydrator at 60°C (140°F). Clean the coral and the meat.

Simmer all the ingredients for the fish sauce, except the basil and olive oil, together for 1 hour. Strain, add the basil and cook for another 20 minutes. Emulsify with olive oil.

To make the brined tomatoes, compress the tomatoes 3 times in the brine with the tomato leaves. Store in iced water.

To make the salad, wash all the seaweed under cold water. Wipe and dress them with a bit of olive oil.

To serve, cut the green tomatoes into thin slices. Heat the sauce. Place the seafood, yellow tomatoes and seaweed around the green tomatoes. Pour the liquid over the green tomatoes. Finish with some drops of olive oil.

SEAFOOD SANDWICH

p. 178

In these days while writing down my recipes, I realized how much I love mussels. In the Adriatic they are considered a food for poor people and when I was a kid, we were picking them every evening, turning them down to delicious Buzara. All you needed was some white wine, parsley, old bread and garlic. I understand mussels as the ultimate sea flavour.

Serves 20

For the mussels
5 kg	cleaned mussels
200 g	garlic
500 ml	white wine
200 ml	water

For the bread
500 g	old sourdough bread
500 ml	mussel stock (half of total)

For the cime di rapa salad
5	organic lemons
50 ml	water
20 ml	fish sauce
50 g	sugar
1 kg	rapini (broccoli rabe)

For the smoked mussel milk
500 ml	mussel stock (see above)
200 ml	milk
1 kg	mussels
100 g	garlic
100 g	mascarpone
30 g	washed capers
4	soaked gelatine leaves ↗

To serve
30 g	pork fat
8	slices of lard

Put all the mussel ingredients together and cook them for 1 hour. Strain and cool down.

Clean the crust of the bread away and cut the bread to perfect 6 cm (2½ in) cubes. Soak them in the mussel stock and let sit until the bread is completely moist but still keeps the shape. Place the bread on oven racks on the top of the oven. Preserve the stock. After 2 hours, place the bread for 1 hour in the dehydrator at 60°C (140°F) degrees.

Peel the lemon for the salad and boil the zest 3 times. Cut julienne. Squeeze the lemon juice, and add the water, fish sauce and sugar and bring to a boil. Reduce by one-third and add the lemon zest. Remove from the heat, keep the lemon zest covered in contact with baking paper. When it is cold, return to the heat and gently bring to a boil again. Never remove the baking paper. Remove from the heat again and let cool again. Repeat this procedure 5 times. Clean the rapini, keeping tender leaves and sprouts. Blanch the sprouts.

Bring all the muscle milk ingredients together except the mascarpone and capers. Cook them for 30 minutes. Strain. Add the gelatine and blend in mascarpone and capers. Blend until smooth, then cold smoke. Fill a siphon.

Fry the bread. Heat 20 g of pork fat and roast the bread on all sides. Place slices of lard on the top so they melt. Add the remaining pork fat and pan fry the rapini spouts and leaves, but they need to remain crunchy. Dress them with candied lemon, some lemon pickling liquid and salt if necessary. Serve with a spoon of the smoked mussel milk.

KAKI p. 183

Persimmons are part of a strong food memory for me. Around 1st November, all the family meet at the cemetery for All Saints (actually the only family occasion where we meet without excuses). My grandmother always brought a few wooden boxes of super ripe persimmons from her garden. In late autumn, when all the leaves have already fallen on the ground, this beautiful fruit still hangs on the trees. Reminding us of the beautiful autumn colours.

Serves 8

For the persimmons
2	super ripe persimmons, matured on the tree

For the persimmon ice cream
200 ml	sugar syrup
70 g	glucose
150 g	caster (superfine) sugar ↗

2 kg   super ripe persimmons, matured on
           the tree

For the almond milk
250 g   raw almonds
2   pinches salt
6   soaked gelatine leaves

For the almond crumble
           blended almonds (see above)

For the tangerine ganache
430 g   white chocolate, ideally Opalys or
           Valrhona
125 ml   cream
20 g   tangerine zest
175 ml   reduced tangerine juice
2   soaked gelatine leaves

For the tangerine gelatine
200 ml tangerine juice
50 g   caster (superfine) sugar
2   soaked gelatine leaves

For the isomalt discs
100 g   isomalt powder
100 ml   liquid glucose
20 g   powdered Earl Grey tea

For the tangerine slices
4   tangerines
100 ml   tangerine syrup

Dry the persimmons in the food dehydrator at 50°C (120°F) for 24 hours. The day after, you will be able to cut them into perfect 1.5 cm (½ in) cubes.

Start the ice cream by heating the syrup at 35°C (95°F). Add the glucose and sugar, bring to a boil then cool down to -5°C (23°F). Clean the persimmons and blend them quickly with the sugar mixture, paying attention that the temperature doesn't rise, as they must not jellify. Transfer to a Pacojet container.

Soak the almonds in cold water for 24 hours, drain, then blend with 1 l water. With the help of a cloth, squeeze out all the almond milk, reserving the almonds for the crumble. Add the salt. Heat 100 g of the almond milk, add the gelatine and mix it together with the remaining almond milk. A few hours before serving, fill the siphon and add 2 chargers.

Dry the almonds at 60°C (140°F) for 48 hours until completely crunchy. Store in a dry place.

Melt the chocolate with the cream at 60°C (140°F) in a Thermomix, then add the tangerine zest. In the meantime, heat the tangerine reduction, fold in the gelatine and add slowly to the white chocolate. Transfer to a bowl and emulsify well with a hand blender. Let cool and transfer to a piping (pastry) bag.

Heat the tangerine juice with the sugar, and reduce for 15 minutes. Filter, add the gelatine and leave to cool.

Mix the isomalt disc ingredients together and bring to a boil. ↗

Cook until it reaches 170°C (340°F). Pour on a Silpat and cool down until hard. Break the crystals and blend to powder. The powder needs to be protected from humidity. Use plastic circle stencils, and with the thin strainer with the help of the spoon, dust the powder over the stencil. Remove the stencil, dust some black tea powder, cover with another Silpat and bake 3 minutes at 170°C (340°F), without ventilation. Let cool and keep away from humidity.

Peel the tangerines and cut them into slices, avoiding the fibres and the seeds. Heat the syrup and remove from the heat, then add the tangerine peels and slices. Cool down and vacuum seal. Store in ice water.

To create the dish, take a bowl, pipe the tangerine ganache on the bottom and place the tangerine gelatine close to it. Put 3 cubes of dried persimmon in the centre.

Put on top 1 spoon of persimmon ice cream. Foam the almond milk and finish with the almond crumble.

MUSSELS, FENNEL AND CHARCOAL-GRILLED GREEN ASPARAGUS

p. 176

There is so much wild fennel growing all around Istria. The fields are painted in green and in yellow. They are very mineral and balsamic and match naturally with salty mussels and smoked green asparagus.

Serves 10

For the mussels and mussel stock
5 kg   mussels
50 g   garlic
500 ml dry white wine
200 g   wild fennel

For the mussel glaze
200 ml mussel-fennel stock (see above)
2.5 g   habanero chilli
200 g   holly leaves
3%   agar agar

For the asparagus juice
1 kg   green asparagus tips
0.8%   gelespessa
7 g   salt

For the oranges
5   bitter oranges
60 g   sugar ↗

To serve
300 g   green asparagus tips
           salt
1%   agar agar
           silver leaf
12   fennel leaves

Clean the mussels and bring them to a boil with the garlic, white wine and 500 ml water. When the mussels are open, remove them from the heat and clean them out of the shells. Strain the mussel water, add the wild fennel and compress. Cook in a vacuum bag for 4 hours at 75°C (165°F). Chill and strain.

Compress the mussel stock, habanero and holly and cook at 75°C (165°F) for 5 hours. Strain and chill. Add the agar agar and bring to a boil. With a thoot stick, coat the mussels in the glaze and cool them down.

Grill the asparagus over a yakitori grill, making sure it is smoky and with embers only. Don't overcook them, as you want the green and bright colour. Juice the asparagus into an iced bowl and keep cold. Thicken with the gelespessa. Compress 7 times to remove all bubbles and season with salt.

Peel the bitter oranges, and remove the white part. Boil 3 times, starting with cold water and changing the water every time.

Squeeze the bitter oranges and reserve the juice. Add the sugar and cook the juice down for 20 minutes. Add the previously blanched bitter orange peel and simmer at 80°C (175°F) for 1 more hour. Keep the orange peels covered in contact with the baking paper.

Grill the asparagus tips in the yakitori, making sure it is smoky and with embers only. Make sure you don't overcook them. Season with salt.

Mix the mussel stock with the agar agar and bring to a boil. Plate when still hot. Place the mussels and asparagus tips on the dish. Pour the asparagus juice and top with bitter orange, silver leaf and fennel leaves.

BASICS

KOBARIŠKI ŠTRUKLJI (ORIGINAL)

Štruklji is one of a few very traditional Slovenian dishes that somehow unifies the country. But every village, town, and housewife makes štruklji in its own way. *Kobariški štruklji* (štruklji from Kobarid) are one of the most unique, beautiful and delicious interpretations of it. Today, the school in Kobarid teaches local children the craft of making them. Štruklji are steamed in Kobarid, while in the other part of the mountain, in Valli del Natione (Italy), people fry them. ↓

Serves 10

For the filling
250 g   walnuts
150 g   sugar
100 g   breadcrumbs
50 ml   milk
50 g   butter
80 g   raisins
20 g   cinnamon
30 g   lemon zest
20 g   bitter cacao powder
50 ml   rum

For the dough
600 g   plain (all-purpose) flour
500 ml boiling salted water

For the dressing
80 g   breadcrumbs
150 g   butter

Blend the walnuts. Roast the walnuts, sugar and breadcrumbs and deglaze with warm milk and butter. Add all the other ingredients and let cool down.

To make the dough, slowly pour hot water into the flour and mix very wildly. Work the dough when it is still hot. Form small balls and flatten them between your hands. Place the filling in the middle, close the wrap and form.

Cook in salted boiling water. When they come to the surface, cook for another 2 minutes and take them out. Dress them with melted butter, in which you fry the breadcrumbs until golden.

ČOMPE S SKUTO (ORIGINAL)

This is one of my favourite shepherd dishes. I could eat it every day, and I am happy to see how much my children enjoy it. The reason the combination of hot potatoes and fermented cottage cheese works is in the sourness and spiciness of ricotta.

Serves 10

1 kg   young potatoes
500 g   fermented cottage cheese
50 g . salt

Brush the potatoes well before cooking. Serve them in their skins, in a boiling temperature with cottage cheese on the side. Serve the salt with them.

Cook the potatoes, unpeeled, in abundant salted water. Remove them when they are cooked, but still crunchy.

FRIKA

It is not pizza, it is frika! This is a shepherd's dish that is shared throughout the alpine world of Slovenia, Italy and Austria. Valter is a frika king and a true ambassador of it. He was the first to propose it at popular events and people fell in love with it again. It is a part of Polonka's menu today.

Serves 6

300 g   potatoes
200 g   1-year-old Tolminc, grated
200 g   2-year-old Tolminc, grated
120 g   Jamar (Valter's pit cheese), grated
100 g   mixed herbs: chives, tarragon, lovage

Peel the potatoes, grate them and steam them for 10 minutes at 200°C (400°F). Dry them. Heat a non-stick pan to very hot and roast the potatoes in it. Cover with one-third of the cheese and let it melt. Turn the frika around and cover with another one-third of the cheese. When melted, turn it around again and start roasting by slowly adding half of the rest of the cheese. Turn it around for the last time and slowly add the rest of cheese and chopped herbs. Serve very hot!

FRANKO'S ROASTBEEF

Franko's roastbeef is one of those things that define Hiša Franko. It is the taste of the past, and is also the taste of the future. Most regular diners would usually never leave the house without having a bite of it. Today it is a part of the menu at Polonka, our little gostilna in the centre of Kobarid. When I was a child, my father used to bring the whole family for Sunday dinner to eat Franko's roastbeef and *štruklji*. We were not the only ones. There was always a long line of people waiting for a table. We serve it with Franko's bread.

Serves 12

1 kg   upper part of beef
100 g   chopped fresh garlic
65 g   rosemary
200 ml olive oil, plus extra for dressing
150 g   mustard
        olive oil
        salt
        pepper
        lemon juice

Clean the meat and spread it with a mix of chopped garlic, rosemary, olive oil and mustard. Massage it for 20 minutes and let rest in the refrigerator overnight. Heat a cast iron ↗

pan to maximum heat and roast the meat from all sides, 3½ minutes on each. Change the pan, heat again and roast the meat for another 7 minutes. Let it set until cold at room temperature and refrigerate for 12 hours before cutting. Cut into thin slices and dress with salt, pepper, lemon and olive oil (in this precise order).

FERMENTED BERRIES

1 kg   berries (blueberries or blackcurrant or redcurrant)
7%   fine salt (no added iodine)

Scale the berries and place in a mason jar with the salt, cover with cheesecloth and let ferment 2 weeks.

FERMENTED CHANTERELLE MUSHROOMS

Step 1
3 kg   chanterelle mushrooms
3 l   water
3 tbsp salt
10 ml   vinegar

Wash and clean the mushrooms. Boil them with water, salt and vinegar until they sink in a pot. Discard the liquid. Rinse the mushrooms in cold water.

Step 2
1 l   water
3 tbsp salt
1 tbsp sugar
4 bay   leaves
1   chopped garlic head
300ml   whey

Make a brine with all the ingredients. Cover the mushrooms in liquid, jar them and put a cloth on top. Ferment for 3 days at room temperature, then store in a cool place.

FERMENTED LEMONS

3 kg   organic lemons
1 kg   salt
5   vanilla pods
30 g   black cardamoms

Cut the lemons in 4 without dividing them. Spread the salt inside. Put the lemons in a ↗

glass or plastic jar, layering with extra salt and spices. Cover with cheesecloth and ferment for 3–4 weeks. Check that the lemons are covered in brine.

PLUM-BERRY VINEGAR

10 kg   ripe organic fruits

Clean the fruits. Mash them with your hands and put in a big container (plastic or glass). Cover the fruit with water and let it ferment, stirring every day until it develops the 'mother'. Keep the barrel covered with cheesecloth, so fruit flies don't go in. Keep fermenting for 3 months, then strain and bottle.

TOMATO WATER

5 kg	ripe tomatoes
300 g	green celery
300 g	onions
1 l	water
30 g	salt
50 g	sugar
50 g	cleaned garlic
50 g	basil
5	soaked gelatine leaves

Bring all the ingredients apart from the gelatine to a boil. Cook for 30 minutes. Strain through a cheesecloth. Add the gelatine and freeze for 24 hours. Hang it in a cheesecloth and let it thaw at room temperature, collecting the liquid. If you need to make the water more intense, don't do the gelatine step.

UMEBOSHI

5 kg	unripe plums
400 g	fine salt (8%)

Wash the plums and soak overnight in water, then discard the liquid. Layer the plums in a plastic or glass container with the salt. Cover with a cloth and a heavy weight (stone). Let rest for 3 weeks. Drying process: drain the plums from the liquid and let them dry under the sun for 1 day, then put them back in the liquid. Repeat for 3 days. Save the brine liquid and vacuum-pack the fruits.

INDEX

Note:
Page references
in **bold** indicate
photographs.

Author Acknowledgments
Three months before the due date for the book material, what you are holding in your hands seemed like utopia. Then the three Slovenian blonde girls met by coincidence. Suzan Gabrijan is one of the most dedicated photographers I've ever met. She has that natural talent to capture spontaneous moments, is very disciplined and very beautiful. Journalist Kaja Sajovic is my favorite writing 'Bridget Jones' and is really dedicated to gastronomy. Kaja is very funny and very beautiful. Working with Kaja and Suzan so closely made me feel addicted to this book. There are no hidden ghostwriters. No translators. I did not want anything to be lost in translation. And finally, a huge thank you to Emily and Emilia, for believing in my work. And thank you to Ariane, the designer, for her patience and amazing results.

Phaidon Press Limited
Regent's Wharf
All Saints Street
London N1 9PA

Phaidon Press Inc.
65 Bleecker Street
New York, NY 10012

Phaidon.com

First published 2020
© 2020 Phaidon Press Limited

ISBN 978 0 7148 7930 7

A CIP catalogue record for this book is available from the British Library and the Library of Congress.

Editor: Emily Takoudes
Production Controller: Nerissa Vales
Photography: Suzan Gabrijan
Design: Ariane Spanier Design

Printed in China.

Phaidon would like to thank Sophie Hodgkin, Manca Istinič, Annie Lee, Lesley Malkin, Eve Marleau, Elizabeth Parson, Andrea Petrini, Rosie Pickles, Kaja Sajovic, and Kate Slate, for their contributions to this book.

Recipe Notes

All herbs are fresh, unless otherwise specified.

All cream is 36–40% fat heavy whipping cream, unless otherwise specified.

All milk is whole at 3% fat, homogenized and lightly pasteurized, unless otherwise specified.

All yeast is fresh, unless otherwise specified.

All salt is fine sea salt, unless otherwise specified.

Breadcrumbs are always dried, unless otherwise specified.

Cooking times are for guidance only, as individual ovens vary. If using a fan (convection) oven, follow the manufacturer's instructions concerning oven temperatures.

Exercise a high level of caution when following recipes involving any potentially hazardous activity, including the use of high temperatures, open flames, slaked lime and when deep-frying. In particular, when deep-frying, add food carefully to avoid splashing, wear long sleeves and never leave the pan unattended.

Some recipes include raw or very lightly cooked eggs, meat, or fish, and fermented products. These should be avoided by the elderly, infants, pregnant women, convalescents and anyone with an impaired immune system.

Exercise caution when making fermented products, ensuring all equipment is spotlessly clean, and seek expert advice if in any doubt.

When no quantity is specified, for example of oils, salts, and herbs used for finishing dishes or for deep-frying, quantities are discretionary and flexible.

All herbs, shoots, flowers and leaves should be picked fresh from a clean source.

Exercise caution when foraging for ingredients; any foraged ingredients should only be eaten if an expert has deemed them safe to eat.

Measurement Notes

All spoon and cup measurements are level, unless otherwise stated.

Australian standard tablespoons are 20 ml, so Australian readers are advised to use 3 teaspoons in place of 1 tablespoon when measuring small quantities.

Ana Roš was born in Yugoslavia, where she focused on skiing and dance as a child. Following her studies in international and diplomatic science at the University of Trieste, she moved to the Soča Valley of Slovenia with her husband, whose family owned the restaurant and inn Hiša Franko. Ana took over the kitchen, and self-taught, over the last twenty years has developed and transformed Slovenian cuisine, working exclusively with local ingredients and producers. Roš has been invited to cook in numerous countries around the world and has participated in the culinary events Cook it Raw, Gelinaz!, Identità Golose and Refettorio Ambrosiano among many others. She has also been featured on Netflix's award-winning documentary series *Chef's Table*. Roš was awarded Best Female Chef in 2017 by the World's 50 Best Restaurants awards and she placed #38 on that list in 2019.